MANCHURIA
CRADLE OF CONFLICT

With a New Introduction by The Author

AMS PRESS
New York

MANCHURIA

CRADLE OF CONFLICT

BY

OWEN LATTIMORE

REVISED EDITION

NEW YORK
THE MACMILLAN COMPANY
1935

Library of Congress Cataloging in Publication Data

Lattimore, Owen, 1900—
    Manchuria: cradle of conflict.

    Reprint of the 1935 ed. published by Macmillan,
New York; with new introd.
    Includes index.
    1. Manchuria.   2. Eastern question (Far East)
I. Title.
DS783.L3   1975   915.1'8'034   72-4435
ISBN 0-404-10632-3

Reprinted by arrangement with Owen Lattimore

Copyright © 1975 by AMS Press Inc.

TO
ELEANOR

INTRODUCTION
TO THE AMS EDITION

When this book was first published, in 1932, Manchuria was very much in the news, after the Japanese invasion of 1931 and later the proclamation of the bogus state of "Manchukuo." Most reviewers commented on it with praise, and the eminent economic historian R. H. Tawney, in his *Land and Labour in China* (London and New York, 1932, footnote on p. 106), said flatteringly that it threw "a flood of new light on the whole subject." More recently my partner of a good many years in research on Mongolia, Mrs. Fujiko Isono (see the Introduction to the AMS edition of Eleanor Lattimore's *Turkestan Reunion*), has said to me that I showed more sensitivity to East Asian ways of looking at things than most Westerners of that time. (She first read the book in 1945.)

Yet I have never been able to turn back to this book with much satisfaction. Mainly this is for a very personal reason. When my wife and I set out for our 1929-30 travels in Manchuria, I took along a copy of the first volume (the second volume had not yet been published in English translation), of Oswald Spengler, *The Decline of the West* (New York, 1926). It was a fashionable book of the time, an "in" book as we would say now, and it infected my thinking. The infection lasted for only a year or two, but it shows in this book, in a tendency to discuss cultures in terms of "youth, maturity, and age (decline)," and a tendency to be, in general, a bit portentous. The effect would have been worse, had it not been for my wife. She kept telling me not to lean too heavily on the thinking of some other man. I had already shown that I could do my own thinking, and sometimes it was not bad. Why not develop it? And after all, she added loyally and generously, Spengler had probably never heard of Manchuria, while I, by that time, knew more about it than any other Westerner.

Another critic of the time I remember with friendly

amusement. I had gone to Hailar (my wife had gone back to Peking) in the corner of Manchuria that is wedged in between Mongolia and Siberia. I was negotiating with the local authorities to find out if it was safe to travel away from the town into the countryside, where "White" (Tsarist Russian exile) bandits were reported to be on the loose. There were certainly elements in the town who were capable of passing information to them about a traveller who might be worth capturing for ransom. In the billiard room of the little hotel where I stayed several of the Russians who played billiards every evening had only the thumb and little finger of the right hand, the three middle fingers having been cut off. The explanation, I was told, was that these were "Whites" who had served as mercenaries in a Chinese warlord army in Shantung. When their side was defeated and they were captured, they had three fingers cut off the right hand, so that they could never handle a rifle, pistol, or sword again.

In the end, being no hero in search of adventure, I did not venture into the countryside, but while gathering local information I thought I would see if I could get anything out of the Soviet Consul. He turned out to be a delightful man, knowing German and English (but no Chinese), and widely read. By the time I got around to mentioning Oswald Spengler with enthusiasm, he could tell, of course, that I was utterly ignorant of Marxism. Being far too intelligent to try, in a passing conversation, to convince me of the superiority of Marx over Spengler, he undertook instead a brilliant, devastating criticism of Spengler, showing that he had read him, but worded more in terms of Spengler's readers than of Spengler's text. The intelligentsia in countries like the United States, he said (politely, he did not say "you capitalists," or "you bourgeois") were swayed by gusts of intellectual fashion. This year Spengler, in a couple of years someone else. Spengler, he said, fitted the disillusion after the 1914-1918 war, and the pessimism accompanying the Great Depression. He did not say anything that sent me rushing to read Marx as soon as I got back to Peking, but perhaps what he said about being swayed by fashion, combined with what my wife said about not learning too much on the authority of one man, had something to do with my not becoming an amateur Marxist when that became fashionable later in the 1930's.

That year in Manchuria, following on my travels through Inner Mongolia and Sinkiang (see the AMS edition of *Desert Road to Turkestan* and *High Tartary*), had started to build up in my mind some ideas about the importance of the Great Wall frontier zone in Chinese history. It was in *Manchuria, Cradle of Conflict*, I think, that I first printed my ideas about "reservoirs" of barbarian power north of the Great Wall—an "inner reservoir" from which barbarian conquerors in China drew military recruits to support their power, and an "outer reservoir" of not fully controlled barbarians always potentially capable of becoming "conquerors of the conquerors," moving in on China to establish a new, upper stratum of empire—as the Jurchid of the Chin dynasty (1115, to some point after 1234) moved in on the Khitan of the Liao dynasty (907, to about 1115), and the Mongols of the Yuan dynasty (proclaimed in Mongolia in 1260, actually ruling the whole of China, 1280-1368), moved in on the Chin, and on the Sung dynasty of South China.

These ideas were set out in, I hope, a more mature way in my *Inner Asian Frontiers of China* (New York, American Geographical Society, 1940). In *Manchuria, Cradle of Conflict*, they are expressed in a more immature, more strident and (again the baleful influence of Spengler), more "portentous" way. There is far too much emphasis on the misleading idea that it is a Chinese tradition that movement toward the north means danger, if not defeat, while movement toward the south means success.

For all its weaknesses, however, I must claim some merits for this book. It is the first, I believe, to show some of the real differences between "old colonization" and "new colonization" in the Chinese occupation of Manchuria; the first to show the real working processes of opium cultivation and banditry; and one of the first to

v

show the important differences between geographical zones: the southern, "old Chinese" zone, the middle and northern Manchu-Tungus zone, and the western, Mongol-inhabited zone.

In conclusion, a word about "Manchuria." This is now an outdated term. There is no evidence that even in the Manchu language a name equivalent to "Manchuria" ever existed. The modern term "Manchuria" was invented by Tsarist Russian and Japanese imperialists who wanted to create the impression that "Manchuria" was somehow different from "China," so that detachment of Manchuria from China would not really be aggression against China. The only proper term is that which the Chinese have always used: Tung'pei; that is, The Northeast (of China). This is correct and appropriate even though one need not, and indeed should not, jump to the conclusion that all of the Northeast has always been a homogeneous part of China. It was, in fact, for centuries a vague area—just as Siberia, for a shorter time, was a vague area. In both cases, however, the name Northeast and the name Siberia have now become firm names.

Owen Lattimore

INTRODUCTION TO THE SECOND EDITION

THE first edition of this book was published only a few months after the violent events which detached Manchuria from China and led to the creation of Manchukuo. The writing of it had been completed before those events: it was therefore a book dealing with Manchuria, not Manchukuo. One of the points most strongly emphasized was that the problems of Manchuria were not new problems, created by the rapid Chinese colonization of the country and the introduction of "modern civilization," but were directly related to a long history and were in fact only modern phases of very ancient problems, complicated by the addition of new factors.

If this was true of Manchuria before 1931, it is even more true of Manchukuo since 1932. Yet it is now almost impossible to find a discussion of Manchuria which is free from bias for or against Manchukuo. It is indeed almost impossible, in treating of Manchuria as it was in 1931, not to take the record of the years 1932–35 and read it back into the record of the years before 1931. Since my original text, whatever its faults, was at least not colored by judgments made after the event, I have thought it best not to make extensive changes. Let it be read as an introduction to the contemporary problems. The later aspects I have dealt with separately, in two new chapters.

The first of these is a summary of the course of events from the 18th of September, 1931, to the present time. In the second, I have discussed the relation between Manchuria, the geographical region, Manchukuo, the political structure, and contemporary history as a whole. These chapters may seem cold and bloodless to some, because they do not embody judgments of right and wrong, but essay only a survey—necessarily brief—of what has happened, together with speculations on the meaning of what has happened and the potentialities of the future. In this, however, I have not departed from the tone of the book as it was first written, for my purpose throughout has been to limit myself to a study of the character of history in Northeastern Asia, and to exclude the political record of rights and wrongs and conflicting claims.

The only chapter that has been extensively rewritten is Chapter I, in which the relation of geography to history has, I hope, been made more clear. To this chapter also has been added a list of the new provinces as established under Manchukuo. Part of this material has also been dealt with in an article in *Pacific Affairs* for June, 1935. The important Mongol province of Hsingan has not been treated in greater detail than the other provinces, since I have separately discussed the relation of Mongol questions to Manchurian questions in my book *The Mongols of Manchuria,* published last year.

Owen Lattimore

Peiping
January 15, 1935

INTRODUCTION

This book is founded on the experience gained during about nine months of travel and residence in Manchuria, in 1929-30, under a fellowship from the Social Science Research Council, New York. Previous experience on the borders of China and Inner Mongolia, and a long journey through Mongolia and Chinese Turkestan, had convinced me that a study of Manchuria must be essential to an understanding of the vast territory that lies between China and Russia. Manchuria, Mongolia and Chinese Turkestan were once important as the lands in which the "northern barbarians" of China's frontier manœuvered in war and migration, working out among their own tribes their destinies of conquest in China or migration toward the West. They are now becoming a field of contest between three types of civilization—the Chinese, the Russian and the Western. In our generation the most acute rivalry is in Manchuria, and the chief protagonist of the Western civilization is Japan—whose interpretation and application of a borrowed culture is of acute interest to the Western world, as on it turns to a great extent the choice which other nations have yet to make between their own indigenous cultures and the rival conquering cultures of Russia and the West.

During our stay in Manchuria my wife and I tried to make our experience as varied as possible, but at the same time to stay long enough in each region studied to insure that our impressions should not be too superficial. Thus we spent part of the winter in one room at an inn, in a mud-walled "boom"

ix

town on the Western frontiers of Manchuria, where Chinese colonists are rapidly taking over Mongol pastures and opening them to cultivation. Then we moved to another one-room lodging in an old thatched schoolhouse, in a small town in Kirin province, where the population was old-fashioned and predominantly Manchu.

In the spring I went up again to the Western frontiers and traveled, first by military motor convoy and then riding with border troopers, among the Mongols. When the ice broke up on the great Sungari river, I traveled on one of the first steamers down to the junction of the Sungari with the Amur —about four hundred miles. As the steamers were afraid to venture into the Amur, no settlement having yet been made of the dispute between China and Russia, I traveled on by cart, with a good deal of difficulty, for some distance along the flooded banks of the Amur, among the "Fishskin Tatars." Later in the summer I visited Hailar, in the Barga region.

In the intervals between traveling, or making long stays in the country, we visited the chief cities—Mukden, Dairen, Harbin and Kirin city—or made short stays at smaller towns, or in villages, or at temples in the hills. In the larger towns we naturally did our best to meet well-informed people of all nationalities, but out in the country we rarely saw a foreigner, and often went for weeks without speaking English except to each other. As we traveled very simply, had no need of an interpreter, used always the same means of travel as the people of the region and lived in the same kind of houses or inns, our contact with the life about us was as close as possible. We were thus able to collect a great deal of local tradition—not only legend and folklore, but the memories of the older inhabitants—besides noting the signs of that "modern progress" which is the chief enthusiasm of the younger generation.

Before leaving for Manchuria, I worked for about six months at Harvard, in the Department of Anthropology and at the Widener Library, so that by the time we set out we knew not only where we wanted to go but what kind of work we wanted to do. As for methods, we knew from experience how we expected to get down to work; and considering the difficulties of banditry, the disturbances consequent on the conflict between China and Russia over the Chinese Eastern Railway, and the local problems that can crop up in so wide a region as Manchuria, we succeeded passably well in carrying out our plans.

This book has been written since our return from Manchuria, in the intervals of further research in Peiping, and I feel that I should say something of the "source material" used. This has been almost entirely Chinese. There exists a great mass of Chinese material dealing with Manchuria, especially from the Ta Ch'ing or Manchu dynasty; but it is not well organized, and what is wanted has to be "dug out."

My principal sources have been the following:

The *Ch'in Ting Ta Ch'ing Hui Tien,* is an encyclopædic compilation of the laws and regulations of the Manchu Empire, printed in 1818, bearing on the multifarious public questions of administration, social organization, land tenure, taxation, military establishment, religion, education, government of the non-Chinese races within the Empire, official and private life, and so on. As much of the "law" concerned is not strictly law, but administrative procedure, recorded in successive edicts and based on precedent and custom, the regular form of entry is chronological, the successive amendments of different reigns being recorded in order, together with many rulings given in disputed cases. The subject matter, however, is divided under many headings, so that whatever bears on Manchuria has to be sought out with diligence. As the whole work is published in sixty *t'ao* or "cases," each containing an average of seven or eight *pên* or separate books, this is not a light matter.

The *Huang Ch'ing K'ai Kuo Fang Lüeh* is the official Manchu account (in Chinese) of the origins and foundation of the Manchu dynasty. It was printed in 1786, in two "cases," each containing eight "books." There is a German translation by E. Hauer (1926).

The *Man Chou Shih Lu* was published by the Mukden Bureau of Records, in 1930, in one *t'ao* of eight *pên*. It was printed from a manuscript in the Mukden Palace, and is apparently the account of the early Manchus as preserved for the imperial household. It differs in some respects from other accounts.

The *Tung Hua Hsü Lu* or *Tung Hua Ch'üan Lu* is a chronicle of the Manchu emperors. The form of compilation is a record, from day to day, of all manner of affairs dealt with by the emperor. It is in twenty-six *t'ao,* each containing on an average seven *pên*. Unless a date is known beforehand, there is no way of getting at the material required except by going right through the whole work. I am at present compiling an extract of all references in this chronicle to Korea, Manchuria, Mongolia, Chinese Turkestan and Russia. The record runs from T'ien Ming (1616) down to the end of the reign of Tao Kuang (1851), and I understand there is a continuation carrying the account to the end of the reign of T'ung Chih (1875).

The *T'ung Chih* or "gazetteers" and *Wai Chih* or unofficial gazetteers of the various provinces are available in a number of editions, of which some are more comprehensive than others. They deal under classified headings with all manners of affairs within the province, and include even biographies of celebrated men and women.

The *Tung Pei Nien Chien,* a new publication, is a yearbook of the Northeastern Provinces, issued for the first time in 1931, by the Cultural Society of the Northeastern Provinces, at Mukden.

The total amount of print in even the few Chinese sources just mentioned is so great that I have not, naturally, been able to search the whole. What I have done is to check, as far as possible, my own conclusions formed in the course of travel and from previous reading.

In the material dealt with in this book I have tried to break new ground. It is, for instance, a common practice to treat the Manchu conquest of China as the beginning of intelligible history in Manchuria, and the entry of Russia and Japan into Manchurian affairs as the beginning of the significant history of the region. As the correction of this estimate has been one of my objects, I have endeavored to bring out the fact that the ancient "tribal" history of Manchuria, so far from being an academic question to be dismissed in a prefatory chapter, should be recognized as the prototype out of which has developed, with remarkably full historic continuity, the modern relation between China and Manchuria, and therefore a great part of the conflict of the present day, with its invasion of colonists and rivalry of civilizations.

Thus, on the foundation of a study of the type and style in action of the old barbarian tribes in their recurrent pressure on China, and the reflex action of China, and especially Chinese culture, on the barbarians, I have tried to build a study of the interacting migrations of peoples and cultures. In Manchuria, I believe, the influence of the region itself has tended always to predominate over the peoples and cultures that turn by turn have exercised the power of the region; so that even now, under the profound alteration of Manchurian life, and the rapid destruction of old Manchurian tradition brought about by the sudden, vigorous onslaught of machine civilization, can be traced the tidal influence of the ineluctable Manchurian regional relation to China, to Mongolia and to Russia—and also to Korea and Japan. The old forces persist, though they work through altered activities.

My thanks are due not only to the Social Science Research Council, but to the American Geographical Society, which, interested especially in pioneer colonization, also gave me encouragement and support, and to the Peabody Museum of Anthropology at Harvard, to which the Social Science Research Council sent me for preliminary study, and which furthered the specifically anthropological side of my work in Manchuria.

After my wife and I had arrived in Manchuria, we met with generous encouragement on all sides. Marshal Chang Hsüehliang showed a personal interest which was of inestimable value in facilitating our approach to officials everywhere. General Chang Tso-hsiang, Governor of Kirin, and General Tsou Tso-hua, Tupan of the great Hsingan Colonization Project, gave us direct aid of the greatest value. Mr. W. H. Donald assisted us with his usual generous disregard for his own time and convenience. The South Manchuria Railway Company, always cordial to research workers, gave us every facility. From the Irish, Scotch and Canadian Presbyterian missionaries in Mukden, Kirin, T'iehling, Liaoning, Hulan and T'aonan, we received unstinted hospitality and help, as also from officials of the Chinese Maritime Customs, Post Office and Chinese Eastern Railway, and from private individuals. In more than one place Chinese residents, on whom we had no claim at all, put themselves out to aid and entertain us, with the most friendly interest.

To my wife, who accompanied me for the greater part

of the time, putting up with inconveniences which can only be appreciated by those who know what it is like to stay for long periods in remote villages and country inns, I owe more than I can say. Finally, it is a pleasure to record once more the name of "Moses," Li Pao-shu, whose humor and shrewdness contributed as much to the success of our work in Manchuria as they had to our travels in Mongolia and Chinese Turkestan.

OWEN LATTIMORE

Peiping
December 10, 1931

MAPS

xvi

CONTENTS

CONTENTS

MANCHURIA
CRADLE OF CONFLICT

Chapter I

THE BATTLEGROUND OF RACE AND CULTURE

DIFFERENCES BETWEEN MANCHURIA AND OTHER UNDEVELOPED LANDS

Popular interest in Manchuria turns on two things: the spectacular immigration of enormous numbers of Chinese (perhaps, in the rapidity of settlement and the numbers involved, the greatest peaceful migration in history), the prospect of commercial exploitation in a field unencumbered by out-of-date industries; and the recurrent political tension which makes it a danger to the international relations not only of Asia but of the whole world. There is a tendency to assume that in Manchuria there is a clear field; that there is almost no necessity of making over an old civilization, with all its vested interests, social and economic, and that it is therefore an ideal territory for the introduction of "modern civilization."

Yet there are striking differences between Manchuria (and the contiguous region of Mongolia) and any other region of pioneer settlement. The tension of international affairs alone is enough to distinguish it not only from Australia, the Argentine, or Northwest Canada, but even from the regions of European settlement in Africa, where the international and racial factors differ not in degree but in kind from those of Northeastern Asia. Historically, Manchuria is a part of the great migration-ground of Eastern and Central Asia. In our time, the form of migration is changing. The great move-

3

ment of population toward Manchuria is paralleled and rivaled by a migration of ideas and cultures. The Western world tends to assume that "modern civilization"—that is, the civilization of Europe and America—is alone worth the name of civilization, and that the process of spreading it and civilizing the rest of the world involves no problem of the proof of superiority; for the inferior nations of the world, once they are confronted with "modern civilization," must obviously recognize its virtues and hasten to convert themselves. Yet, in point of fact, Manchuria is a focus of conflict in which meet three antipathetic styles of civilization: the old but still vigorous civilization of China, the newer but materially more powerful civilization of the West, and the newest of all, a force still largely incalculable, the civilization which is being created in our time in Russia and, rejected by the West, is turning with great vigor toward the Orient.

So far from being a "virgin" country, Manchuria is a vast territory with an important regional, racial and cultural history of its own. The problems of modern colonization cannot be dealt with simply in terms of the numbers of colonists who settle annually, and the number of new commercial opportunities created. Historical forces, which influence the affairs of the living, must be taken into consideration; the importance of the region, in its bearing on culture, and of culture, in its effect on races: above all, it is necessary to hold in mind the importance of ideas and the way of life of different peoples, as opposed to purely material factors of climate and geography. To elucidate these manifold and often conflicting forces, and to set forth, with as sympathetic an understanding as possible, the point of view and way of life of the different nations and cultures involved is the object of this book.

Manchuria is a storm-center of the world. In actual colonization, China is overwhelmingly in the lead; but on either flank stand Russia and Japan, in strategic positions which we are accustomed to describe as "dominating," but which are really more than that—they are imperative. As far as can be seen from present conditions the pressure of these two nations on Manchuria, unavoidable because inherent in their positions, has not yet reached its maximum. It is commonly held that the Chinese are proving that in the basic fact of colonization, by occupying Manchuria with a Chinese population, they can put themselves beyond competition from Russians or Japanese, and far beyond competition from the non-Chinese indigenous races. If, however, Manchuria is in this respect primarily a field of Chinese colonization, yet China is handicapped by the difficulty of asserting its power and control over Manchuria as an integral part of China, or even as an outer dominion, for China is weak in its relation to any alien power. The power of united China is growing, undoubtedly; but that growth depends to a gravely dangerous extent on the good will of foreign nations, so that the Chinese are not yet fully masters of their own destiny. The incorporation of alien principles with the traditional culture of China itself has not yet been successfully completed; a critical period has yet to be faced in which China must prove that its reconstructed culture can develop the power of fresh social growth, and it must therefore be considered still an open question how far Manchuria may come to be a colonial region occupied by Chinese but in some degree dominated, and correspondingly exploited, by non-Chinese governments.

The grave weight of the historical factor must also be considered. In Africa, for instance, in the regions affected by actual settlement of Europeans on the land, the indigenous tribal populations offer problems which are often difficult enough. They have a history, of a sort, but it is emphatically not a history of dynamic growth and really dangerous assertion. There is a problem of how to deal with them, but there is not a problem of whether they can be dealt with at all.

In Manchuria, on the other hand, the factor of history is one of the most powerful living forces in the present. Time and again races emanating from Manchuria, and still to a certain extent represented there (of whom the most important are now not the Manchus but the Mongols), have led or shared in conquests of China, and have established in China dominions of greater or less territorial extent, in which the Chinese became politically a subordinate race. In fact China's immediate title to Manchuria derives historically from the conquest of China by the Manchus. In earlier periods, however, China had exercised a certain sovereignty over parts of Manchuria. Signs of the influence of Chinese culture can be detected in the remotest parts of the country, and must often antedate by generations the actual arrival of Chinese colonists in decisive numbers. One of the important tasks of future research in Manchuria and Mongolia must be to determine how far Chinese influences were carried and actively propagated by the Chinese, and how far they were brought back as part of their plunder by admiring non-Chinese raiders and conquerers—who would naturally be guided by non-Chinese criteria of what was admirable and imitable, and what was merely luxurious.

We can appreciate to some extent the importance of this long historical relationship if we imagine that the various wars against native tribes in North America and Africa were not merely the overcoming of difficulties in the way of establishing the white man, whose ultimate triumph was a foregone conclusion, but were vital decisions of recurrent problems of whether the colonist was to rule the native or whether red or black dynasties were to be set up, ruling over and exploiting the colonists. The fact is that however empty of "natives" the part of Manchuria in which a Chinese colonist settles, and however ignorant he may be, it is not to him an empty land historically. While he was growing up in China, long before he thought of emigrating, he was familiar with legends and hero-tales of battles and stratagems in which victory often wavered between the mighty but stupid barbarians and the champions of his own people, often weaker but always more astute, often resigned to defeat but always confident of their superiority in culture. He has come to settle in and identify himself with a land into which, even in the glorious past, his own people always ventured at their peril, and in which was always latent a threat of dominion over China.

There is no single Chinese name for Manchuria as a unit, in inevitable common use, corresponding to our use of the *non-Chinese* term "Manchuria," to which Chinese object because it does not suggest that Manchuria is an integral part of China but, on the contrary, implies a distinction between Manchuria and China proper. Even the term Three Eastern Provinces is comparatively modern, has been deliberately fostered by publicists, and is on the whole unsatisfactory, owing to the fact that at present, with the inclusion of the Jehol region of Inner Mongolia in the Manchurian military-political group, there is some uncertainty as between Three Eastern Provinces and Four Eastern Provinces. Consequently the simpler term Eastern Provinces is now preferred. The commonest vernacular terms for Manchuria are *K'ou Wai,* which means Outside the Passes (of the Great Wall) and applies to Mongolia and Chinese Turkestan as well as to Manchuria, and *Tung K'ou Wai,* which means Outside the Eastern Pass (at Shanhaikuan) and applies to Manchuria in a general sense, but perhaps more specifically to the southern districts with which the Chinese have been most familiar from ancient times. These names have a certain ring of hostility, but there is no doubt that they evoke for Chinese an impressively rich association of ideas. To the emigrating European "the Colonies" mean, in one aspect, the sadness of separation from home; in another, the adventure into the unknown—but a triumphant adventure, not an intrusion into the territory of the conquerors of his people. The comparable emotions of the emigrating Chinese, when it is a question of migrating beyond the Great Wall—but *not* when it is a question of emigrating to, say, the South Seas—are, in the first place, a feeling of *risking* himself beyond the Wall (the *defensive* Wall) and, in the second place, after he has once become established, a feeling that he is now in a superior position with regard to China. He is no longer defended by the Great Wall frontier; it is China that is defended by the Wall from him and his compeers. In other words, there is a partial and curious, but most significant substitution of regional feeling for race or national feeling; the phenomenon, in fact, of the permanence of a certain social psychology within a region, governed by the conditions of the region and paramount, intermittently at least, over the conditions of race, culture or nationality of the different peoples that successively hold the region.

CHINESE CIVILIZATION AND "WESTERNIZATION"

If the psychology of regional feeling is a powerful motive running through Manchurian history, cultural motives are also of high importance. There is the unitary tribal feeling (from almost the beginning practically a caste-feeling) of the Manchus; the multiple tribal feeling of the Mongols; and above all the cultural and racial feeling of the Chinese.

The most important thing about the civilization of China, in itself, is its age. It is not only a mature and an old civilization, but a decidedly "late" civilization; and it is correspondingly difficult for any population saturated with its feeling and oriented by its standard to modify either its instinctive feeling or its intellectual methods. The Chinese migration to Manchuria long ago passed the stage of the "Pilgrim Fathers" or "pioneers of the frontier," though pioneer elements do survive. It is, one may say, not a naïve but a sophisticated migration. This is a truth too much obscured by the poverty, ignorance and general social depression of the migrants as individuals. Yet the fact is that, however "primitive" as individuals, they are, as a group, under the pronounced control of "civilized" feelings. If the European-American pioneer colonist of the present day is psychologically biased by such artificial considerations as railways, motor roads and the accessibility of towns, *so is the Chinese*. That is, he has no longing for the wilderness as such; he is reluctant to move beyond the reach of the civilization that he knows, and on the whole, as a community, he looks up to the city and down on the village and the farm.

It must, however, be also always borne in mind that there is a profound difference between our civilization and that of the Chinese. The difference is one both of underlying feeling and conscious point of view, a subjective difference in the mode of every process, and an objective difference in every result that is planned for.

The cleavages between Orient and Occident are prolific sources of prejudice and nonsense, and must therefore be handled with extreme wariness. It would be grotesque to study Manchuria, where so many powerful "modern" factors are at work and where technical borrowings from the West probably play a more important part than in any other part of China of equal area, with an imagination biased by popular conceptions of "Orientalism." At the same time the problems of Manchuria are, in spite of their international bearings, a specifically Chinese study, in view of the colonization now taking place and the overwhelming racial dominance and great cultural vigor of the Chinese. These problems therefore would also be distorted if the pronounced individuality in style of the Chinese culture and civilization were not considered at all.

The mere fact that the Chinese have a highly developed, individual civilization is enough to place Manchuria, with Mongolia and Chinese Turkestan, in a different category from all the other great regions of the world that are now being settled and civilized for the first time. This ought to be a glaring truth, but it has never been so treated. As a spectacle, the Chinese colonization of Manchuria is so magnificent, the millions taking part and the rapidity of their spread have such a dramatic appeal, that there cannot but be a tendency among Westerners—especially in a nation like America with a strong and highly sentimentalized pioneering tradition—to regard it as a spectacle *in our own manner*. We tend to stress the resemblances to the great colonizing migrations of our own people and kindred peoples—the filling up of America and the advance across the continent, and the parallel phenomena of the colonial expansion of European countries in the nineteenth century. What is amazing, however, is that the colonial problem of Manchuria should be so commonly discussed as if it were a subsidiary phenomenon of our own world, and nothing else—a mere incident in the spread of our own technical methods and style of expansion and exploitation, which began to dominate our society in the late eighteenth century and is now reaching out to grasp the rest of the world. Time and again discussions not only of

Manchuria but of all Chinese questions are vitiated by such
misleading references to what *may* be happening, but what
we cannot yet be sure *is* happening, as: "When China has
added Western technique to her own ancient civilization . . ."
"When the modernization of China has been completed . . ."
"The latest scientific methods are now being employed
in . . ."—as if the *only* question at issue were that of the rapidity with which China can be converted into a second and
greater Japan. And the folly of describing "the relief of con-
gested population in China by emigration to Manchuria and
Mongolia"—as if such relief were a solution of the population
problem of China—is constantly repeated.

For there can be no doubt about the radical divergences
between China and Japan. Just as the difference between
America and Spain is one of degree but that between America
and China one of kind, so the difference between Japan and
China also is one of kind, that between Japan and Germany
essentially one of degree only. Japan, as an imperial and
colonial power, must be ranked as one of our own group of
Western nations; and that not merely in method, as is so
often postulated, but in character. This must not be lost sight
of when considering the pressure of Japan on the Chinese
who are colonizing and governing Manchuria.

If there had been any real, any valid drift toward Westernization in China, the Chinese could easily and long ago—in
the eighteenth century, for instance, when the Jesuits stood so
high at the court of the Manchu emperors—have forestalled
the rise of Japan as the leading Western nation of the East.
As things are, such Westernization as has taken place cannot
definitely be rated as the beginning of a transformation from
within of the Chinese culture; it can only be discussed as a
question of the degree to which the Chinese instinct has succeeded in adopting Western inventions without subordinating

itself to the Western technique or the Western mental attitude in using them. The differences between Japan and China
strike very deep. Japan, in the past, *voluntarily* reformed its
own culture (which already contained a diversity of elements
of widely differing provenance) by selective borrowing from
the high civilization of China. A strong precedent therefore
existed for a fresh voluntary reconstruction through selective
borrowing from the West. The culture of China, on the other
hand, was autochthonous and monopolistic, accustomed to
cultural lending but not to cultural borrowing—for even such
an apparently important borrowing as, for instance, the introduction of Buddhism from India, was essentially a *fashion,*
which did not involve any radical revaluation of society or
culture. The pride which the Japanese feel in their own skill
in synthesis and constructive borrowing does not therefore by
any means automatically stimulate admiration or respect in
China for the way that Japan has jumped ahead in Westernization; on the contrary, there is a strong disposition in China
to belittle Japanese "progress" as mere servile imitation, and to
impute to Japan a weakness in the faculty of organic growth.
China, it is felt, ought not to *imitate* either Japan or the
West; to do so would be surrender. Westernization, so far
as it is to be adopted at all, ought to be introduced as a subordinate element, never as a controlling element.

What is true is that the necessities of Manchuria are imposing on the Chinese an increased use of Western borrowings
—which explains the relative material "progressiveness" of
Manchuria in comparison with the rest of China—and that
parallel with the Chinese expansion, in a characteristically
Chinese manner, throughout Manchuria, there is a direct application of Western methods, in the full Western manner, by
Japan, in the zone of the South Manchuria Railway, and by
Russia, in a somewhat modified manner, in the zone of the

Chinese Eastern Railway. A crisis can therefore be foreseen, and is in fact near at hand, the upshot of which will be a decision as between the mastery of the Chinese by the Western methods, and the survival of the Chinese manner in spite of the Western methods which the Chinese tradition is increasingly forced to employ. This may completely alter the complexion of the colonizing and colonial problem in Manchuria. In the meantime Westernization is not, as is too generally assumed, the solution of all the problems of the rapid Chinese expansion, but is in fact the most ambiguous of the problems raised by that expansion.

Still, different as are the factors of tradition and temperament in East and West, it ought to be possible to assess Manchurian values in terms convincing to Western students. The essential requirement is a faculty of sympathy, which allows for states of feeling as well as for matters of fact. The living phenomena of society must be followed out and revealed in their relation to facts, which is like the relation of living motion to physical structure. Manner is as important as cause and effect. The study of the way in which things are done must be added to the catalogue of things that happen. Therefore, in all that follows, an effort has been made to balance the citation of facts and material circumstances with constant reference to cultures and the living style of different societies, as far as an outsider can penetrate them, in order to illuminate, wherever possible, the importance in all social and historical processes of the mode in action.

ECONOMIC, HISTORICAL AND RACIAL GEOGRAPHY

Manchuria is closed off from China, except for the narrow corridor along the sea entering China at Shanhaikuan, by the mountains of Jehol. These are the eastern end of the escarpment which divides Mongolia from China. Farther to the west, this escarpment is comparatively abrupt; there is a clear distinction between the plateau of Mongolia and the mountains and plains of China. In Jehol, the edge of the plateau breaks up into a confused mountain system, which reaches far enough to the east to divide Manchuria from China, but does not offer a sharp escarpment dividing China from Mongolia. There are thus two approaches to Eastern Inner Mongolia; from the south, through the long mountain valleys, and from the east, across the plains of Manchuria.

Manchuria itself consists of a huge plain, open to the sea on the south, but on all other sides walled in by mountains. On the southwest are the Jehol mountains, which link up on the west with the Great Hsingan, forming the western frontier, except where the Barga Mongol territory extends beyond the mountain barrier. Around the curve of the northern frontier, the Great Hsingan massif links up with that of the Little Hsingan; east of the Little Hsingan the great corridor of the Sungari breaks through northward to the valley of the Amur, but east of this again, and reaching back to the south, stand the Eastern Manchurian mountains, the core of which is the Ch'ang Pai Shan, dividing Manchuria from the Maritime Province of Siberia and from Korea.

Each part of the ringing mountains has its own racial, historical, cultural, and economic associations, and the influence of each mountain section reaches out into the central plain. On the south the association is with the Chinese; on the west, with the Mongols; on the north, with the Tungus tribes from which, at a comparatively late period, the Manchus emerged, and on the east with the

Koreans. The curious triskele formation of the Willow
Palisade, an ancient frontier system now almost obliterated
but still important as a key to historical problems, defines
the older relation of the different mountain frontiers to
the central plain.

The Willow Palisade ran northeastward from the Great
Wall near Shanhaikuan to a point a little beyond the Liao
river at T'ungchiangk'ou, some seventy miles north of
Mukden. From this point it continued northeastward as
the Outer Willow Palisade, reaching the Sungari twenty-
five miles or so to the east of the point where the South
Manchuria Railway now crosses the river. From the point
near the Liao river where the Willow Palisade became the
Outer Willow Palisade, the old frontier which may be
called the Inner Willow Palisade diverged to the southeast
and south, eventually reaching the sea at a point west of
the mouth of the Yalu river.

Thus the Willow Palisade and Inner Willow Palisade
together formed an enclave, through which flowed the Liao
river in its lower course. This enclave, through communication across the sea with Shantung, and along the Shanhaikuan corridor with Chihli (now Hopei) province, was
from very early times predominantly Chinese in population
and thoroughly saturated with Chinese culture, presenting
the typical Chinese landscape of walled cities in close
association with village agriculture. The artery of its life,
its culture, and its economy was the Liao river; for the
essential Chinese society, before the period of Western
maritime contact, was inseparable from systems of inland
water transport. Cities drew their food from comparatively
short distances, from the surrounding countryside, and
distributed their manufactured products over the same restricted regions. Animals pulling loads of either agricultural

or manufactured products ate up the value of the load within a journey of not very many days; the export of surplus agricultural produce, which alone could provide purchasing power for staple manufactured commodities, therefore depended on coastal and inland water transport. Beyond the range of rivers and canals, there was a rapid change from trade in staples, the prices of which were necessarily limited in scale, to trade in such luxuries as could stand the high cost of overland transport.

For this reason Chinese penetration of such regions as Mongolia and Northern Manchuria was throughout history a trade penetration, associated more with luxuries than with necessities, rather than a colonizing penetration. Northern colonization never became dynamic until railways made cheap long-distance transport possible; and as railways were forced on the Chinese in the first instance for the sake of promoting the trade expansion of Western nations, their advantages in such enterprises as colonization were offset by the permanent threat of foreign penetration.

At a later date, the use of the Luan river in Southern Jehol duplicated the use of the Liao river within the Willow Palisade, leading to the formation of a "Chinese Pale" in Southwestern Jehol quite different in character from the settlements in Southeastern and Northern Jehol. In Southeastern Jehol, in the Jo-oda League Mongol territory, the Chinese originally interpenetrated the valleys and mountains as laborers working for the Mongols; they were subsistence farmers whose lower standard of living eventually squeezed the Mongols into helplessness, but they did not drive out the Mongols. In the northern, more open country of Jehol, Chinese colonization did not succeed at all until the modern period, and then it succeeded by virtue of the railway approach from the east, from Manchuria, and immediately took the form of driving out the Mongols.

West of the Willow Palisade and Outer Willow Palisade, occupying at one time the greater part of the vast Manchurian plain and reaching back westward to the Hsingan range and the true Mongolian plateau, lay a region that was not "Manchurian" at all, as the term is now understood, but Mongol. In earlier times this region had been occupied alternately by tribes with Mongol and with Tungus affiliations. The Khitan, who founded the Liao dynasty, controlling a large part of North China in the tenth and eleventh centuries, were based in part on the Manchurian Plain and in part on what is now Northern Jehol, and were more Mongol than Tungus in racial character. The Nüchen or Juchen, who succeeded them in the twelfth century and were definitely of Tungus rather than Mongol affiliation, and were in fact closely akin to the Tungus stock from which the Manchus later sprang, were based on the eastern side of the Manchurian plain and on the mountains reaching back into what is now Northern Kirin. They took over and extended the conquests made by the Liao in China, and were then themselves overthrown at the beginning of the thirteenth century by the tribal movement which formed the modern Mongol nation under Chingghis Khan.

Most of the modern Mongols of Manchuria came into Manchuria at this time. Their main line of penetration was undoubtedly through Northern Jehol, around the southern and lower end of the Hsingan range. They then spread eastward and northward, occupying almost the whole of the Manchurian Plain, and reached right up into the Nonni valley. In this region, and in the northern part of the Hsingan, there were also Tungus groups that survived the Mongol conquest—chiefly by virtue of the forested mountains, which were an impediment to the Mongol pastoral way of life—and from these groups were formed, or re-formed, after the Manchu conquests at the beginning of the seventeenth century, such true Tungusic tribes as the forest Solons and such mixed Mongol-Tungus groups as the Daghors and the plains Solons. The Mongol tribes of the Barga region, west of the Hsingan range and therefore outside of the natural mountain walls of Manchuria, stand apart from the rest of the Manchurian Mongols. Their association with Outer Mongolia and with the Buriat Mongol region in Siberia is close; but they formed an eddy in the tribal movements originating in Outer Mongolia and resulting in the great conquests of Chingghis, because these movements did not strike directly east across Barga to reach Manchuria, but swept to the south before turning eastward through Northern Jehol.

The historical and geographical associations of the Manchus are with the north and the Outer Willow Palisade, where it extends to the Sungari. The Tungus, of whom the Manchus were a southern offshoot, were a people of the northern mountains and northern forests. While ethnically related to the Mongols, they were a distinct people; and the cultural distinction was as important as the racial. The Mongols were riders of horses and herders of sheep and cattle; the Tungus were forest hunters and herders of reindeers. In the east and south, some of these Tungus, in the valleys of the Amur, Sungari, and Ussuri, took to the use of dogs and dogsleds instead of reindeer, and to a garden agriculture (not an extensive, exporting agriculture) as a supplement to the hunting economy. Those who moved farthest south gave up the use of dogs also, and elaborated their agriculture until it approximated to the level of Chinese agriculture, with numerous villages centering around small walled cities.

The Tungus, both in Manchuria and in Siberia, have

always been distinguished by their cultural adaptability. In the Mongol regions of Manchuria, they tended to merge with the Mongols; on the lower Amur, they took on many of the characteristics of such Palaeo-Asiatic tribes as the Gilyaks; when they reached the Chinese, they conformed rapidly to Chinese standards. At the same time, they retained the mobility and aptness for military organization of their forest nomad history. They founded cities, but they did not mind abandoning one city to found another. The river valleys by which the Tungus-Manchus advanced into Manchuria flow northward—with the exception of the Nonni, which joins the Sungari and then turns northward—so that their valleys afforded an approach toward the Chinese, while the flow of their water did not favor a merging with the economic-social "bloc" of the Chinese in South Manchuria. It is possible that the rapid adoption of a Chinese economy and culture, together with lack of inland water and seacoast trade to bind them to the Chinese, accounted largely for the border bickerings which finally resulted in the Manchu Conquest. If the forms of transport and trade which went with the Chinese economy and culture had been there, the Manchus might have become simply an extension of the Chinese; as it was, they made conquest take the place of trade, and superimposed themselves on the Chinese as a conquering people.

This was quite late in the history of the formation of the Manchus, and the Tungus group from which the Manchus were formed was quite small. It is usually taken for granted that Middle and Southern Kirin—the region of Kirin City— was their "country of origin"; and this idea was indeed fostered by the Manchus themselves. As a matter of fact, however, they undoubtedly came from the north; they took off from the lower Sungari, and the line of their drive toward

Southern Kirin and the region from which they emerged as conquerors was from Ilan Hala (now Sanhsing) on the middle Sungari, up the Hurka or Mutan to Ninguta and thence across country to Kirin City and the upper Sungari.

In this country, the people with whom they had first to deal were the Koreans. East of the Outer and Inner Willow Palisades, throughout Middle and Southern Kirin, the Koreans were until recent centuries the sole inhabitants. In the seventh century, under the T'ang dynasty, the Chinese had attempted to drive across Southern Manchuria into Korea, but neither then nor later did they thoroughly succeed, and the Inner Willow Palisade marked a very real frontier between Chinese and Koreans. The Korean population in this region was perhaps not very large, because of the forested mountains; but its importance cannot be doubted. Some of the cultural influences among the early Manchus are certainly Korean rather than Chinese. Moreover the Manchus, while definitely expanding the frontiers of "Manchuria" up to the Yalu river, did not entirely drive out the Koreans. In the Chientao region, where Manchuria, Korea, and the Maritime Province of Siberia now meet, the Koreans continued to hold a recognizable enclave within Manchuria. In the southeastern part of Kirin province, east of the Inner Willow Palisade, it is probable that there was also always a recognizable Korean element among the population. Many Koreans also were enlisted among the Manchus in the early seventeenth century, and counted thenceforth as Manchus, becoming gradually absorbed among the Manchu Bannermen.

It was from the comparatively small foothold of the Chinese Pale within the Willow Palisades that the Chinese reached out to make all Manchuria Chinese. Manchu policy obstructed Chinese colonization until the end of the nineteenth century, but even so the Chinese had already spread from Southern Manchuria into Kirin, had made considerable advances westwards into the Mongol territory of Manchuria, and had begun to move up the valley of the Nonni and down the valley of the Sungari toward the northern frontiers. Still, even at the turn of the century, the total population of Manchuria (excluding Jehol, where the population probably did not exceed a million) was probably not more than ten million at most. By 1910 it was estimated at 14,917,000,[1] but this estimate was probably too high. It was arbitrarily calculated from the number of families. In China the number of individuals in a family was reckoned at 5.5. In Fengt'ien, the most heavily populated province of Manchuria, the number for some reason was set at 8.38. If the 1,780,308 families then counted in Manchuria had been tallied at the not unreasonable figure of 5.5 individuals to a family, the population figure for Manchuria would have been less than ten million. As colonization gathered momentum with the building of railways the population increased with startling rapidity, and according to the latest Japanese figures[2] it has now reached the total of 30,959,164, divided as follows:

Fengt'ien	15,143,420
Kirin	7,125,542
Heilungchiang	3,672,777
Hsingan	920,400
Hsinching Special Municipality	126,309
Harbin Special Municipality and District	553,364
Jehol	2,054,305
Japanese Leased Territories .	1,353,047

[1] *China Year Book,* 1934, p. 2.
[2] "Handbook of Information" on Manchukuo, 1933, quoted in *China Year Book,* 1934, pp. 3 and 213. The figures are as of 31 December, 1932, and 31 May, 1933 (for the Kuantung Leased Territory and S.M.R. zone).

The non-Chinese population included within these figures may be estimated at about two million Mongols (not all of the Mongols in Manchuria being included within the autonomous Mongol province of Hsingan, since many thousand agricultural Mongols live within the new "Chinese" provinces); about 750,000 Koreans, about 150,000 Russians and about 300,000 Japanese. It is probably not possible even to estimate the numbers of the true Manchus; moreover the Manchus, by loss of their language and cultural assimilation to the Chinese, now constitute a special class, rather than a separate race. The distribution of the Chinese population is extremely uneven. The largest single expanse of territory in Manchuria is still held by the Mongols, in the vast western province of Hsingan; the Koreans form a solid racial and economic group in the Chientao region, and thousands of square miles of territory stretching across North Manchuria, north of the latitude of Tsitsihar in Heilungchiang and Sanhsing (Ilan Hala) in Kirin, are virtually unoccupied. While, therefore, it is perfectly correct to point out that the population of Manchuria is overwhelmingly Chinese, it is far from correct to assume that the majority of the territory of Manchuria is inhabited by a predominantly Chinese population. This is of the greatest significance in considering attempts at Japanese and Korean colonization. It is not in the least likely that colonization will relieve population pressure in either Korea or Japan; but it may yet prove possible, by the use of Japanese and Korean colonists, and the Mongols of the western territory, to consolidate strategic areas of non-Chinese population which, while not rivaling the Chinese in actual numbers, can be used to dominate and control the numerous but politically and militarily weak Chinese.

The increase of the Chinese population, from the latter

years of the Manchu dynasty to the eve of the Japanese conquest, represented a spread westward and northward from the old Chinese Pale. By the building of Chinese railways to the west of the South Manchuria Railway and to the south of the Chinese Eastern Railway, a "core" of Chinese power was built up in the center of the great Manchurian Plain, and the center of gravity of the Chinese population tended to shift from the valley of the lower Liao into the Great Plain. While the dynamic energy of this period of expansion was derived primarily from the use of railways, older economic factors were by no means entirely superseded. The use of inland waterways (with steamers to offset the unfavorable direction of the current) established "ribbons" of Chinese settlements leading out from the main body of the Chinese population into the valleys of the Yalu, Nonni, Sungari, Ussuri, and Amur rivers, and colonization continued to seek primarily the regions in which long-range export of agricultural produce could be balanced by the building of cities, each of which maintained a short-range exchange of trade with a surrounding rural area.

The river system of Manchuria radiates from the center of the country toward both north and south, and with the construction of supplementary canals could be made to serve the whole of the interior. The chief cargo traffic is the export of agricultural produce, with timber as an important secondary export. For such freights the rivers are conspicuously well adapted, as all of them flow outwards, favoring export as against import trade. The Liao river made possible the earliest Chinese penetration of Manchuria. The Yalu was not so favorable, in the early period, partly because of its strong current and partly because of the mountainous and forested character of its valley. In the modern period, the most important potential waterways are the Amur and

Ussuri, both of which are frontier rivers with one bank held by the Soviet Union, and the splendid Sungari, with its great affluents, the Nonni and Hurka or Mutan. The whole of this northern river system, including also the Tumen, on the frontier of Manchuria and Korea, is oriented toward the Soviet Union; above all, the Russians hold the entire lower course of the Amur, below the infall of the Ussuri, which gives them absolute control of river communication with the sea. During the summer, seagoing vessels can ascend the Amur as far as Habarovsk, in Soviet territory; but it is doubtful if seagoing vessels could ever reach Manchurian ports on the Ussuri or Sungari.

The most economic method of handling such bulky freights as grain and timber would be to float cargoes down the Sungari, Amur, and Ussuri to Habarovsk, with a minimum expenditure of fuel and labor, and there load them direct into seagoing vessels. Timber, in particular, cannot be towed upstream at a profit to reach the Manchurian railways. While, therefore, the present railway system of Manchuria is oriented toward the south and east, to favor trade through the Korean port of Seishin and the Manchurian ports of Dairen and Hulutao, the railways largely pull against the natural economic direction of the rivers, instead of supplementing them. If, therefore, at any future time, the Soviet Union should gain an ascendancy over Japan, it would be perfectly simple to switch the orientation of the railways so that they would work together with the rivers, diverting the economic communications of all North Manchuria toward Siberia. For the same reason, any speculations about possible Japanese conquest in Eastern Siberia must take into consideration the natural economic orientation of North Manchuria as well as the economic and strategic characteristics of the Russian Far East itself.

THE GEOGRAPHY OF FOREIGN PRESSURE

The Japanese position in Manchuria before 1931 derived from treaties following the Sino-Japanese and Russo-Japanese wars, modified subsequently by treaties between the three governments, and by agreements entered into by the South Manchuria Railway acting as a corporation. This railway was designed to define and dominate a Japanese sphere of influence in Southern Manchuria. One of the categorical safeguards was a stipulation that no railway should be built, with either Chinese or foreign capital, parallel to the South Manchuria system. No distance at which a parallel railway might be constructed was defined. The Japanese Government never explicitly abandoned this treaty safeguard, but the South Manchuria Railway, acting as a corporation, did make liberal concessions, both in allowing the construction of Chinese lines and in financing them.

The Russian position was also founded on treaties following the Sino-Japanese and Russo-Japanese wars. This position was also modified by subsequent treaties between the three governments, and by agreements between the Chinese Eastern and South Manchuria Railways as corporations. The Russian position was additionally complicated by events following on the fall of the old Russian Government and the establishment of a new one. This in turn led to difficulties because of the anomalous and ill-defined international relation between the Soviet Union and China, and because of often conflicting negotiations between different Chinese interests and the Railway as a corporation, and between the Soviet Government and the provincial authorities of Manchuria, as well as between the Soviet Government and the Central Government of China, whose unstable authority and fluctuating interest sometimes coincided and sometimes conflicted with those of the provinces.

The international factors, acting sometimes in the way of pressure and at other times in the way of more or less inert resistance, made it necessary for the Chinese to work within a sort of fence. Although necessarily they proceeded often by temporary expedients, yet there was a certain continuity and drift in their policy, as a result of which a solid Chinese core in Manchuria was formed, with a "Japanese front" on the southeast and east, a "Russian front" on the northeast and north, and a "Mongol front" (complicated by Russian interests) on the west. Although Chinese colonization and many Chinese exploiting interests did spread beyond the railway fence of the Chinese Eastern and South Manchuria lines, yet these lines formed recognizable frontiers impeding the full effect of Chinese expansion. The Chinese core which they enveloped from east to north was the scene of the most confident Chinese activity, and by inevitable consequence the "Mongol front" on the west, where non-Chinese interests were least positively defined, was the outlet toward which Chinese expansionism pressed most assertively.

The railways of the "core" of Manchuria, in spite of Japanese financial interests which extended the influence of the South Manchuria Railway, were dominated by the most solid expansionist force of China. Their function was to round the southern escarpment of the Inner Mongolian plateau and then to reach northwestward, approaching the Hsingan range and the grasslands of Outer Mongolia. They would thus, in time, have turned the flank of the Gobi, which has always been the chief bar to a decisive Chinese expansion from the south, and have opened up a vast new scope for Chinese action both in Manchuria and in Mongolia. This in turn would have reoriented the triple interests of China, Japan, and Russia in northeastern Asia. From this it can be seen how devastating was the effect of the Japanese blow at Mukden in September, 1931. It completely shattered the Chinese "core" of Manchuria, and by eliminating Chinese initiative in the affairs of Manchuria, from within Manchuria, it destroyed the buffer between Japan and Russia.

THE NEW MAP OF MANCHURIA

Until 1931, Manchuria consisted of the three provinces of Fengt'ien (for a while called Liaoning, until the name of Fengt'ien was restored after the Japanese conquest) and Kirin and Heilungchiang. Jehol had been added to the Manchurian group of provinces in 1928, when it was made a province, its governor being one of the original adherents of Chang Tso-lin, the "Old Marshal." Its historical connections with Manchuria were close; it had once been almost entirely held by the Mongols of the two Leagues of Jo-oda and Josoto, whose alliance with the Manchus at the beginning of the seventeenth century had opened the way to the conquest of China. In the southern part of the province, the Mongols had long since been outnumbered by the Chinese, but in the northern part, although Chinese colonization had recently begun to gather momentum, chiefly through the use of a railway approaching Jehol from Manchuria, the Mongols still predominated.

The State of Manchukuo was created in 1932, following on the Japanese invasion of 1931. In 1933, through the exertions of a special expeditionary force, Jehol was definitely added to Manchuria. Even before 1933, however, a new provincial organization had been started. The first step was to take those parts of the great Mongol domain in Western Manchuria which still remained recognizably Mongol in population and interest, detach them from the provinces which had been absorbing them, and form them into a separate Mongol province, with a special relation to the new Central Government, different from that of the "Chinese" provinces.

Within this province, to which the name of Hsingan was given, the tribal, territorial, and historical divisions of the Mongols themselves were recognized by the formation of four subprovinces. The Northern, or Barga, division consists of that part of the province of Heilungchiang which lies west of the Hsingan range, with the exception of the territory in the north draining to the Amur. The Eastern, or Nonni, division consists of the eastern slopes of the Hsingan range, draining to the Nonni. The Southern, or Jerim, division consists of those parts of the Jerim League of Mongols which had not as yet been smothered under Chinese colonization, the heavily colonized districts being left within the provinces of Fengt'ien, Kirin, and Heilungchiang. The Western division consists of the majority of the territory of the Jo-oda League, in Northern Jehol; part of the Jo-oda territory, and all of the Josoto League, being left within the province of Jehol. Mongol communities that were left out of this autonomous Mongol province were granted some degree of protection through local "offices of Mongol affairs" within the Chinese-populated provinces of Jehol, Fengt'ien, Kirin and Heilungchiang.[3]

At the end of 1934 a further administrative reorganization created eleven new provinces out of the five provinces of Jehol, Fengt'ien, Kirin, Heilungchiang and Hsingan. These provinces are as follows:

[3] For fuller discussion of Hsingan Province, and of Mongol questions in Manchuria, see *The Mongols of Manchuria,* by Owen Lattimore (New York: John Day, 1934).

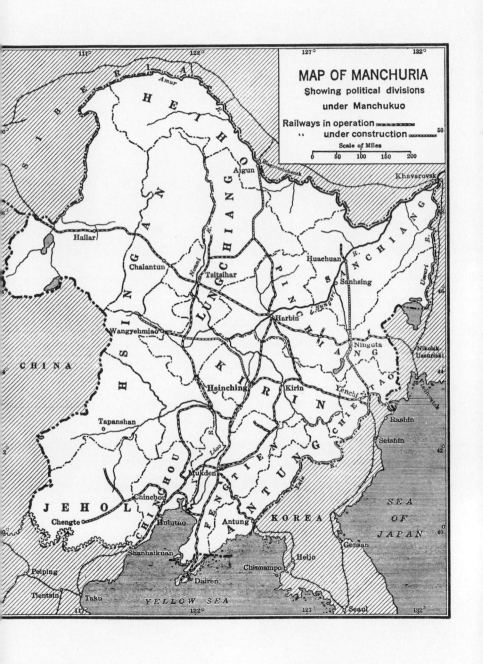

MAP OF MANCHURIA

Showing political divisions
under Manchukuo

Railways in operation ══════
" under construction ═══════ 50

Scale of Miles

0   50   100   150   200

SIBERIA

Amur R.

HEILUNGCHIANG

Aigun

Blagoveshchensk

Khavarovsk

Hailar

Chalantun

Nonni R.

Tsitsihar

PINCHIANG

Huachuan

Sanhsing

SANCHIANG

Ussuri R.

Usuri R.

46

HSINGAN

Wangyehmiao

LUNGCHIANG

Harbin

Sungari R.

Ninguta

Nikolsk
Ussuriski

CHINA

KIRIN

Hsinching

Kirin

Yenchi

CHIENTAO

44

Tapanshan

Rashin

Seishin

42

JEHOL

CHINCHOU

Liao R.

Mukden

FENGTIEN

ANTUNG

KOREA

SEA

OF

JAPAN

Chinchou

Chengte

Hulutao

Antung

Heijo

Gensan

40

Shanhaikuan

Yalu R.

Peiping

Chinnampo

Tientsin

Taku

Dairen

YELLOW SEA

Seoul

Hsingan, consisting of four subprovinces, as already described. Additional Mongol territory, south of the Shira Muren or upper Liao river, was taken from Jehol and added to Hsingan at the time of reorganization.

Jehol. At the expense of China, a certain amount of territory has been added to this province on the south, in order to make its frontiers march with the Great Wall. On the north it has been cut down by the allotment of territory to the western division of Hsingan, and on the east a stretch of territory drained by the Talingho, flowing eastward out of Jehol to the Gulf of Liaotung, has been allotted to the new province of Chinchou. The present territory of Jehol is therefore restricted to the mountainous country which forms the southern front and eastern end of the Mongolian plateau escarpment.

Chinchou. This new province stands astride of the Willow Palisade. It includes on the west the basin of the Talingho, taken from Jehol province, and on the east the Shanhaikuan corridor, the strip of coastal plain leading from Manchuria to China, taken from the province of Fengt'ien. It is a strategic province, in which meet the lines of communication between Jehol and what may be called Manchuria proper, and between Manchuria and China. Its importance in the sphere of communications is emphasized by the port of Hulutao, on which converge the railways of the western part of Manchuria.

Fengt'ien. This province, greatly cut down in area, now contains the region in which the maximum concentration of Chinese population is to be found, including both the main part of the old Chinese Pale between the Willow Palisade and Inner Willow Palisade, and the region adjacent to the Willow Palisade on the northwest, which was earliest and most completely assimilated to the Chinese Pale. By straightening the Kirin frontier, a little bit of Kirin territory has been allotted to Fengt'ien. The reduction in the size of Fengt'ien province is due to the cession of territory to the new provinces of Chinchou on the west and Antung on the east, but above all to the cutting off of the great Mongol territories in what used to be the northwestern extension of Fengt'ien, which have been allotted to Hsingan province.

Antung. This new province has been formed out of the mountainous eastern and northeastern part of Fengt'ien province, including the whole western side of the Yalu valley and extending over to the western side of the watershed. A large part of the territory is forested. The southerly part of it includes a region into which Koreans have penetrated during recent years. The new province is a kind of halfway house between Korea and Manchuria, and can easily be used for spreading Korean population into Manchuria. A port of its own, at Antung, at the mouth of the Yalu, gives it an economic focus.

Kirin. This ancient province has been deprived of much more than half of its former territory, out of which have been formed, in part, the new provinces of Chientao, Pinchiang and Sanchiang. In the area that remains are concentrated most of what may be called the "typical" Manchus—those who can now be distinguished from the Chinese only by class characteristics, rather than racial characteristics. Even these Manchus are greatly outnumbered by the Chinese; but the Chinese of this region derive in the main from the old period of infiltration, not from the modern period of mass-migration. They are socially conservative, and are on the whole well assimilated to a kind of Manchurian regionalism. The western part of the province includes a good deal of old Mongol territory in which the Mongols, though still numerous, are outnumbered by Chinese.

Chientao. This new province is, as a region, old and distinct. Within it, the Korean population probably outnumbers the Chinese. Most of the Koreans are not recent immigrants, but the descendants of a long-established population which held the region at the time of the rise of the Manchu dynasty, at the beginning of the seventeenth century. Once a rear-guard of the Koreans who were being driven out of Manchuria by Manchus and Chinese, they are now a vanguard of Korean penetration into Manchuria. The southerly part of Chientao includes a certain amount of territory taken from Fengt'ien. The province reaches right down to the sea, at the mouth of the Tumen river; and at this point the frontiers of Korea, Manchuria, and the Vladivostok region of Siberia meet.

Pinchiang. This new province has been formed out of a belt of territory stretching across the middle of what used to be Kirin province, on both sides of the Eastern line of the Chinese Eastern Railway, together with the basin of the Hulan river and its tributaries, which has been detached from the province of Heilungchiang. Most of the territory of the new province is fairly well settled and, being well served with railways, is open to further development. It consists largely of the economic area tributary to Harbin.

Sanchiang. This province, also new, has been formed out of territory on both sides of the lower valley of the Sungari, taken from the provinces of Heilungchiang and Kirin. The Sungari flows right through it, the Amur along its northern frontier, and the Ussuri along part of its eastern frontier. While the land adjacent to the Sungari, and to a lesser degree the land near the Amur and Ussuri, has been well settled by Chinese within recent years, the majority of the province is open to new development. Japanese colonization has already been tried at one or two points, and it might be possible, if the funds are available, to establish an important Japanese and Korean population which, without running into overwhelming numbers, would alter the general balance of populations within Manchuria. Weight of numbers is not necessarily the deciding factor in population; it can be offset by advantages of position and organization.

Lungchiang. The name of this province has been abbreviated from Heilungchiang, the Chinese name for the Amur. The new province is simply the central part of Heilungchiang, the Barga Mongol region and part of the western side of the Nonni river valley having been detached and made over to Hsingan province, and the northern territory, draining to the Amur, having been formed into the new province of Heiho. The province as now constituted is a natural geographical and economic unit, occupying almost the whole of the Nonni river basin. It includes important Mongol, Daghor, and Manchu racial minorities, but the bulk of the population is Chinese, and the trend of development favors the predominance of the Chinese.

Heiho. This new province has been formed out of the fringe of northern territory in the valley of the Amur detached from the former province of Heilungchiang. The province is mountainous and almost entirely forested. Many of the short streams flowing into the Amur are gold-bearing. While there are villages along the Amur, the only considerable town is Aigun or Heiho. The province as a whole is more suitable for development through forestry and mining than through colonization.

Kuantung Leased Territory. This territory, while not a province, deserves separate treatment. The narrow ribbon of land through which the South Manchuria Railway runs, and the railway concessions adjoining several important towns, are usually listed together with the Leased Territory. Their status derives from the treaties following the Russo-Japanese War, and they are directly administered by Japan, not by Manchukuo. The port of Dairen, the key to the approach by sea to Manchuria, stands in the Leased Territory. It may well be said that these Japanese vested interests are the root from which sprang the great and sudden tree of Manchukuo. The fruit of this tree, whose value is bitterly disputed, has not yet been plucked.

CHAPTER II

THE "RESERVOIR" OF TRIBAL INVASIONS

OLD NON-CHINESE POPULATIONS

THE modern Chinese colonization of Manchuria began in the eighteen hundred and nineties, following on measures adopted by the Imperial (Manchu) Government, which modi-fied the theory and practice of land tenure, and imparted in important respects a fresh character to the process of colo-nization. The rate of colonization did not however accelerate for many years, and it was only about 1926-28 that spectacular newspaper accounts of the "millions" migrating from China to Manchuria began to draw popular attention in the Western world.

When the modern period began, population elements in Manchuria were comparatively static, and their distribution was well defined. In Liaoning province, east of the Liao river, was a Chinese population, typically Chinese in culture, but with a peculiar social status, owing to the large numbers of Han Chün or Chinese Bannermen, politically and socially identified with the Manchus. Numbers of true Manchus were also settled in this part of Liaoning (Fengtien) province.

It may be as well at this point to clarify to some extent the use of the terms "Banner" and "Bannerman." The Manchu Ban-ner may have been originally the military levy of a particular tribe, contributed to the army of all the Manchus. Later it became a military administrative unit, the tribal association being replaced by a regional association. In every suitable region, a system of eight Banners was formed. As young men reached the military age of sixteen, and passed the military tests, they were assigned to Banners. Thereafter they drew a military subsidy, and could be called upon for active service. Each family was associated with a Banner, but the Banner was not a tribe, and members of the same clan might be associated with different Banners. For instance, the "Bordered Blue Banners" of Tsitsihar, Kirin, and Peking, respectively, had no connection with one another, tribal or administrative.

In Southern Manchuria, when the Manchus began to enroll Chinese troops, they introduced the same regional militia system of series of eight Banners. In such regions, where both Manchu and Chinese troops were enrolled, each banner would have two "battalions" (so to speak)—one Manchu, one Chinese. In Peking, each Banner was in reality a triple formation, with Manchu, Mongol, and Chinese "battalions." In the Chahar region of Mongolia, which came under the Manchus by conquest, not by alliance, the Mongol princes were deposed and the Manchu Banner system substituted.

The Mongol Banner in regions which came over to the Manchus by alliance, or where the conquest was not thorough enough for the Manchus to depose the princes, is something quite different. It is a compromise between the Mongol tribal system and the Manchu military system. Hence it still retains a tribal connotation which the Manchu and Chinese Banners did not have. This type of Mongol Banner has always remained an hereditary tribal unit, ruled by an hereditary chief.

In the western part of Liaoning was a Mongol population. These Mongols also extended into the western plain of Kirin province (west of Ch'angch'un) and northward to Petuna and Tsitsihar. The historic boundary between Mongols on the west and Chinese and Manchus on the east was the Willow

Palisade, which ran from north of the Great Wall through Ichou and Fak'umen and Ssup'ingkai, then a little east of Ch'angch'un and on to the Sungari. At Tungchiangtze, where the Palisade crossed the Liao, a branch went off east and southeast, defining the most ancient "pale" of Chinese penetration and settlement. The Mongols west of the Willow Palisade derived from the migrations of the great Mongol conquests in the twelfth and thirteenth centuries..

In Kirin province, not, in the first place, in the Sungari valley but in the valley of the Mutanchiang or Hurka, as far north as its junction with the Sungari at Sanhsing, was the true country of the Manchus. Their oldest centers were at Sanhsing and Ninguta, from which they later spread to the upper Sungari in the region of Kirin city, and still later, with the growth of their military power, all along the western slopes of the Ch'angpaishan until they overlooked and dominated Liaoning province, where they established a capital at Mukden in the first half of the seventeenth century, prior to their conquest of China.

The Manchus appear never to have penetrated in numbers east of the Ch'angpaishan. This eastern country, not only in Kirin but in Liaoning (Fengtien, or Mukden Province) was "old Korean." The Koreans must once have been well established, and the popular name for ruins of cities and fortifications is still "Korean cities"; but they left little ethnic trace, and their withdrawal must have been practically complete by the rise of the Manchus at the beginning of the seventeenth century. Only between the Ch'angpaishan and the Yalu, in heavily forested, mountainous country, is it probable that Koreans then lingered; and they, from the nature of the country, cannot have been numerous. The establishment of Korean settlers in eastern Fengtien (Hsingching region) and eastern Kirin (Hunchun region and Ussuri valley) is a modern phenomenon. The Koreans, however, did leave certain cultural traces, notably in the type of dwelling house, and it is a question, not clear but all the more interesting, how many of the non-Chinese characteristics of the Manchus may be of Korean derivation. The question is further complicated by the fact that the Tungus, from whom the Manchus were differentiated at a late period, appear to have had an early influence in Korea.

In northern Kirin and Heilungchiang, in the valleys of the Ussuri and lower Sungari, and generally speaking all the forested lands draining to the Amur, as well as in the Nonni valley, were tribes racially connected with the Tungus and thus with the Manchus. After the rise of the Manchu power, the kinship of most of these tribes was recognized by including them as auxiliaries in the Manchu military Banner organization, under the designation of New Manchus. These tribes were never numerous, and the chief interest of their distribution is historic and schematic.

In the Nonni valley, from the lip of the Amur basin southward to Tsitsihar, were tribes that showed a merging of the characteristics of Tungus hunters (originally, most of them, without doubt reindeer owners as well) and Mongol pastoral nomads. Thus the Solons, who within living memory extended as far down the Hsingan range as the T'ao river headwaters, where the town of Solun preserves their name, now survive as only a few wretched families—except west of the Hsingan, where the almost completely Mongolized "Mongol-Solon" would hardly be recognized as kin of the original Solon forest hunters. Of the mixed Mongol-Tungus tribes the most important were the Daghurs, whose ready acceptance of Manchu influence made them important instruments of Manchu policy. As Manchu Bannermen some of them migrated west of the Hsingan, where they are still important

as officials and traditional leaders among the predominantly
Mongol population.

Finally, west of the Hsingan, in a region so large and important as to continue at the present time a recognizable political sub-division of Heilungchiang province, is the Barga
country. In the fringe of forest west of the Hsingan watershed a few Tungusic elements are still distinguishable, but
the great plains are decidedly Mongol, and political questions are Mongol-Chinese-Russian. The Mongols of Barga
are tribally and politically separate both from the Eastern
Mongols of Liaoning province and the Mongols of Outer
Mongolia. Their country is a sort of bay of Mongolia, which
appears to have been comparatively little affected by the great
upheaval of the Mongol tribes in the twelfth and thirteenth
centuries, not being swept by the migrations, but receiving
the backwash and sheltering the fragments of many tribes.
There is evidence, in the different structure of the aristocracy
and the comparative weakness of the monastic lama hierarchy, of the late impact of alien influences. The reluctance of
the Barga tribes, during the recent years of political unrest, to
associate themselves definitely with either Inner or Outer
Mongolia is also the result of long isolation and lack of association with the tribal affairs of other groups.

The conglomeration of Barga tribes includes, besides groups
related to the Khalkhas of Outer Mongolia and to the neighboring Leagues of Inner Mongolia, a few descendants of a far
western group, the Ölöt or Jungar Mongols, of whom some
were deported to Barga after the Manchu-Chinese conquest
of Chinese Turkestan. There are also a few Buriats, whose
ancient habitat was east of Lake Baikal in Siberia, who migrated to Barga some generations ago; and there are the
Mongol-Solon, Daghur, and other mixed groups. In recent
years there has been a secondary immigration of Trans-

Baikalian Buriats, dissatisfied with Soviet rule, which further complicates the interest of Soviet Russia.

The pressing problems of Barga are modern, and date from the construction of the Chinese Eastern Railway, which broke in on the old isolation. Since the eighteen hundred and nineties and the beginning of Chinese reaction against the advance of Russia, the Barga tribes have been threatened with submersion under a wave of Chinese immigration; in face of which they have distinguished themselves among the "native" elements in Manchuria by the effectiveness of their resistance. Several risings, with more or less open support from Russia, have staved off the Chinese advance, but have by no means decided the issue. In the effort to break down this resistance there have been several abortive attempts at asserting a Chinese "forward policy." It can now be foreseen that the "Barga question" will become acute again with the progress of the new T'ao-an-Solun Railway, which in time is to be projected toward the Siberian frontier. This railway, taking off from the Chinese system in the "core" of Manchuria, will cut off a large part of Barga from Outer Mongolia, will flank the Chinese Eastern Railway, and will provide a new route for Chinese colonists and Chinese troops to support them; for at present the transport of Chinese troops along the Chinese Eastern Railway is hampered by recurrent disputes between the Russian and Chinese interests concerned over the question of fares to be paid.

THE TRIBES AND THE "RESERVOIRS"

Wherever the old populations and old social conditions of Manchuria can still be detected, it is easy to discern the effects of a well-defined historical process; the periodic assault on China of barbarian tribes from the north, alternating with

Chinese reactions which threw back the invaders and extended Chinese authority and influence into barbarian territories. Manchuria, sometimes as an appendage of Mongolia, occasionally through the independent action of Manchurian tribes, has for more than a score of centuries been concerned in this cyclical process.

The process itself can be concisely described, for it has followed a curiously regular, almost stereotyped course. At different periods barbarian tribes north of the Great Wall have descended on China, establishing kingdoms and sometimes empires of greater or less territorial extent. Thus in the fourth century the Hsiungnu, after capturing two successive Chinese emperors, forced the Chinese to move their capital to the site of Nanking. In the fifth and sixth centuries the Wei dynasty, founded by the Toba Tatars, ruled a great part of North China, with its capital first at Ta T'ung (Northern Shansi) and then at Loyang in Honan. The T'ang dynasty of the seventh, eighth and ninth centuries was founded with the aid of tribal allies, and its power depended essentially on its tribal policy north of the Great Wall. In the tenth and eleventh centuries the Liao (Khitan) dynasty, originating in Manchuria, conquered China as far as the Yellow River, with a capital first at Liaoyang in Manchuria and then at Peking. In the twelfth century the Liao were overthrown, not by the Chinese but by another Manchurian horde, that of the Chin (Nüchen), who extended the conquest of China as far as the Yangtze. The Chin, in turn, were overthrown by other barbarians—the Mongols, who established the Yüan dynasty and completed the conquest of China. The Mongols, under Chinghis himself, had already overthrown the Western Hsia or Tangut kingdom (a non-Chinese state), which had occupied what is now Kansu in Northwestern China.

Thus when the purely Chinese Ming dynasty drove out the Mongols in the fourteenth century, China within the Great Wall was cleared of tribal dominance for the first time in many centuries; and even so the Mongols were still so strong that within a hundred years they were able to return, invade China and carry the Ming emperor into captivity, holding him for eight years.

Owing, however, to the fact that each alien dynasty, as it matured, became more and more Chinese, the reflex action of Chinese culture north of the Great Wall was never lacking. Invariably the conquerors took over the Chinese dynastic model for their ruling families and Chinese forms of government for their new territories; and, gradually losing the characteristics of conquering aliens, became essentially a Chinese ruling class. Just as invariably, when the power of the dynasty waned, a Chinese reaction, tinged with racial animosity, took place. The dynasty was overthrown, the Chinese power moved north once more, sometimes as far as the Great Wall, sometimes even north of it, and an effort was made to define afresh the boundaries between civilization and barbarism. Whoever seized the power after the overthrow of the alien dynasty established a new dynasty; and when this in turn decayed the next invasion from the north swept over the Great Wall.

During these fluctuations of conquest, a remarkable stratification became established, which may be schematically described as Great Wall–Inner Mongolia–Outer defense walls–Gobi–Outer Mongolia. While it is not possible here to go fully into the profound significance of the Great Wall, it can be pointed out that the frontier line it represents is the most ancient and fundamental line of cleavage between a highly individual civilization and a form of tribal barbarism only less individual and persistent. It is the country immediately north of the Great Wall which most urgently needs the attention of the historian. This region appears to be considered most commonly as the area of maximum effect of outward-spreading Chinese culture. While its historic position in this respect is obvious enough, it has another function of at least equal importance. It is the "reservoir" area of the successive northern invaders of China.

The Manchu conquest demonstrates most clearly a process which must have accompanied every previous conquest of the Manchu type. In this "reservoir," dominating the Great Wall by virtue of the plateau formation of Inner Mongolia, was repeatedly established a population composed of tribal followers of the conquest, who remained outside of the conquered territory but were identified with the alien dynasty within the Great Wall. It supplied officials and troops to participate in the rule of China, and drew from China a great deal of wealth in the form of subsidies to the tribal chiefs. The Banner tribes of Inner Mongolia, who extend eastward into western Liaoning province, are a living survival of the "reservoir" system.

North of the "reservoir" lay another great zone, of which the part most easily recognized at the present day is Outer Mongolia. Here lay the lands of the "unregenerate," the tribes which had not participated as allies or auxiliaries of the conquest in North China. The Gobi from west to east, and the Hsingan range from south to north, mark the physical distinction between the "reservoir" and the lands of the unregenerate; but the geographical cleavage was emphasized by a system of frontier defenses, which may still be detected south of the Gobi and east of the Hsingan. The fact that these defenses are Chinese in type has led to their being considered chiefly as *outworks* of the Great Wall system. Outworks they were, in truth, during the periods of Chinese ascendancy; but at every period of the domination of an alien dynasty in China they became *rearguard defenses*. For one of the most important duties of the "reservoir" population, and the duty which explains why they did not all enter China, was that of staving off possible rival invasion on the part of "unregenerate" tribes not associated with the new dynasty.

It cannot even be considered certain that the outer defense systems were first constructed as outward-facing Chinese frontiers. Nothing is more obvious than that establishment in the "reservoir" as privileged tribesmen had a pronounced effect on the territorial and social organization of the tribes. It is also beyond dispute that some at least of the ruined cities of Chinese type which characterize the "reservoir" zone, and have led to its being considered the region of maximum Chinese impact, were not constructed during periods of Chinese ascendancy, but were in fact "luxuries" which the tribal chiefs allowed themselves as part of their share of the spoil of China. If, as is quite certain, tribes associated with the "reservoir" system tended to become stabilized and decreasingly nomadic, while their chiefs tended to convert the prerogatives of chieftainship into the powers of a fixed hereditary aristocracy strongly affected by Chinese ideas, and to build Chinese towns and import Chinese craftsmen and traders, then it is highly probable that they also emphasized their new static position by constructing static defenses of the Chinese type between themselves and the "unregenerate" tribes.

Naturally, during periods of Chinese ascendancy, these towns of Chinese type, with partially Chinese populations, must have tended to become more active centers of the radiation of Chinese influences. It should, however, be a prime object of future research in Mongolia and Manchuria (and Chinese Turkestan as well) to determine as clearly as possible how far the spread of Chinese cultural elements is to be re-

garded as an assertive and positive expression of Chinese advance, and how far as "loot" brought back by the barbarians
themselves. It is even probable that the elements brought by
the Chinese themselves as indispensable and the elements
chosen by the barbarians as forms of plunder can often be
distinguished.

What emerges from all these considerations is a principle
of the very highest importance. The "reservoir" region, both
during periods of barbarian ascendancy and periods of
Chinese ascendancy, is to be regarded as the key to the
sovereignty of North China—often of all China. It therefore has a *regional* importance which transcends both its
racial and its cultural importance. However triumphant the
northward spread of Chinese power, any Chinese population
flowing into the "reservoir" region inevitably becomes even
more conscious of the fact that it can now exercise a control
over the affairs of China behind it than that it can press
forward to fresh conquests of barbarian territories. The overthrow of the Mongol dynasty of the Yüan and the establishment of the Ming was the last great resurgence of the Chinese
power. Yet the Chinese population established in South Manchuria under the Ming became so regional in consciousness
that it allied itself with the rising Manchu power and turned
back to the conquest of China. Even at the present time, the
disastrous defeats of the Manchurian armies in the quarrel
with Russia over the Chinese Eastern Railway in the winter
of 1929–30 had far less effect on the imagination of the mass
of the population in China than any one of the incursions
within the Great Wall of the racially and culturally Chinese
but regionally Manchurian armies of Chang Tso-lin and his
son Chang Hsüeh-liang—not to mention the fact that the
quasi-dynastic succession of political power in Manchuria is
of deep significance. The crucial importance of such a region-

alism, oriented as it is *toward* China with a tenacity apparently not to be overcome by any rise of nationalistic feeling, can hardly be exaggerated in a study of Chinese colonization beyond the Great Wall.

MONGOL, MANCHU AND CHINESE

The historical distinction between Manchuria and Mongolia is not nearly so sharp as that of modern times. The stratification of defense lines, "reservoir" and outer unregenerate territory is more easily illustrated by Mongolian examples, because Manchuria is the dead-end of the great migration ground of Eurasia. In Manchuria, of necessity, the currents of migration have turned and eddied. There is a little-known and almost uninvestigated frontier fortification which is a key to the warping of the historical strata. It runs from some point north of Jehol, follows the eastern watershed of the Hsingan, and extends almost to the Amur—perhaps all the way. In spite of the extreme northern extension of this wall, probably to be explained by the far northward reach of power under the Liao and Chin dynasties of the tenth and twelfth centuries—both of which originated in Manchuria —the "reservoir" area of Manchuria, roughly and on the average of history, may be defined as all of Liaoning (Fengtien) and Kirin provinces lying south of latitude forty-six degrees North. This "reservoir" is contiguous with Inner Mongolia, though it reaches farther to the north, and has the same historical function. Northernmost Kirin and all of Heilungchiang, which lie north of this latitude, are an ancient no-man's-land, with an historical importance comparable to that of Outer Mongolia.

The peculiarity of "reservoir" Manchuria is the triple balance that was established there, as an essential preliminary to the Manchu conquest of China, between Mongols, Manchus and Chinese. Without going into detail, it may be stated that the Manchu military power was based on an *alliance* between Manchus and Mongols, and an *amalgamation* between the Manchus and the highly "regional" Chinese of the "reservoir." This early grouping was perpetuated in regional sub-divisions which had much of the character of "spheres of interest," which persisted up to the beginning of the modern period, which can still be traced, and which had an important bearing on local conceptions of the bases of land tenure and social organization.

One of the remarkable points of interest of the outer defense walls of the ancient "reservoir" is the fact that, though they are locally attributed to different dynasties or culture-heroes, like Yao Fei (Yüeh Fei) or Chin Wu-chu, or Chinghis Khan they almost everywhere are still recognized as tribal or sub-tribal boundaries. It is significant that the Mongols concerned in the Manchu Conquest (whose heirs in modern Manchuria are the Banners of the Cherim, Chao-uda and Chosotu Leagues) held a territory south of the Gobi and east of the Hsingan and the Hsingan Outer Wall. On the east, the boundary between them and the Chinese and Manchus (confirmed under the Manchu dynasty) was the Willow Palisade. Thus they belonged not to the outermost barbarians of the "unregenerate" lands, but to the ancient tribal "reservoir"; in fact they were, in the main, descendants of the Mongols of the Yüan dynasty, who had been displaced in China by the Ming. For this reason (a fact never sufficiently emphasized) there were elements of hostility in their alliance with the Manchus. There was in fact a close race for power between Manchus and Mongols, and the later Manchu policy, throughout the "reservoir," was confronted with the double problem of preserving the usefulness of the Mongols

as military auxiliaries, while preventing the recrudescence of
a Mongol power that might rival their own. Thus by trick-
ery and coercion, and occasionally by planting Chinese colonies, they edged the Mongols away from certain strategic
points overlooking the Great Wall barrier; but on the whole
they supported the tribalism of the Mongols and maintained
the integrity of Mongol tribal domains. Thus the Mongols
even in our own time continue to be a tribal people, while the
Manchus long ago became Chinese; and not only is it difficult
to distinguish Manchus from Chinese, even in the remotest regions, but the very bases of distinction, from a comparatively
early period, ceased to be racial and became wholly social.

The Manchus were, from the beginning, without either
the strong tribal consciousness or the strong historical traditions of the Mongols. They appear to have filtered in from
the outer no-man's-land to the "reservoir" and though they
endowed themselves offhand with a tradition of descent from
the Nüchen-Chin,[1] they rose to power with such rapidity
that they never thoroughly absorbed the tradition and spirit
of the "reservoir"; they rather created a new, modified "reservoir"-regional tradition of their own.

This very immaturity facilitated their extraordinarily rapid
and thorough assumption of Chinese characteristics. Indeed
nothing could be more evident (though the fact is usually
given very little weight) than that the Manchus, from a very
early period, not only looked on China as a country to conquer, but on Chinese civilization as something to aspire to.

---

[1] While there was no political continuity between the Nüchen and the Manchus,
there was a certain racial kinship, in that they both derived from the same
general Tungusic stock. Out of this tribal group the Nüchen emerged, to found
the Chin dynasty; on the fall of the dynasty, at least part of them fell back into
the wilderness and merged again with the tribes. Centuries later the Manchus
emerged from the same tribal group; and had it not been for the impact of the
West, breaking up the cycle of Chinese frontier history, the most northerly of the
Manchus left in Manchuria would, on the fall of the dynasty, have relapsed in
the same way into a "tribal" state.

There is some reason to suppose that the Manchus derived from a stock which originally owned reindeer, but lost the reindeer on moving south. If this is so, then the *necessity* of reorganization consequent on the loss of the reindeer economy may explain in part their rapid development toward the Chinese standard.

The Chinese then in southern Manchuria must have been in the main the immediate descendants of those who had participated in the last great Chinese expansion, under the Ming; although the Chinese foothold in southernmost Manchuria was already very old, and the larger body must therefore itself have been informed to a certain extent by the tradition of the oldest local Chinese elements. While characteristically Chinese in culture and social organization, they had taken on a strong "frontier" color, which is quite understandable in the light of the historical forces already elucidated. Thus they were, for their part, willing to accept the authority, and identify themselves with the drive, of the rising and aggressive Manchu group, which promised them a share of the power and wealth to be garnered in China— the rich land, the land of civilization and luxury; a land whose promise altogether overshadowed any promise of growth and expansion toward the barbarian wilderness.

It has never been sufficiently emphasized how *Chinese* the Manchus were by the time they entered China. Still less has it been realized how far they were outnumbered, in Manchuria itself, by the Chinese, or how easy it would have been for these Manchurian Chinese, had there been any genuine social motive power urging them toward outward expansion, to exterminate the Manchu tribes on their first appearance. Yet, in point of fact, Chinese were willingly incorporated, from the very beginning, in the Manchu military system, and thoroughly identified themselves, politically, with the Manchus. No one who has visited both the old Manchu and old Chinese regions of Manchuria and noticed the number, distribution and known age of towns and villages can doubt that, long before the Conquest, the largest numerical element in the Manchu armies must have been Chinese.

The Manchus, for their part, had taken on a thoroughly Chinese color. Their two emperors who ruled from Mukden before the entry into China were emperors in the Chinese manner. It is not too much to say that the final Manchu conquest of China was less an alien invasion than the triumph of the strongest regional faction in a colossal Chinese civil war. This is borne out by the fact that the Manchus actually passed through the Great Wall as a result of negotiation, and in alliance with one Chinese faction against another, which had already desecrated the Ming tombs and occupied Peking, where the last Ming emperor had hanged himself. It is further borne out by the rapidity and success with which the Manchus assumed the administration of China and carried it on in the Chinese manner.

It cannot be doubted that the *racial* character of certain laws of privilege passed by the Manchus has been greatly overemphasized. There was a residuum of racial feeling in some of these laws, but all of them, in operation, had an almost purely social function; and in any case their nominal racial character is vitiated by the fact that, from the beginning, Chinese Bannermen were counted as Manchus. The Banners themselves were purely a military, never a racial formation. The organization of distinct Chinese Banners must have been due initially to the overwhelming preponderance of Chinese in the southern part of Manchuria, who associated themselves politically with the Manchus; and although thereafter Manchu and Chinese Banners continued to be found frequently side by side, there were no grave distinctions between the races. Not only was intermarriage free (between Manchus and Chinese Bannermen), but it was certainly possible for a Chinese Bannerman, moving north into a district so preponderantly Manchu that no Chinese Banners were maintained, to change his registration to a Manchu Banner; although technically the change of registration was supposed to be only temporary. Thus the distinction between the Bannermen as a group and non-Bannermen as a group included Chinese among the privileged as well as among the unprivileged. In discussing "Manchu" history, the term "Bannerman" should in the great majority of cases be substituted for the term "Manchu"; and if this were done, the social intention of many laws and privileges would become clearer.

Thus, in the case of laws prohibiting Manchus from intermarrying with Chinese, it ought to be much better known that in fact there was no restriction on marriage between Manchus and Chinese Bannermen, and that at an early period Manchus began to marry non-Banner Chinese girls, although not giving their own daughters in marriage to non-Banner Chinese men. The laws forbidding Bannermen to engage in trade or agriculture [2] had the same intention as the marriage laws; the maintenance of a self-conscious class associated with the dynasty.

Among the most conspicuous Manchu laws were those restricting the immigration of Chinese into regions outside the Great Wall, and especially forbidding women to pass beyond this traditional frontier. Undoubtedly many individual Manchus felt that such laws maintained their privileged position in the "reservoir"; but equally there is no doubt that these laws, far from striking the generality of Chinese as

[2] Manchus within the "reservoir" in Manchuria, especially in Kirin, continued of course to engage in agriculture; these laws applied only to garrisons in China.

oppressive, satisfied the underlying feeling of Chinese state-craft, with which the Manchus had entirely identified themselves. The very nature of the Great Wall and the outer frontier fortifications was defensive. Throughout history it can be seen that the fundamental aim of Chinese statecraft was to control the border territories, not to occupy them. Colonies were planted always as expedients to control strategic points. There was no general urge toward the complete occupation of outlying territory; for a general spread of population toward the north would have upset the balance of the State, which was identified with a very ancient drift toward the south and east. *The north was, in general, the rear; only exceptionally the front.*

LAND TENURE AND TRIBAL ORGANIZATION

While there has apparently been a revolution in the Chinese feeling toward northward expansion, the effect on basic notions of land tenure of the different social organization of Mongols, Manchus and Chinese can still be detected, and has an important bearing on the methods of colonial expansion in the different "spheres" of the ancient "reservoir."

The relation of Mongol tribe to Mongol land emphasizes the profound cleavage between Mongols and Chinese. Undoubtedly the basic feeling of the Mongols is that the land belongs to the whole tribe. Neither individuals nor the chief may establish a prescriptive claim to personal ownership of any part of the land. Even the tribal ownership is probably to be understood according to a psychology different from that involved in any modern "state" ownership. We have undoubtedly to deal with ancient pure nomadic instinct, although the Mongols are now no more than semi-nomadic. The Mongol attitude toward the land is guided by an instinctive reluctance to identify people with land. It seeks to gratify the feeling that the tribe ought, on occasion, to be able simply to pick up and move off, flatly abandoning the old land. Except where tribal frontiers are defined by ancient walls, which basically do not govern the tribe as a tribe, but the tribe in its relation to China, even Mongol frontiers are curiously inexact. They are marked erratically by landmarks at conspicuous points, and govern, in the last analysis, not limits of ownership, but relations of war and peace. To pass between two of the landmarks of a tribe is not, essentially, to encroach on its land, but to challenge its freedom of movement.

When a tribe comes within the "reservoir," however, the attitude toward boundaries is necessarily modified, because it occupies thenceforth a "station" governed by the relationship with China. When the tribe is an auxiliary ally of an alien dynasty ruling in China, the machinery of recruiting tribal levies requires at least a rough knowledge of the fixed distribution of population according to territory. In order, therefore, to regularize the relations between the sovereign dynasty and the "reservoir" tribe, there is a distinct tendency to transform the chieftain, originally the leader of a horde, with powers fluctuating according to necessity, into a petty territorial princeling. This tendency, however, is not a manifestation of inward, spontaneous tribal feeling, but is produced by the pressure of its external relations. Thus we find that in modern times there is a distinct cleavage between the interests of princes and tribes, and that the closer the relations between the tribe and China the more stable and regular are the functions, rights and powers of the prince.

Under the Manchu dynasty, the princely families and the religious hierarchy were the elements most easily modified into regular channels of intercourse between the tribal "reservoir" and the civilized government of China. When colonies were planted to assure Manchu control of the passes overlooking the Great Wall, the necessary negotiations were conducted through the princes; and following this precedent Chinese colonization at the present time in Mongol lands continues to be regulated by negotiation between Chinese officials and Mongol princes or high ecclesiastical authorities. The inevitable consequence is that the princes play the double part of leaders in the occasional rebellions against China, and of profiteers who, when resistance is futile, take payment from the Chinese for the cession of tribal land, to the detriment of the tribe as a whole, making use of a kind of spurious title to *territorial* sovereignty which is only a modern fiction.

At the same time the older instinct still preserves the abhorrence of individual ownership of land within the territory occupied by the tribe. The idea that it is "impious" to cultivate land is merely a late "rational" explanation of the innate aversion for permanent, fixed identification of man and land. Thus historically and at the present time the Chinese penetrating into a region where tribal administration has not yet been replaced by direct Chinese administration is forced to modify his activities to conform with Mongol ideas. The result is that the Chinese frontiersman of the Mongol frontier is quite different, socially, from the frontiersman of the old Chinese and Manchu spheres within the Manchurian "reservoir."

The attitude of the Manchus toward the land was from the beginning essentially different. In the first place, even during the generally postulated nomadic period of their history, they were forest nomads, hunters and fishers; and it is much easier for the nomad of this type to establish a fixed holding than it is for the pastoral nomad with a "vested interest" in valuable herds which require at the minimum a winter and a summer range. The Manchus, at the time they emerge into history, appear to have had a loose social organization of villages by the side of streams in forested country. They had lived by fishing and hunting, before they began to practice conquest as a form of exploitation, and the garden-patch agriculture, found on the edges of their villages, though apparently it had been practiced for a considerable period, had not risen to a more than ancillary status.

The clan was the most important unit, notably for the control of marriage; but members of the same clan lived in different villages, and this weakened the importance of the villages, and of the identification of society and locality.

Under such conditions, land ownership can hardly have been of great importance, especially since land was both rich and plentiful along the streams. Nor was their relation to "wild" land the same as that of a tribal people like the Mongols. The intrusion of one pastoral tribe on the lands of another, or even on lands merely used by them when in migration, does not necessarily mean the eating up of pastures of which they stand in imperative need for their flocks, but it does mean interference with their scope of movement and control of their flocks. Among a people of riparian villages, on the other hand, hunting parties that strike away from the river settlements may well converge on the same group or range of hills, and the general interest is therefore best served by the principle that hills, forest and unsettled land are *public,* but that private ownership could be established by the settlement of an individual or a village. The social organization of the Manchus was obviously one that had not been so thoroughly worked out as to become rigid. With the assertion of a central military authority, they became at once a young nation, not a group of tribes, with a tendency to establish fixed communities in preference to ranges of migration—

and, in consequence, an initial sympathy for Chinese as against Mongol ideals. The Manchus, from an early period, worked on two lines of endeavor: to establish a political superiority over the Chinese, and to raise themselves to an equality of civilization with the Chinese. The first result of military unity was the establishment of a dynasty on the Chinese model, closely followed by the assumption of the whole Chinese conception of society, both in agricultural and town communities. The individual ownership of land was thus confirmed, and it became easy for "wild" lands to pass from a somewhat vague "public" classification into the much more definite category of "state" lands, to which a prescriptive right was affirmed on behalf of the sovereign.

The consequence was that when, in later times, the need of land was felt by either Manchus or Chinese "squatters," it was an easy matter to encroach on state lands, the officials being either indifferent or venial. "Uncontrolled" settlement at the present time can only be regarded as a continuation of this old process. It is extra-legal rather than illegal. The clearing of wild land is tacitly regarded as establishing a respectable claim. In such cases, as the country fills up and land boundaries become more important, it is necessary to legalize the tenure of the squatter; but he is far more likely to be accommodated by some form of compromise than to be summarily ejected.

CHAPTER III

EARLY CHINESE EXPANSION: CONQUEST AND COMPROMISE

CHINESE AND MONGOLS

THE fundamental divergence in social orientation between Mongol and Manchu explains the fact that two distinct types of Chinese frontiersman are to be distinguished in the early Chinese penetration of Manchuria. So essential is the disparity between Chinese and Mongols that Chinese, when penetrating the Mongol sphere of the "reservoir," have never become Mongol in their point of view; even when very decidedly influenced by the political atmosphere of the "reservoir," *unless they have "gone native."* On the other hand, when penetrating the Manchu sphere, it is evident that the Chinese never had to abandon or modify anything that was essentially Chinese in their outlook on life. The mark of success was a status of privilege, and there was nothing in the form of the privilege, or the way it was exercised, that was anything but satisfactory from a Chinese point of view.

Because of the gulf between Chinese and Mongols, the formation of mixed groups has always been an essential preliminary either to the absorption of Chinese by Mongols, or of Mongols by Chinese. Mongol borrowings of Chinese cultural elements are strongly reminiscent of plunder. The Mongols have always taken from China only what they like, and used it as they like. Thus quantities of Mongol clothes, hats, boots, saddles and so forth have for centuries been made

in China; but they have always been made to Mongol speci-
fications, and Mongol costume, in spite of borrowed Chinese
elements, continues to be recognizably Mongol. This is in
striking contrast to the manner in which the Manchus modified their own society in order to conform to Chinese standards. It is therefore axiomatic in the study of the racial and
cultural migrations north of the Great Wall that every
Chinese element among the Mongols is recognizably *alien,*
while every pure Manchu element that survived the amalgamation with the Chinese is recognizably a *survival,* and is
felt in the social consciousness as a survival.

The formation of mixed classes intermediate between
Chinese and Mongol, being the only method of bridging the
gap, definitely slowed down the rate of advance of Chinese
colonization, and, paradoxically, though in itself an expedient for obliterating frontiers, did much to preserve the existence and meaning of frontiers. The underlying cleavage continued to affect every kind of activity, official and mercantile,
as well as the progress of agricultural colonization.

Mixed classes are found, for instance, not only among the
advanced squatters and colonists scattered through Inner
Mongolia and western Fengtien, but among caravan traders,
trading-post merchants, pedlars, and interpreters, artisans
and scribes employed by Mongol princes and lamaseries. In
practically every case the Chinese engaged in these frontier
activities either has Mongol blood or, perhaps more frequently, comes from a family which has a definite tradition
of activity among the Mongols. Success, in every case,
depends to an important extent not only on learning the
Mongol language, but on "going native" to a certain degree—
perhaps taking a Mongol wife, certainly conforming to Mongol customs. *Something Chinese has to be surrendered.* The
importance of this, in view of the intense racial and cultural

self-consciousness of the Chinese, has never been properly emphasized.

Easy, quick and substantial profits have always been the essential inducement to any Chinese activity among the Mongols. This has always been necessary, because there has never been any guarantee of permanency. Caravan traders and trading-post merchants, like the Jews of medieval Europe, carried on hereditary businesses on credit terms at usurious rates, collecting the cattle and wool of the grandson against the interest owed by the grandfather. At the same time, they worked without social guarantees. One year they might be bullying and wheedling, threatening and promising, bent on the collection of their "just dues"; the next year many of them might be slaughtered and the rest plundered and driven out; a year more, and the survivors, with recruits from their families and relations, would be back again: the individual ran hazards, but the trade was inevitable. In the circumstances it it easy to understand that the universal Chinese assessment of the Mongol closely resembles the Jewish estimate of the Gentile: brutal and violent and unreasonable, yet on the whole not only honest, but an honest fool.

As for squatters and colonists beyond the actual reach of definite Chinese control and administration, they could only cultivate land under Mongol sufferance. They could never obtain a title to their land. Land ownership was a gauge of the respective military strength of Mongols and Chinese; if the Mongols were strong enough, they expelled Chinese who threatened to establish too definite a claim to the land they occupied. If the Chinese were strong enough, they ended by expelling the Mongols. Thus land policy lies at the bottom of every outbreak of massacre and war between Chinese and Mongols.

The curious thing is that when the Mongols are expelled

and the Chinese move in, the true frontiersman, whether trader or farmer, *moves on with the Mongol.* That the trader should do so is easily understandable; that the farmer should do so can only be explained by the fact that during the period of uncertainty he has so far "gone native" that his interests have become largely Mongol. Apart from the fact that he may have a Mongol wife and half-breed children, he has commonly accumulated sheep, cattle and horses, the pasturing of which would be inconvenient in a closely settled region. The original accumulation of property in the Mongol form might be due in part to the business instinct of the Chinese; but it must also have been due in part to the necessity for insurance against the possibility of being forced to discontinue agriculture.

The prevailing ignorance of the lives, methods and traditions of the traders, frontiersmen and squatters in advance of the obvious front line of Chinese colonization accounts for the general impression that the chief phenomenon, when Chinese meet Mongols, is the turning of Mongols into Chinese, and has obscured the importance of the formation of advanced mixed groups. Thus frequent reference is made to the "agricultural Mongols" of Chosotu and Chao-uda, east and north of Jehol; notably the Kharachin. In the eighteen hundred and nineties there was trouble between Mongols and Chinese over land policy in this region; numbers of Mongols were massacred by the Chinese, and several thousand Kharachin migrated to Cherim League, in western Liaoning province, where they now form an important agricultural element. In the true manner of the advanced frontier, they made their own terms with the local tribes, occupying and cultivating land without being granted title of ownership. They live in houses of a Chinese type, but frequently possess also felt *yurts* put up on permanent foundations; as the felt wears out it is plastered with mud, and eventually becomes a round mud hut, which is commonly used as a storeroom, while the family lives in a house. They pay a portion of the grain they harvest to the chieftain of the local tribe, to whose winter food supply it forms a welcome supplement. At the same time they continue to own livestock, and members of the family are frequently away from home for long periods, camping with the flocks. In spite of their houses, they set great store by a certain measure of Mongol freedom, and frequently move from one valley to another.

These Mongols are very much mixed in physical type. They are almost all bilingual from childhood, but the women are less fluent in Chinese than the men. Their clothes are a mixture of Mongol and Chinese, but those of the men are more Chinese, and those of the women more Mongol. Their family shrines are also a mixture of Mongol and Chinese, with Chinese elements predominating, as is natural to people living in houses; but they are as hospitable to lamas as are other Mongols. Most significant of all, they frequently have a Chinese family name, as well as Mongol clan name and personal names. All of these indications point to the fact that many of them must be descended from Chinese frontiersmen who "went native"; and whose descendants elected to migrate with the Mongols rather than remain in the land permanently occupied by the Chinese advance.[1]

Such people are obviously of extraordinary interest in the history of Chinese colonial expansion. Their social equivalence to such precursors of American and Canadian colonization as the *coureurs des bois* and *voyageurs,* and the men of

---

[1] There are instances, however, of the reversal of this process of "going native." Thus in the Jehol region numbers of families can be found which were originally Chinese, but "turned Mongol" after penetrating well into Mongol territory. Since the overwhelming advance of the Chinese in that region in the last thirty years, these "Mongol" families are now "turning Chinese."

the Missouri "fur brigades" is probably closer than that of, for instance, Oklahoma "land-stampeder" to Shantung "coolie" immigrant in the modern phase. The influence of the "reservoir" is to be discerned however in the fact that such mixed groups function alternatively as a rearguard of the Mongols and an advanced guard of the Chinese; whereas the frontiersman of American colonization was prevailingly conscious of being in the front of the advance, and comparatively seldom "went native" completely. The difference is due to the fact that there is no "reservoir" in American history, and no alternation of political ascendancy. It is distinctly noticeable that semi-settled Mongols of the Kharachin type are frequently massacred or driven out with other Mongols during periods of Chinese aggression; yet at the present time in the Cherim League, where the advance of Chinese colonization is producing a bandit class of dispossessed Mongols, bilingual Kharachins are willing to serve in Chinese irregular levies of cavalry engaged in checking banditry. On the other side there is no doubt that pastoral Mongols, too, regard them as a separate class; and also no doubt that in the event of a Mongol advance they would be found on the Mongol side. At present, with Chinese colonization proceeding vigorously in Cherim League, I know from personal observation that the Kharachin form potentially an element valuable to Chinese administration; for frequently, where pastoral Mongols take up agriculture under pressure of Chinese regulations, they turn over the cultivation of the lands allotted to them to Kharachin tenants or managers, and continue themselves to be interested primarily in their livestock.

There is still another type of frontiersman to be found on the Mongol border. This is the man who first moves in to land taken over from the Mongols, when the pastoral people and semi-settled people of the Kharachin type have moved out. In this class also a marked tradition is to be discerned. It is a class of farmers, among whom knowledge of the Mongol language is not common, but who have a special knowledge of frontier conditions and a special experience in the cultivation of raw land. They own more livestock than the farmer working under typical Chinese conditions, and though land is the basis of their society, they are not rooted in a particular tract of land. They may move only once in a generation, but they tend to move. As the land about them fills up, and values rise, they sell out the land they have developed and move forward to the next belt of newly opened land, there to invest once more their experience and special knowledge. This class, like that of the mixed groups of the extreme advance, is now being swamped by the mass immigration of people from China proper with little tradition behind them; but they are of great interest as being the class probably most nearly comparable to the pioneer of the Western type of colonization.

As for the traders, they are recruited almost entirely from certain towns many of which now lie far within the borders of solid Chinese population, and from families which have maintained for generations a tradition of Mongol trade. Firms and families often have a history of several centuries of trade among the Mongols. The young men begin very early to serve an apprenticeship, in which the acquisition of the Mongol language plays an important part. Almost invariably, when they can afford it, they marry or keep a Mongol woman; but just as regularly, after many years of work in distant regions, they retire to their own towns to spend their old age. Their lives are in two compartments, Mongol and Chinese, and though in the course of their active career they may often almost completely "go native," they never lose the feeling of superiority and distaste, and retire with relief at the appointed period. It is men of this class, based on the towns, who dominate the caravan trade also, as owners and capitalists; but among the caravan men themselves is a large proportion of the men of the advanced "mixed groups," born in the "reservoir" and knowing no other home.

CHINESE AND MANCHUS

It has already been pointed out that the Chinese penetrating into the Manchu sphere of the "reservoir" was never called on to make any surrender of the kind implied in "going native." In addition there was the fact that the different status of land tenure allowed a more sporadic and spontaneous form of penetration and settlement, which must at an early period have obliterated any idea of a linear "front," if it ever existed. Nor was there any basic hostility to be overcome as between races or instinctive ideas of social order. It might be thought, from the nominal character of the Manchu laws discriminating between Manchus and Chinese and Bannermen and non-Bannermen that Chinese penetrating into the "reservoir" would be confronted with a social order to which they would be instinctively hostile. On the contrary, such was the character of the "reservoir" itself, and so important was the number of Chinese already identified with it, even before the establishment of the Manchu dynasty, that the normal ambition of the newcomer was not to form a group hostile to the prevailing order, but to qualify himself individually for admission into the ranks of privilege in the order as it stood. This brings to the fore a fact which has never, so far as I know, been pointed out: the criterion of success, for the adventurer starting out with his back toward China and his face toward the wilderness, became the ability to *turn about* and, as a member of the privileged population of the privileged "reservoir," face toward China; which thus took the place of the wilderness as the "promised land," the source of wealth and the proper field for the exercise of power. The significance of this phenomenon, reversing the direction of an originally expansive movement like colonization, cannot too strongly be emphasized.

The Chinese Bannermen formed a natural gradation between Chinese and Manchus. Some distinctions were maintained in theory between Manchu and Chinese Bannermen, but Chinese Bannermen were definitely ranked, socially, with the Manchus and apart from other Chinese. Manchu and Chinese Bannermen intermarried freely; but in the south of Liaoning (Fengtien) province, where the weight of numbers had an effect, the two groups tended to remain distinct, as groups, though practically identical in function. In the north, on the other hand, wherever the weight of population was in favor of the Manchus, there was undoubtedly a tendency for Chinese Bannermen to become actually Manchu Bannermen. This was facilitated by the fact that the Banners were not clan units, but territorial military cadres; and military mobilization groups they remained, in spite of a tendency (apparently stronger in China than in Manchuria) to merge the hereditary organization of military service with the social unit proper, the clan.

During the rise of the Manchu power, any Chinese who shaved his forehead and grew a queue (thus making it difficult for him to desert at short notice to an anti-Manchu political faction) could be recruited into a Chinese Banner. This method of social transformation continued to be recognized in later years, though it was invoked with decreasing frequency both in regions where the Bannermen hardened into a caste which was jealous of enlarging its privileged membership, and in regions where the Chinese ceased to find it an advantage to pass from the subject "race" to the dominant "race."

It was, however, certainly possible, in Manchuria, for a Chinese from China proper to become, in his own lifetime, an out-and-out "Manchu." An instance of this phenomenon came within my own experience when I formed an acquaintance with a Chinese military officer and his old father. The father, born in Honan, had gone to Manchuria as a young man, had traveled over the most remote parts of the three provinces, and had finally settled at Tsitsihar. One day I said to the young man, "Why is it that you, who were born in Tsitsihar, speak just like the generality of Manchurian Chinese, while your father, who was born in Honan, has not only the speech, but exactly the manner and even gestures of the old-fashioned Manchus of Manchuria" [which differ somewhat from those of Peking Manchus]. He laughed, and said, "When my father was a young man, it was difficult for a *min-jen* [non-Banner Chinese, "a civilian," "one of the people"] [2] to get on in the world, up in the northern regions. The Manchus dominated everything, and they harassed the *min* Chinese. In Tsitsihar, where he settled down, they had a custom

---

[2] The fact that the word "Manchu" was and is almost never used in conversation, and comparatively rarely in writing, is of distinct significance. The term in commonest use was *ch'i-jen*, "Bannermen," which included both Chinese and Manchu Bannermen. The corresponding term for non-Banner Chinese was *min*, "a commoner," "a civilian." This bears out the point I have made that the Manchus had become Chinese and retained not a racial, but a social distinction.

Another term still in use in Manchuria for non-Manchurian Chinese and newcomers not yet identified with the still persisting "regionalism" is *Man-tze*. This peculiar term has a great psychological interest. It is a very ancient north-Chinese term for the non-Chinese "barbarians" south of the Yangtze. Its continued use both by the people of Manchuria and the Mongols can only be referred to the basic cleavage and antagonism between the Chinese of the north and south; and it indicates the extent to which the peoples of the "reservoir" identified themselves with the power of the north, and the true ancient direction of the driving force of Chinese national and cultural expansionism—toward the south, not the north.

of "chasing out the *min*" twice a year. All the Chinese who
had filtered in were liable to be driven out, and often beaten
and robbed. Of course, many of them came back; but the
only way to become secure was to "follow" [as the phrase
went] the Manchus and become so like them as to be un-
detectable.[8] So my father, when he had learned their ways,
"entered the Banners" and married a Manchu [which of
course was against the strict law] and has always remained
like them. But when I was growing up, it was no longer of
any use to be a Bannerman, and therefore I became like all
the other young men of my generation."

This is a story which illustrates the processes of the present
as well as of the past; for the young Manchus of Manchuria
are becoming rapidly indistinguishable from Manchuria-
born Chinese. As for the practice of "harassing" (*ch'i-fu*)
the under-dog, it cannot by any manner of means be construed as an attempt to differentiate the Manchus *racially*
from the Chinese. It can at the present time be observed in
any region which contains a self-conscious dominant element
and an intrusive element whose competition is feared. The
identification at which the newcomer had to aim was one of
regionalism and social status. Even the tricks of manner and
language which he had to acquire, though tinged with survivals of Manchu characteristics and a few transformed Manchu words, were on the whole Chinese. If newcomers had
been faced with the necessity of acquiring the Manchu language, amalgamation would hardly have been possible until
the second generation.

Indeed, there is a great interest in the contrast between the
rapid extinction of the Manchu language, and the strong

---

[8] This however is obviously not the same thing as "going native," which is a
form of *conversion*. It is merely a climbing from one class to another—a form
of *promotion*.

power of survival which the Mongol language has always shown. Thus the Manchu language was already in decay, and Chinese undoubtedly already the dominant language of administration, even before the Manchus entered China. The repeated efforts made by the Manchu emperors to keep the Manchu language artificially alive are themselves a proof of its complete decay. Yet Mongol is still spoken in Mongol families living within a hundred miles of Mukden, where they have been settled in the Chinese manner and surrounded by Chinese for several generations. The contrast can further be seen in the manner in which the Manchus, from the beginning of the modern Chinese advance, have surrendered their outworn social privileges and identified themselves with the Chinese; whereas the tendency of Chinese who have "gone Mongol" is distinctly to move on with the Mongols who retreat before the Chinese advance.

So many of the old processes in the Manchu-Chinese sphere of Manchuria survive at the present time that it is possible to gauge the phenomena of the infiltration period of Chinese penetration. The migrant might be a Chinese born in southern Manchuria, or a borderer (there is still a slang name distinguishing Chinese from the part of Chihli province adjacent to Manchuria) or a man from one of the districts in Shantung which, as will be seen, had an established tradition connecting it with Manchuria.

The attraction of Manchuria was the prospect of a life more free from competition than in China proper, and more free also from restrictions, because it was a land of privilege, and governed accordingly more in a spirit of easy prosperity than of any urgent necessity of exploitation. The prospects of finding immediate work were facilitated by the existence of numerous families, both of Manchu and Chinese Bannermen, whose ambition was a life of leisure. The "reservoir" was full of families which lived on the wealth that some relative had acquired or was busy acquiring, as an official in China, and who were glad to turn over their lands to an industrious and paying tenant. Indeed, the fall of the Empire revealed the fact that many Manchus had moved to Peking, leaving their lands in the hands of tenants; then, being interested in official careers, they had neglected these lands, and finally the tenants usurped them and, when the Empire fell, were able to maintain their claims against the lapsed interests of the original owning families.

The activities of outsiders who penetrated the "reservoir" followed fairly regular courses. If they came among Chinese Bannermen they had only to prove themselves industrious and generally acceptable members of society. Then, by marrying into one of the established families, or by some other form of social negotiation, their position was quietly regularized. Undoubtedly many of them "became" Chinese Bannermen; but this was not necessary, for in southern Manchuria large communities of non-Banner Chinese existed, deriving from that part of the population which had passively accepted, rather than actively participated in the Manchu conquest. On the whole, however, though permanent settlement was easier and more rapid in the south, only a fractional residue of the migrants (as is most conspicuously shown in the "Shantung" type of migration) took up permanent holdings. This was due not only to the formal prohibition against the emigration of Chinese women beyond the Great Wall, but to the fact that the recognized ambition of the established families was the marriage of their daughters, not to promising pioneers, but to members of the governing classes, who were oriented toward China.

Farther to the north, in the markedly Manchu regions of the "reservoir," infiltration was distinctly slower and more difficult. Newcomers were almost invariably single men, and formed so distinct a class that they received an appropriate slang name, which their counterparts of the present day still bear—*p'ao-t'uei'rh-ti* or "leg-runners"—drifters, wanderers, masterless men. This is distinctly a pejorative term, and it is worth noting that in other border regions it is the term applied to bandit spies and go-betweens.[4] Even Chinese born in Manchuria, when venturing into an unknown region, were likely to go without their families. In other words the northward drift was in character a tentative and uncertain *spread,* not the instinctive and urgent *drive* of a spontaneously expanding nation. Whether or not the adventurer returned later for his family depended not only on whether he succeeded but on the manner of his success; and on the whole the prevailing tendency was for the successful man to return, not to settle.

The adventurer might strike into the forest and make a clearing for himself, like a true pioneer. The terms *wo-p'eng* and *wo-p'u,* incorporated in many place names in Manchuria and Eastern Inner Mongolia are legacies of this form of settlement. Both terms mean not only "outlying farmer," or "outlying village" or "inn or shelter by the wayside" but—and this is undoubtedly the earlier meaning—"base camp of a hunting party." To this day a *ting wo-p'eng-ti* is "a settler" as opposed to "a newly arrived member of an already established community."

It was comparatively difficult for such a settler to obtain a recognized status. He might succeed, by purchase or negotiation or even theft, in getting a wife from one of the established communities. If he did not steal her, she would have to

---

[4] Indeed, it is significant that there is no old-established vernacular word in common use, which has the same proud and honorable connotations as "pioneer" in English.

be written off the clan lists as "dead," in order to evade the Manchu marriage laws; and such an evasion in itself emphasized the non-acceptance of the newcomer by the community. If he did steal her, he outlawed himself. He might in time return to his native village for his wife; but on the whole the man who could afford the double journey was more likely to retire from pioneering.

The pioneer of this type almost never worked alone, but in groups of single men. The crucial moment of such a settlement arose when either it came within the cognizance of an official or into contact with an earlier-established community. If the new group was able to strike up terms, the settlement had passed the crisis; after a period of toleration it would be absorbed into the general group of communities and the settlers would be likely to "graduate," so to speak, into the Banner class.

If, on the other hand, the squatters failed to hit it off on coming into contact with official or community, or if they encroached on local interests, they would be driven away, thus becoming outlaws. The history of spontaneous colonization in Manchuria and Mongolia is closely interwoven with the history of banditry. Indeed, the pioneers were often squatters, wanderers and outlaws by turns. Their original quest might be for such valuable medicinal materials as ginseng or elk-horn in the velvet; or for gold (more often washed from streams than mined); or for sables (which were an article of imperial tribute and could be disposed of to the Manchu tribute officials even by illegal hunters); or other valuable furs. Now the State in China has from of old had a prescriptive interest in minerals and treasure. The mere act of prospecting for gold put a man beyond the law; and even if a party struck up an arrangement with the nearest official, on the quiet, they were no more than outlaws under temporary toleration. This explains the remark which I once heard of a region in Heilungchiang where the predominating influence is still that of the spontaneous period of colonization: "All the villagers there have the flavor of banditry." Nor was this a haphazard epigram; remarks of the same purport crop up in casual conversation all over the thinly settled north.

The career of the adventurer who did not strike out for the wilderness, but made for an already established community, was commonly more decorous. His immediate object was to find work under an employer, and usually his ambition was, as has already been pointed out, not to settle but to make money and return to his home. The Manchu of leisure who wanted to have his land worked for him was likely to be affable to the non-Banner Chinese, up to a point, because the outsider, having no legal status, was not likely to make trouble; whereas the local Bannermen, receiving government subsidy, were all anxious to rise above manual labor. The industrious immigrant would cultivate an agreed acreage for his landlord. Then, if out in the country, he would add a piece of land "of his own" whose harvest was his private profit. Or, if on the outskirts of a town or village, he would be likely to add a market garden, "his own" in practice if not in theory, selling the produce in the village. The landlord had the tenant well under control up to a point; but if too much bullied the newcomer would either look out for another landlord or decamp to join the forest adventurers.

The successful man of this type, if he did not retire to his own home, would gradually pass from a status of toleration to one of higher social recognition. If he were aiming at permanent establishment he would be on the whole more likely to look for a wife locally than to bring his own from his old home. If he had become recognized as a sound man, a poor local family might evade the marriage laws and provide him with one of its daughters.

Even at this level, however, he had not freed himself from a certain element of hazard. Too much assertion on the part of an individual, or too rapid growth of an intruding "tolerated" element, threatening the interests of the established community, might arouse the resentment of the privileged. Then the traditional process of "harassing" would begin, and the newcomers, except those whose ties in practice were strong enough to protect them, would be driven away to join the outlaws and adventurers. These intermittent purgations, obviously, played an important part in giving banditry the curious social status which still distinguishes it in Manchuria.

The fully successful pioneer of this type (if pioneer he can be called) was the man whose social value in terms of wealth and ability became so convincing that he stood at last possessed of all the privileges, most of them conferred on him indirectly and unofficially. Thus if, after due private negotiation, a son of his appeared at one of the periodical musters of the Bannermen, and was accepted without protest as qualified for the retaining subsidy of a Banner soldier, the whole family would quietly be inscribed on the rolls of a Banner, and perhaps at the same time, by the same type of private negotiation, the family would by change of surname merge into one of the local clans.

The most significant result of this method of tacit social graduation was that the family which had succeeded became divorced from all the interests of the "pioneers." It not only was ranked above them, socially, but was oriented in an opposite direction. The tide of infiltration, the people sometimes tolerated, sometimes harassed, was definitely directed toward the frontier; it was on the edge of the wilderness that they had to qualify. But once a family had graduated into the corps of the elect, it faced about toward China. The people of privilege, the lords of the "reservoir," were oriented toward Peking. Official preferment was the norm of ambition. The wealth and power to be derived from the potential new sources of the "reservoir" itself were distinctly secondary; they merely contributed to the ease of life. The richest prizes were to be had in China, and to be gained through careers in the imperial service. That this was the standard of social values is proved by evidences not yet obliterated. The villager in China is familiar with old legends and names of far-away regions; but their geography is curiously vague. On the whole, "the border" is all the same border to him, whether the land beyond be Turkestan, Mongolia or Manchuria. But the old-fashioned villager of "old" communities in Manchuria (a fast-vanishing type) was familiar with many names and their geography; for even in a small community there would be Banner families whose members had held high office all over China and its outer dominions.

MANCHURIA AT THE FALL OF THE MANCHU EMPIRE

At the close of the Manchu period we have, therefore, a Manchuria which, in spite of the triumph of Chinese civilization over the barbarity of the "outer tribes," still fulfills the ancient function of the "reservoir." It is not an outlet for Chinese expansionism and a field for the growth and development of the power of China, but the key to the exercise of power within China itself. Within Manchuria itself, however, while the Manchus have amalgamated themselves with the Chinese, there persists an emphatic cleavage between the Manchu-Chinese amalgamation and the still practically intact Mongol mass. What emerges from this is a realization of the

profound power of culture—the way of life—in comparison
with the factors of race and environment (including climate,
soil and natural vegetation, but not relative regional position,
under the heading of environment); and of the equally remarkable power of geography—regionalism—in determining
the social and historical orientation of culture itself; whether,
that is, the culture is oriented toward civilization and cities
or toward the frontier and the wilderness.

What mattered most profoundly to the Manchus was not
the way of life itself, nor the details of political conceptions,
but the mere exercise of power. During the two generations
of extraordinary activity leading up to the occupation of
Peking in 1644 they practically took Chinese civilization in
their stride. It has already been pointed out that the "conquest" itself was not, in its essential aspects, an alien invasion
but the last campaign in a series of Chinese civil wars. The
quasi-"caste" structure of Manchu society, and the military
Banner organization, were in the ultimate analysis nothing
but a method of safeguarding the "reservoir" as the key to
strategical power; and this is none the less true from the fact
that in the popular opinion of both Chinese and Manchus, the
distinctions that existed were racial. Popular misapprehen-
sions of the meaning of "race" are, however, common enough
in all histories. In point of fact, within the "reservoir" and
through the Banner organization, and in China proper
through the examination system, it was possible for the Chinese to participate on terms of equality in the Manchu exercise
of power; and this they did, to the point of outnumbering
the Manchus.

The Chinese beyond a doubt outnumbered the Manchus
within the "reservoir" itself; but so far from resenting the
Manchu dominion, they participated in it enthusiastically;
the Manchu dominion could, it is obvious, have been most

easily overthrown by a revolt within the strategic regional stronghold—yet when revolt came, it came from far to the south, beyond the Yangtze. Not only was the whole of the North late in turning against the Manchus, but in Manchuria itself there were no massacres of the "tyrants." Indeed, the Manchu overlords not only did no violence to Chinese culture or Chinese ideals, but their rule, because of the ancient orientation toward the Yangtze of the power of the North, was generally welcome. It was only with the decay of the ruling house, the growth of the power of revolt in the South, and the desire to find a scapegoat on which to hang the blame for all the ills of China, that a quasi-racial hatred was worked up against the Manchus, which is now being perpetuated in textbooks and political doctrines. While locally and in particular cases the Chinese were treated by the Manchus as a subject race—and the tendency to do so increased with the decay of the dynasty—it can hardly be affirmed that they were in State theory regarded as an inferior race. On the contrary they seem to have been regarded, in the light of what may be called (since Chinese political terminology does not correspond with ours) "unconscious theory," as "the political party out of power." It is curious and interesting that Chinese officials referred to themselves, when received in audience by the emperor, as *ch'en* (an official); it was the Manchu officials who used the term *nu* (a slave); thus emphasizing that they were regarded as the emperor's personal, or "party" followers.

Language is primarily a vehicle of culture, not a symbol of race; and no more important contrast can be distinguished, as between Manchus and Mongols, than the use and fate of their respective languages. From the beginning, Chinese was the language of Manchu administration; the Manchu language, although used parallel with Chinese in decrees, as a matter of form, rapidly lost all significance except as the nominal vehicle of communication between the emperor and his personal following—and even here Chinese was really the living language. The Manchu presented in audience to his emperor learned a few Manchu phrases, without necessarily understanding their meaning, which he repeated as a matter of form; but Chinese was the language of thought. Within eighty years of the Manchu conquest there was produced, under imperial patronage, the great dictionary of K'ang Hsi—one of the greatest monuments of Chinese scholarship. The survival of Manchu, as a dead language confined to the schoolroom use of a social class, is to be compared not with Norman French as used at the courts of the successors of William the Conqueror, but with Greek and Latin as taught in the eighteenth century and at the English public schools of the nineteenth century.

Among the Mongols, on the other hand, during the most brilliant period of their empire in China, such totally alien languages as Persian and Arabic seem to have been quite as important at court, if not more important, than Chinese. Marco Polo stood high at the court of Khublai Khan; he spent the prime of his life in China, made journeys of extraordinary length, and served as an official—yet in his account there has not survived one reference to the Chinese written character. This indifference, to be appreciated, must be contrasted with the overwhelming preponderance of Chinese elements in the accounts of the Jesuit Fathers at the Manchu court in Peking; who also made important journeys in Manchuria and Mongolia. Some casual reference to Chinese writing may have been lost from Polo's account; but if it had been dealt with at length, as important and marvelous, it could hardly have been lost entirely. Friar Rubrück, although he did not visit China proper and does mention Chinese writing, is often a better observer and more apt commentator than Polo; and his account, too, bears out the comparative unimportance of Chinese civilization to the Mongols.

For to the Mongols the way of life is everything. The Chinese have always looked on the Mongol culture as rude and barbarous, and something of their contempt has been passed on to Westerners. Moreover we, obsessed by one critical method, look all too uncritically for "evolution" in every phenomenon, and therefore dismiss Mongol nomadism as a "lower" form of society awaiting evolution to something "higher." Yet the Mongol nomadic society is a phenomenon complete and independent. It resists "evolution" into the "higher" form of settled agriculture not passively but positively. It is, in fact, so complete that it is incapable of evolution, it can only be replaced. Nor can its origins be attributed entirely to environment. Both Russians and Chinese have proved in the modern period that the Mongolian environment does not everywhere forbid agriculture, and ruins of "pre-Mongol" cities prove that agriculture was also possible in the past. Environment plays a part, and change of climate may have acted as an impetus in launching the migrations of the Huns, and again in the sudden emergence of the Mongols of Chinghis Khan; probably the true importance of the environmental factor, on the average, is that the regions of the Mongolian plateau where agriculture and city life are possible have always lain open to, and been dominated by, the great regions which favored a pastoral life.[5] But even allowing for the full influence of environment, the devastating expansion of the modern Mongols in the twelfth century as an assertive conquering people must have been in the main a spiritual phenomenon, rooted in a passionate conviction of

[5] See "Caravan Routes of Inner Asia," *Geographical Journal,* LXXII, No. 6, Dec. 1928.

the nobility and superiority of the free life. Too wide a dispersion and—which is far more important—a profound contempt for the structure of power in settled communities, lost them their empires; but even in decline they are still instinctively satisfied with, and proud of, the pastoral life and the free life. Indeed, the most important modification of Mongol society is the result, not of the direct action of the obviously superior Chinese civilization, but of the introduction of monastic lamaistic Buddhism. The foundation of monasteries has to a great extent undermined both the instinct for free movement and the idea of conquest as a career; and it is undoubtedly this influence of the lamas, and not the frequently alleged cessation of increase in population "as a result of (nominal) celibacy" which accounts for the present decay of Mongol society. It is my opinion that the Mongol conquests did not, in the ultimate analysis, originate in pressure of population, whether due to change of climate or any other cause, but in an attitude of mind. They did not set out to conquer because they had to, but because they wanted to. The idea of freedom, free movement, free migration, developed to a point where conquest became an exaltation, the only career for noble souls. When this inspiration was sated, the Mongols declined. In 1242 they were at the gates of Vienna; nothing could stop them. Then came the news of the death of Ogotai, the Great Khan. This demanded the return of Batu, commanding the host in Europe, to take part in the election of a new supreme Khan. There was no reason at all why he should not have arranged to hold the new conquests he had made; but he did not. The truth is, he did not want them. The act of conquest had been enough. He and Subutai, his great marshal, turned around with all their host and rode back. The high point of the expansive energy of the Mongols had been passed.

In the lethargy that followed the great conquests, lamaism was introduced. The present decay of the Mongols is not due to "monastic celibacy" but to change in the attitude of mind, of which lamaism was, originally, not the cause but a result. Even at the present day, and in spite of the damage done by lamaism, the average attitude of Mongol communities to the advance of civilization is avoidance. Some Mongols do settle down and "become Chinese"; but even when they do their language (the index of pride in non-Chinese origin) shows a power of survival extraordinary in comparison with Manchu. On the whole, in spite of the superiority of the Chinese, it is still necessary for Chinese to "go Mongol" when penetrating among the Mongols in a sense quite different from that of "going Manchu" during the period when Chinese entered Manchu regions of old Manchuria.

It is all the more striking that, whether the social condition was one of amalgamation, as between Manchus and Chinese, or irremediable disparity, as between Mongols and Chinese, the influence of the region continued paramount. At the same time that the Manchus were becoming Chinese in culture, the Chinese of Manchuria were becoming Manchu, or perhaps it would be better to say Manchurian, in politics. At the same time that a Chinese population was driving out a Mongol population, and pushing back the "Mongol menace" from the plateau overhanging North China, it did not produce a new regionalism, but perpetuated the old. So long as the colonizing frontiersmen were establishing a territorial foothold, they represented a Chinese advance; when they had succeeded, they faced about. The Mongol front became defensive, and the escarpment of the plateau between them and China became "the frontier."

A regionalism of this kind enters into the blood, it survives changes in the type of civilization, and defies intellectual definitions of policy and expansionism. That this regionalism does survive, and that it produces an inner discord in Manchurian affairs, is proved by the categorical differences in temper and execution between contemporary Manchurian frontier policy, whether the frontier is Mongol, Russian or Japanese, and the policy of that other, inward-facing frontier still essentially defined by the Great Wall. The fall of the Manchu dynasty has altered only the names, not the facts, of one of the radical problems confronting the statesmanship of China—the problem of so controlling the inevitable and now very rapid expansion into Manchuria that it will effectively alter the balance between China and other nations, without precipitating fresh crises in the ancient opposition between North and South within China, and without strengthening the ancient power of regionalism and the "reservoir." The fact that the problem of regionalism as a dangerous obstacle is instinctively appreciated is borne out by the strong feeling among Chinese that the regional term "Manchuria," used in all foreign languages, ought to be discontinued.

Western opinion generally has been misled by the extraordinary acceleration in contemporary colonization and exploitation in Manchuria into the belief that "the Manchurian question" is essentially a problem of the new world; that Manchuria is in the forefront of the development of a new China, and that its problems are chiefly those of Chinese expansion, affecting external frontiers. In point of fact the crux of all Manchurian affairs is still the relation of Manchuria to China. The policies of the inward-facing frontier of regionalism still take precedence over the outer frontiers of the nation. It is not sufficiently realized that the growth of wealth and power in Manchuria still increase the pressure of Manchuria on China far more than they increase the pressure of China on

Mongolia and the wilderness or on Japan or Russia. The frontiersman still has his back to the frontier.

What is in fact taking place is the revaluation of a still vigorous regionalism in terms of new categories of power—of which the chief are Western mechanics and the railway. Because of the comparative emptiness of the land, the Western factors have had a freer play and more immediate effect than in other parts of China, and this in itself accounts for a great deal of the superficial resemblance of colonization in Manchuria to colonization in Western lands. This very resemblance, however, obscures the underlying conflict between the civilization of China and that of the West. The "progressiveness" of Manchuria is, in fact, part of the impact of the West on China; and while Westernization is now accepted as inevitable, and the achievement of Western technical standards is regarded by the most active public opinion in China as an end to be striven for, Western civilization as a whole is considered to have a number of menacing qualities. In the process of modernizing Manchuria there is, therefore, a struggle to subordinate Western technical methods to Chinese ideals of civilization; a struggle to master the West, not to become Western. It is therefore necessary to consider two aspects of the complex of problems in Manchuria—the derivation of the modern phase from a historical process of great vigor and distinct individual character, and the contemporary struggle between two civilizations totally alien to each other.

Chapter IV

THE LIVING FORCE OF CHINESE CULTURE

EAST AND WEST

No MORE fruitful breeding ground of fallacies exists than the comparison of the civilization of China and that of the modern West. One thing, however, is certain: the civilization of China is not only the oldest living civilization in the world, but it is in itself extremely "late," in the full Spenglerian sense of the term. It is the final expression of a culture which long ago fulfilled and matured every potentiality of growth inherent in its own powers. While, therefore, the radical problem of modern China is frequently defined as the adaptation of Western forces to Chinese culture, what is more commonly to be observed in the contact of the two civilizations is not a process of blending but a struggle in which Western elements either kill off and replace Chinese elements or are successfully subdued and so transvalued that they no longer have their own meaning; in other words, are themselves defeated.

So imperfectly has the West as yet comprehended the spirit of Chinese civilization, that it is probably not yet possible to interpret the whole of Chinese civilization in terms which are valid for Western understanding. I should like, however, to discuss two Chinese characteristics which, while they cannot begin to "explain" the total character of Chinese civilization, may serve to illuminate some of its working processes. The two characteristics are interdependent; one is the attitude toward responsibility, the other the attitude toward definition.

The Western attitude toward responsibility is characteristically defined in terms of will and activity. The individual assumes and asserts responsibility; and equally, when there is a legal question of the determination of responsibility, it can only be defined in terms of intention and action. In accordance with this instinct, even a negative attribution of responsibility must be defined in terms of what a man has not done, or not decided. Moreover, in sympathy with the respect for will inherent in the Western concept of responsibility, we judge the ability of a man by his capacity to "do things" with the forces of nature, and to "make things happen" in the world of men. The type of the settler in the wilderness, the pioneer colonizer, that emerges against the background of this tradition of assertive personal responsibility is obvious and to us familiar; but there can be no doubt that he differs from the frontiersman nourished by the Chinese tradition.

For the Chinese tradition inevitably tends to appear, to the Westerner, one of passivity. It is probably, in truth, more neutral than passive; there seems to be a profound instinct for adjusting the forces of nature and of humanity—and, in the affairs of humanity, active forces and negative forces, in order to produce a pure harmony in which any conflict of negative and positive is as completely eliminated as possible. So impatiently assertive is the West, however, that it invariably assesses as negative this method of "canceling out."

To begin with the Chinese method appears, in practice, to fix responsibility not in terms of "who has done something," but of "what has happened." When something has once happened, responsibility must be assigned; and hence there is always an underlying tendency to try to prevent decisive things from happening, and to diffuse responsibility. In legal practice, for instance, this leads to the convention that when a murder has been committed, a murderer must be produced to match the corpse. If the individual cannot be apprehended by the police, the family or the village or some larger community must be made responsible and made to produce "satisfaction." Similarly, when a murderer has been apprehended, the fixing of responsibility on him by the official prosecution is not in itself sufficient, because it is assertive, one-sided and unbalanced. The murderer must be made to confess, thus bringing the whole process into harmony, canceling out the assertion of the prosecution with the acquiescence of the defense.

Naturally such conceptions often led, in the old typical tradition, to such evasions as the hiring of a victim to replace the actual criminal, or the production of a scapegoat by a community within whose bounds a crime had been committed by someone totally unknown. This conception of responsibility, leading apparently to such working theories as the idea that a conviction for every crime is even more important than proving that the convicted man is the actual criminal, and that an employee can, for instance, be made to bear the penalty that should have been allotted to an absconding principal, have led Westerners to liken the Chinese system to the Hebraic canon of "an eye for an eye and a tooth for a tooth." It is, however, in the ultimate analysis, something different.

Be that as it may, the fact emerges that an instinct which tends to work in terms of what has happened rather than in terms of who assumes the responsible initiative for making things happen, must produce a type of conquest of the wilderness, a type of colonization, and a type of colonist totally strange to Western ideas. Thus in the Empire builder, the administrator and the great official the type to be looked for is not the type of Clive or Cecil Rhodes, but the type of the negotiator, the mediator, the man who adapts the change of the old to the progress of the new. In the colonist the type to be looked for is not the man who goes off in search of loneliness and "room to be free," but the man who adapts himself to the necessities of a spreading society. In the suppression of bandits, extermination is only exceptional; negotiation is the typical process—usually, and very significantly, by merging the bandits, through enlistment, in the ranks of their enemies the troops. Some of the bandits, or their leaders, may subsequently be exterminated through treachery; but that is a secondary adjustment; the antecedent negotiation is the primary process.

A comparable contrast distinguishes Western and Chinese ideas of definition. To the Westerner, definition is a primary thing. So urgent is the assertion of personality and control that all definitions must be carried out to the remotest extreme —even to extremes of absurdity, as may be seen, for instance, in the multiplicity and arrogant assertiveness of American laws, which are not unique or different from the laws of Europe, but merely carry further the general tendency inherent in all Western codes. In China, on the other hand, definition is often avoided, and even when used is purely secondary. No matter how elaborate and specific the declared theory, all working processes are consciously carried out in a spirit of compromise between fact and theory. In the West, any such compromise is felt to be a failure of the system; in China it is the system. No greater contrast could be imagined than the fact of a liquor traffic and the theory of liquor prohibition in America, and the fact of an opium traffic and the theory of opium prohibition in China. In America the connivance of officials in violations of the prohibition law is felt to be a failure of the system, and efforts to perfect the system, however futile, are incessant. The situation arises from a conflict of individual wills with the official will. The connivance of individual officials is merely one of the incidents of the struggle. Even were the system perfect, the official will would still conflict with innumerable private wills.

In China, on the contrary, the whole opium traffic depends on the fact of official participation; the official prohibition is merely one of the incidents which contribute to the profits of the trade. Official participation is so real that the very officials who are theoretically responsible for the suppression of opium frequently enforce in practice the cultivation of the poppy. The difference between this method and venial connivance ought not to have to be pointed out. In the same way, in spite of strenuous efforts at reform, new theories of the functions of the officials still conflict with the living tradition that the official is not expected to *execute,* but to *manipulate* the policies with which he is entrusted; and, specifically, that he does not rely on pay and promotion, but on the profits of his actual office and private negotiation for the acquisition of higher office.

All this does not prove, what Westerners frequently think, that the Chinese tradition, and the family system especially, tend to the suppression of personality. In no country in the world is the personality of the individual more potent than in China. The working of personalities of great depth and power may be seen in every turn of Chinese events. It is only that the modes of personality differ in China and the West. In the Western style, the individual strives to realize every potentiality within him; he defines his courses, assumes responsibility for them, and stands or falls by the successful implementing of his own assertions. In China, on the other hand, the individual holds every potential power and resource of his personality in reserve; he negotiates warily, and deploys all his resources, before allowing responsibility to be allotted to him and thereafter displays his personality, and wins approval or condemnation, by his manipulation of events as they occur.

Thus in Western crises leading to war, the justifications which are cited by the responsible leaders are based typically on asserted responsibilities or policies, and are even so of secondary importance; public commendation and public support depend primarily on the assertion of what is going to be done during and after the war. In China, on the other hand, the justifications for entering on a war are of the most profound importance; they are designed to show that the responsible leaders are making the most skillful adjustment possible to inevitable events. The announcements of policy during the war and after victory are secondary; public opinion is far from being outraged when the war itself is carried on by shifts and expediencies, and the terms of peace arrived at turn out to be quite different from those postulated. Unrest in Europe is very largely due to the fact that the results of the Versailles Treaty are different from the objectives responsibly announced. Unrest in China proceeds not from the terms of peace at the conclusion of any given civil war, but from the feeling that the "inevitables" postulated at the beginning of the conflict are not genuine but merely disguise personal ambitions.

Even the Great Wall, which appears at the first blush to be one of the most magnificent monuments in history of definite assertion and definite policy is in fact nothing of the sort. It is indeed the symbol of perhaps the most passionately asserted attitude in Chinese history; but that attitude was not declared in a single gesture. The Great Wall is not the result of a military conception dynamically carried out. It is the outgrowth of the discovery of a type of defense that was of unique value in stemming the force of barbarian invasions, and graduating the steps of necessary adjustment. The system was gradually built to suit current needs, and though largely unified under the great Ch'in Shih Huang-ti, it could be shown, were the records complete enough, that in any given generation the frontier was not absolute, but a basis of adjustment, the balance wavering to one side or the other. In the same way, the greatest conquests of expansion beyond the Great Wall have a character of defense; they belong in the category of British operations beyond the Northwest Frontier of India, and the Younghusband Mission to Lhasa.

CHINA AND JAPAN

The modern history of Japan illustrates the fact that, in a region like Manchuria where the civilizations of East and West are abruptly opposed to each other, the resulting unrest proceeds not from the mechanical difficulties of amalgamation, but from a struggle for domination. Underlying the profound Chinese antagonism toward Japan there is a hostility, not of race but of culture. For Japan is now essentially a Western nation. Though it retains its national characteristics, these modify its essential Westernness not very much more than, say, the "Latin" characteristics of France modify the position of France in the Western group. The eagerness with which the Japanese took over the Western civilization, in spirit as well as in fact, is to be compared with the rapid assumption of Chinese characteristics by the Manchus; while the profound distrust which the Chinese feel for the civilization of the West is to be compared with the traditional avoidance of the civilization of China by the Mongols.

The first approach of the West was resisted in Japan as in China; but when Perry demonstrated that the West "amounted to something," the effect approximated to a revelation, and was so accepted. It is now evident that the really important subsequent conflicts of opinion within Japan itself turned, in the main, not on questions of the desirability of Westernization, but on the methods to be adopted in accomplishing Westernization. There was a latent power of growth within the nation which was released by the West, which welcomed the West, and has flowed eagerly since then into the Western outgrowth grafted on to the original stock. Characteristics that are merely national have survived with little modification; but cultural characteristics that are incompatible with the spirit of the West tend to fall into the category of survivals, respected and preserved for the sake of tradition, but no longer governing the national life.

There is, it is true, a gap between Japan and the West which is very important. Japan, viewed from China, may well seem more Western than when viewed from America. It may even be that the Japanese are more Western in Manchuria than in Japan itself. Some critics hold that Westernization in Japan is only a veneer. It has, however, affected Japan too vitally, I think, to be called merely superficial. It is the Westernization of Japan, above all else, that conditions its international relations—that is to say, its life in the world, as distinguished from its private life. Even if it be conceded that Westernization in Japan itself is imperfect, that does not materially affect the truth that Japan in Manchuria functions as a unit of the group of Western nations.

Perhaps what is most important, and to the Japanese most dangerous, in the difference between Japan and the West proper, is the chronological "lag." The pace of development in the West itself is so rapid that Japan has never, in many important respects, really caught up. Technical inventions and improvements drag behind the progress of the West, and the processes of Westernization have been much more thorough in some departments of the national economy than in others. Under the stress of keeping up with the West and trying to cut down the handicap of a late start, much that is "modern" in Japan is, perforce, more imitative than creative. It can be argued that Japan, in converting itself, has abandoned to a great extent initiative and latitude of choice, being forced to follow the majority lead of the West. This, however, is true also of the less "developed" European nations.

The commonly accepted statement that Japan adopted the technique of the West in order to preserve itself from subjugation by the West misses a great part of the truth. Undoubtedly this was the overt aim of many leaders of reform in Japan, and to this end they staved off the West as best they could while schooling the nation in its assumption of the qualities of the West. But the spirit of the nation itself realized innumerable fresh possibilities; its unfulfilled powers of growth reached out toward the new dispensation. The nation that emerged after the schooling was not an Eastern nation with an external Western armor but a nation which has integrated itself with the West, has continued to be a vigorous member of the West, and has carried on, in the East, the work of the West.

It is China, on the contrary, which has endeavored to use the weapons of the West to preserve itself from the West. Misunderstanding of the cleavage between China and Japan has done a great deal to pervert Western judgment, and above all has led to the fallacious and self-flattering expectation of an "awakening" of China which is to be comparable to the "awakening" of Japan. Contact with the West was established earlier and more gradually in China than in Japan, and for a long time, so far from there being any threat of Western domination, the governments of the West were respectfully cautious in dealing with China as a great power of unknown quantity. Yet such curiosity as China displayed in regard to Western civilization was only the curiosity of fashionable diversion. Chinese interest in the West only became serious when the foreign nations, finding that China, in spite of its impressive potential power, was vulnerable to Western methods of attack, became aggressive. The interest then awakened was primarily defensive, and it has remained essentially defensive. While the power of many Western inventions has been recognized, and the profit to be realized from many Western methods, no single quality of the West, no subjective conviction, has truly appealed to the Chinese. The Western style, for the Chinese, reveals no new dispensation, nor any opening up of fresh and desirable or morally superior worlds of inspiring possibilities. There is nothing in it that, from the standard of Chinese spiritual values, it would be disgraceful to have to go without.

While Japan manœuvered for time to adopt Western characteristics and catch up with the West, the whole history of Chinese relations with the West implies an underlying instinctive playing for time, in the hope that the West would exhaust itself and China be able to assert once more the superiority of which the Chinese are morally convinced. The normal type of the Chinese "employment of Western methods to defeat the West" has consistently been not the adoption of Western methods in order to attain Western standards, but the interposition of Western methods between China and the West, in order to stave off the West; and this type of manœuver can only be explained, viewing the conflict from the standpoint of China, by postulating as ideal some such eventual solution as the sloughing off of the West and the survival of the Chinese tradition in its full integrity.

Had the Western spirit possessed any such true appeal for the Chinese as it had for the Japanese, China would have been ideally situated for receiving and adopting it. It is true that

China, on account of its territorial mass [1] and innumerable population offers great difficulties to the penetration of alien ideas. Japan, in comparison, with its limited area, accessible from all sides, its numerous ports and small population, could be approached and penetrated at many points simultaneously. This consideration is frequently brought forward by both Chinese and foreign critics, when comparing the problems of Westernization in China and Japan. It is a sound point, but in emphasizing the material difficulties it begs the question of cultural feeling. As against this point, it may be said that other factors might have been expected to favor China. The Western approach to China was gradual, was in the first instance highly conciliatory (as is shown by the histories of the early embassies) and was for long restricted to a few coastal ports. Had Western inventions been adopted and developed in China as rapidly as Chinese inventions were adopted and developed in the West, it would have been easy, in the vast hinterland, to marshal the latent forces of the nation during a period of transformation, making it possible for a formidable and well-integrated nation to emerge and participate in international affairs.

The West, however, was at first regarded as an intrusive element which had to be subordinated, then as an importunate element which had to be accommodated, and is now still regarded, on the whole, as a violent but stupid element which may yet be neutralized, as a forest fire is defeated by counter-fires. The consequence is that every "advance of Westernization" in China tends to have the character of an aggression.

The period of doubt and struggle in Japan turned on the

---

[1] It may not be out of place to point out, in respect of the great size of China, that if we subtract Mongolia, Chinese Turkestan and Tibet, where the Chinese provide only a fraction of the population, but which are usually marked and colored on maps as if they were homogeneous with China, we are left with a China reduced in size by nearly half.

question of whether Japan was to be "run" by foreign interests, or whether the Japanese could "run" their own country as a Westernized State transformed by themselves. The process of Westernization was directed by the men who had Westernized themselves; they had full responsibility and full initiative. In China, on the contrary, policy and control are still in the hands of men who are not Westernized. Men with railway training may be directors of railways, but they are themselves controlled by men who understand the functions of railways in Chinese, not in Western terms. Western military training is not an essential but an incidental qualification for a commanding general. Western military science, in fact, affects only the tactics, never the strategy of Chinese warfare. Not only do Chinese commanders with foreign training altogether discard Western ideas of strategy, but even foreign military advisers, called in to train armies, are jealously restricted from any voice in the conduct of a campaign as a whole.

So irrational is all Western civilization when assessed by Chinese standards that Chinese statesmen of great ability have repeatedly and regularly handled the question of "Western power" not as if it were subject to rational analysis but as if it were some kind of knack or trick, which could be used without having to be understood. The problem of understanding the West is repeatedly abandoned in favor of an experimental search for the "secret" of Western power. Japanese military training is tried; maybe that will do the trick. The Russian combination of military units and propaganda units is tried; maybe that will do the trick. German staff organization is tried; maybe that will do the trick. All kinds of formulæ are tried; it may be that one day one of them will suddenly provide a universal, a quasi-magical solution of all problems, and the "problem of the West" will have been mastered. The whole career of the great Dr. Sun is a kind of quest of a philosopher's stone. Not only do his analyses of political, social and economic forces appear weirdly irrational to Western thought, but they never affected, by any power of reason, the political thought of China. He was always distrusted while he was alive by the majority of his countrymen. He will be remembered in time as an historical figure of tragic irony. When his working life was at an end, his name suddenly was invoked all over the country, as if it were magical in itself; for he had won a following, not by intellectual persuasion, but because his latest, weirdest and least understandable formula seemed for a moment to have turned the trick, to have captured the knack. Since then his name and his formulæ have been invoked only for tactical purposes; his method of modernization has no more been followed out than that of any other philosopher, and the quest for a magic formula that carries the secret of Western power but does not demand the price of Westernization is once more pursued in doubt and conflict by two-and-seventy jarring sects.

The tragedy of Dr. Sun's devoted life is that his ideas, as expounded in the *San Min Chu I* or "Three People's Principles," and elevated to the authority of dogma, serve chiefly to stultify original thought in the generation that is now maturing. Exegesis of the *San Min Chu I* has, to an appalling extent, superseded original thought. To outquote a rival in terms of the *San Min Chu I* is better than to out-think him; to quote Dr. Sun on foreign aggression or economics has, for the student generation, practically replaced the quest for methods of defeating foreign aggression, or for a new economics. So authoritative is the canon that independent utterances on public problems, foreign affairs and political economy can be as dangerous for Chinese politicians as are independent judgments on Russian affairs for American public men. If a quotation from Dr. Sun can be made to apply to any situation, with intent to obstruct, the handling of that situation on its merits can usually be prevented. In the meantime, the world of affairs lives from hand to mouth, convinced neither by the teachings of Dr. Sun, nor by the "new dispensation" of the West, nor yet wholly confident of its own autochthonous tradition.

In the world of affairs the struggle still turns on the question of whether Western activities are to remain essentially Western, or whether they can be transvalued into Chinese terms. Thus foreign interests advancing the capital, undertaking the construction and initiating the administration of railways owned by and operated on behalf of the Chinese Government have consistently found it necessary to stipulate for safeguards of foreign control. All questions of control, and all controversies affecting private investment, Central Government control, Provincial Government control, and so forth, can be reduced to one simple statement of an ultimate antagonism: Are railways in China to be what Westerners think a railway should be, or are they to be what the Chinese think it is enough for a railway to be permitted to be?

In railways which are not safeguarded by some element of foreign control, "capital investment," "operating expenses," "maintenance," "director," "shareholder" and all other technical terms lose their Western significance. The whole enterprise, except for the fact that it was fashioned in the image of a railway, and is called a railway, becomes as unintelligible to a Westerner as are the operations of a Chinese tax-monopoly or the machinery of a Chinese parliament. The chief residuum of fact, from the investor's point of view, is defaulted payments on capital and interest.

On the other hand, every railway or other comparable enterprise which is protected by safeguards, however tactfully disguised, for the benefit of the foreign interests concerned, inevitably affronts the Chinese as an aggression. In other words, what appears to the investor to be the minimum protection insuring a fair return on the investment is construed in the country of investment as "foreign aggression"; and the mere existence of this concept obliterates distinctions of detail between the "aggression" of individuals, corporate firms, or nations. It is all "foreign aggression"; because the whole thing would be done differently if the Chinese had a free hand.

There is no denying the substratum of bitter truth in Dr. Sun's bitter description of China as a "semi-colonial" country. There can be no doubt that only the accident of geographical situation saved China in the past century from being accorded full colonial treatment. Other parts of the world were reached and dealt with first, and by the time China was reached, there was enough tension among the Western nations to make them impede one another in the subjugation of China. The process went little further than the establishment of Western safeguards for processes of Westernization.

WESTERN PRESSURE ON CHINA THROUGH MANCHURIA

The fact that the Chinese instinct still seeks, not to become Western but to use Western methods for holding off the West, is of cardinal importance in the frontier problems of Manchuria, Mongolia and Chinese Turkestan; and above all in Manchuria, which is accessible from the West both by land and sea. In China proper the clash with the West is one of cultures, not of populations. In Manchuria there is a threatened pressure of mutually unassimilable populations.

There is an accelerating spread of Chinese populations, largely made possible by an accelerated introduction of Western methods of transport and exploitation. The strategic position of the nations across the frontiers is becoming decidedly stronger; economic pressure is increasing, and it can hardly be doubted that while direct political pressure is being abandoned, it will as it were inevitably be replaced by increased indirect political pressure.

All of these factors result in a reflex action exceedingly difficult to analyze, but potent in itself, within the "Manchurian situation." The increasing Chinese population represents a Chinese expansion, nominally comparable to the nineteenth-century spread of people of European stock into the American West. Yet on the other hand this Chinese population, worked on both by direct Western pressure and the indirect influences of a Westernization distinctly higher in dynamic power than the parallel forces of Westernization in China proper, itself serves as an intermediary in the increasing general Western pressure on China.

For the pressure of the West on China is not diminishing, but undergoing a transformation of phase. Recent developments in the situation as between China and Russia clearly point out the type of transformation. Direct political pressure is being relaxed, and the privileged position of foreigners, of which "extraterritoriality" is the stronghold and catchword, is being abandoned. The experience of the Russians after the abandonment of extraterritoriality, the uneliminable antagonism between Chinese and Russians over fundamental ideas of the functions of a railway, the dispute of 1929–30, distinguished by the comical avoidance by both sides of the name "war," and the subsequent negotiations, not yet completed, all point to the replacement of "privilege" by something else—"vested interests" or whatever it may be.

The essential processes of Westernization, in defiance of all conciliatory phraseology, continue to be carried on chiefly in forms of aggression; and the status of individuals and corporate bodies associated with an aggressive process cannot be other than "privileged," however earnestly legal definitions of privilege may be avoided.

Moreover, while the direct forces of pressure and privilege are being transformed into activities of different form but equivalent function, there is an inevitable tendency, in the case of a region like Manchuria, toward the taking over of many of the functions of political pressure on China by the Manchurian Chinese themselves. This tendency is reinforced by the political and social tradition of the "reservoir," and facilitated by the employment of such Western instruments of power as the railway, the factory and the arsenal. The obvious and frequently asserted aim of the Chinese in Manchuria is to employ Western methods to hold off the West; to transform Manchuria from a colonial region into a part of China proper, and to support the Chinese front against Russia and Japan. As against the execution of this ideal, however, the reflex action of which I have spoken works in such a manner that, in practice, the mere borrowing of Western technique is enough to prompt the assertion of the power of Manchuria, as a quasi-autonomous unit, in China. The situation, restated in its most simple contradictions, is that the mass colonization of Manchuria by Chinese is in the main made possible by Western methods which were first introduced as a form of aggression (the Chinese Eastern and South Manchuria Railways are good examples) and are in great measure hostile to the spirit of Chinese culture; and that the power inherent in the methods encourages the Manchurian Chinese to reassert against China the ancient domination of the "reservoir"—thus providing a channel which conducts toward China the increased pressure of forces destructive of the essential Chinese civilization.

THE OLD AGE OF CHINESE CIVILIZATION

The civilization of China, as has already been pointed out, is not only extremely old but extremely "late." The period of growth and of dynamic expansion must have been completed before the time of Confucius, for Confucius was no creative thinker, but the didactic tabulator of formulæ already sanctioned as the wisdom of the sages of antiquity. It is the quality of age and fulfilled growth which lies back of the "static" or "repetitive" appearance of Chinese life which very commonly impresses Westerners. Except for the conflict between Western introductions and the old tradition, there seems to be little movement that is not in the manner of variations on old themes. Conservatism not only tends to do the old things in the old way, but the new things, as far as possible, in the old manner. The really crucial problems, in face of such an assertive encroaching power as the civilization of the West, though they are called problems of development, turn more truly on methods of destruction and replacement than on methods of adaptation. That is why the processes of Westernization, though they are felt to be imperative by leaders of Chinese thought and the type of statesman who tries to rule performance by theory, meet with an inert but living opposition in the body of the nation—there is a feeling that reformation is not a triumph, but a defeat.

For this very reason the greatest danger which hangs over China, which disturbs the leaders of all factions and is rapidly coming to be realized as a menace even by the solid, untheoretical classes that have kept China going through the hazardous years of the revolutionary phase—the classes that stick doggedly to practical measures—is the danger of total revolution and chaotic destruction. This danger is generally called Communism, but the label is more convenient than accurate, for Chinese Communism is different both from Marxian theory and Russian practice. It is the embodiment of the danger that all alternatives of adaptation may be abandoned and swept away in a total collapse, with all the violent phenomena of defeat and despair. If the conflict between East and West should end in such a catastrophe, the nation that would at last emerge might be a China dominated and exploited by the West, or it might be something totally different; but it certainly would not be either an "evolved" nation like Japan, in which the old currents have been turned into new channels, or a nation vigorously preserving in all its integrity the old civilization of China, fortified externally by borrowed Western methods.

This latter ideal, that of Western methods adventitiously used but not incorporated into the old tradition nor allowed to modify the essential point of view—an "adaptation" which would preserve the old currents running in the old channels, but would fortify the banks of the channels by the latest modern methods—was the result which all the great modern statesmen of China, from Li Hung-chang to K'ang Yu-wei and Dr. Sun, attempted to achieve by widely differing methods, all of which failed.

The problem of colonization in Manchuria is therefore the problem of assessing an apparently vigorous expansive movement in its relation to the equally apparent and contradictory fact that the expanding nation is shaken down to its roots by an offensive and defensive struggle over the most fundamental conceptions of civilization and instincts of culture, and in the light of the fact that the very factors which make possible a rapid colonizing expansion are in themselves manifestations of forces which threaten the whole of the living Chinese tradition.

Now the civilization of China, it is generally agreed, grew up in the Northwest, in the basin of the Yellow River. The period of its positive expansion is undocumented, for old as Chinese written history is, it only begins at a period when philosophers, historians and statesmen were taking stock of a situation the broad lines of which had already been permanently determined. The driving power of the Chinese, in the period which, though undocumented, must have been the most creative in their history, was directed toward the South and Southeast. China south of the Yangtze was a conquest—a total conquest in terms of civilization, a partial conquest in terms of population. It is for this reason that the center of gravity of the most truly Chinese policies has always lain in the North. The military vigor characteristic of the North, during the long period of documented history, is based on the survival of the ancient domination. It is not, as is occasionally postulated, the result of the incorporation among the northern Chinese of barbarian invaders. These invasions merely reaffirmed a military superiority, in relation to the South, which had always existed, and carried on a political tradition which had long been established.

It is because the ancient center of gravity lay in the North that novel ideas and alien borrowings have always been more welcome in the South, for in the South the Chinese civilization was not quite so ancient, nor so fully worked out; it had undergone initial modifications in the process of establishment, and above all it was not autochthonous. This is so profoundly true that it is axiomatic in Chinese affairs that the less characteristically Chinese any new social or political movement is, and the more it contains of drastic innovation, the further south is its point of initiation and center of gravity.

As for the regions north of the Great Wall, the instinctive attitude toward them was long ago manifested. A positive expansion does not build limiting walls. There are no Great Wall systems in the South. For at least twenty-five centuries, every extension of Chinese authority beyond what is now the line of the Great Wall, even when backed up by a move of population, has had a peculiar lack of vitality. Strategically and politically, as has already been shown, expansion beyond the Wall was defensive. The prime object was to secure the frontier; the acquisition of extra territory was incidental. The social equivalent of this defensiveness can be detected in the substitution of amorphous phenomena of mere spread for phenomena of drive and directional energy. Emigration beyond the Wall is bound up, in the consciousness of the people, with proverbs and legends of lament and despair. The most important positive attitude in such a vaguely spreading population is always the "inward facing" characteristic of the "reservoir"—a characteristic which apparently has no important equivalent among Southern Chinese migrating to, for instance, Malaysia. These emigrants contribute largely to Chinese political funds[2] but they do not exercise a pressure on South China equivalent to the pressure of the northern "reservoir" on North China.

THE MANCHURIAN PRESSURE ON CHINA

It must be evident that many of the forces already considered run counter to generalizations on Manchuria, and on China and Chinese policies, that are based on Western formulæ or on analogies with Europe, America or Japan. If these

---

[2] It is even doubtful how far political contributions from Chinese overseas are spontaneous, since it appears that they are to some extent elicited by threats of reprisals against relatives still in China, or by "racketeering" methods of secret societies.

forces have been correctly appreciated, we shall have to look at the territorial question, not as the eager occupation of "virgin" lands in which an impetuous nation is clamoring to demonstrate its vigor, but as a wary manœuvering to maintain control over lands which dominate North China strategically, and in which Chinese authority has ebbed and flowed for centuries. The immigrants arriving in such numbers are not spontaneously and competitively thrusting forward to find room in which to release their pent-up energies; they represent in the main a reluctant, eddying backwash from a stream which, after flooding its ancient outlet, has backed up sullenly, obliterating its own current. Psychologically, the colonists are less pioneers, carrying with them a young and confident tradition, than refugees, looking over their shoulders at a homeland unwillingly abandoned, and burdened with everything they can save of the old tradition.

Nor, in spite of what Manchuria owes to rapid Westernization, can it be said that, in the popular consciousness, Western technique is regarded as a new dispensation. Western methods are only expedients; the more detached and adventitious the manner in which they can be used, the better; and the reward of successful exploitation with the use of Western means is the ability to live better by the old standard. All exploitation and industry bear the marks of an old society. That most significant phenomenon of a young society, the man who has grown up with an industry and risen to command it, is comparatively rare. On the contrary, the men who dominate the use of the new techniques are generally men who do not understand them and do not want to understand them: they are interested in the profits, not in the thing itself, and they employ subordinates to look after the incomprehensible details. And—which is highly illuminating—this is generally regarded as natural and right.

"Progress" is dominated by "big interests," absentee land-lords and distant capitalists. It distinctly does not spring from the roots of the nation, and is not carried on by ardent pioneers, working spontaneously with their own hands to further the promise of their new home.

Politically, the outlying provinces do not regard themselves as primarily the outposts of a growing empire, in spite of the fact that they inevitably function as outposts. Their forward positions they occupy tentatively, and maintain by shifts and compromises, and forward movement is hesitant. The ambition of the most able and energetic men looks backward, toward China. Here tradition is at its strongest. Subconsciously, much more than consciously, men are powerfully affected by the unbroken tradition of the "reservoir" where, throughout history, the tendency to expand the authority of China has been overborne by the tendency to turn and assert authority in China. I do not see how a man can merge himself at all in the popular feeling of Manchuria and not detect this urgent counter-drift; of which the meaning is, in practice, that a comparatively strong policy of advance, no matter how well planned at headquarters, tends to dwindle, on the front of advance, into a comparatively feeble spread; while, conversely, a relatively slight pressure from beyond the frontier inevitably develops into a relatively strong Manchurian thrust toward China.

This is in many respects the most obscure and the most important riddle of the future. The balance between a forward frontier policy in Manchuria and the domestic relations between Manchuria and China affects the status of all Northeastern Asia, not only in terms of population but of social system and civilization. It is commonly held that China's enormous reserves of population predetermine the final result; but nevertheless the balance at present swings against China.

Thus there was a period of minimum Russian initiative in Russo-Manchurian affairs, following on the death of Chang Tso-lin in 1928. Russia may have been induced by the disappearance of the greatest personal figure in Manchuria—the "Old Marshal," Chang Tso-lin—and perhaps also by the expediency of cultivating good relations in Japan, to try the policy of allowing the Manchurian situation to develop itself. This period was marked by the rapid acceleration of the Chinese spread into North Manchuria, and the attainment of a maximum rate of development of Chinese exploiting enterprises of all descriptions. The projection and initiation of new railways was perhaps the most striking index of expansion. The first sign of trouble from an over-hasty expansion was an outbreak among the Barga Mongols; but as the Young Mongol party in Barga received no strong support from either Outer Mongolia or Russia, the trouble subsided, and the warning was disregarded. It may well be that the Russian attitude of deference to Chinese ambitions was construed as an indication of weakness. At any rate, the Chinese "forward policy" became still more assertive, until the crucial Russian interest in the Chinese Eastern Railway was jeopardized. Russia then called a halt, took up the challenge of the bold Chinese intervention on the Chinese Eastern Railway, and forced the crisis to a definite issue. The Chinese "forward policy" collapsed. No serious effort was made to measure the power of China against that of Russia. The initiative was once more surrendered, and a policy adopted which amounts in practice to a feeling out of the Russian strength and a manipulative adjustment to it—a policy, not of deciding what is to happen and proceeding to make it happen, but of waiting until things have happened and then dealing with the situation defensively.

The consequences of this precipitate abandoning of the initiative can hardly be exaggerated, although the challenge and conflict were so brief and quasi-unofficial, the underlying issues so carefully obscured, and the name of war so disingenuously evaded by both sides. The whole northward drift has almost openly been acknowledged to be a negative policy, profiting opportunistically by every indication of lack of resistance, but not itself informed with inward dynamic power. The streams of colonization in the North have withered, and even those in the South have shrunk. More important still, the whole of Manchuria has frankly faced about toward China once more. The question of the hour is not the technical rectification by treaty of Russo-Manchurian questions, but the potential assertion of the power of Manchuria in China proper. The troops and material which were held in reserve at the time of the Russian conflict have been freely deployed in China: and in spite of the modern names given to many Chinese problems, the essential situation reveals the cleavage between North and South China, and the power of the "reservoir" impending over North China, in a form more pronounced than at any time since the decay of the Ming dynasty and the rise of the Manchus. The fact that Manchuria is still a comparatively empty and undeveloped country, with an inexhaustible supply of settlers from China, and with railways to bring them in and distribute them, and capital to launch them in many enterprises, merely heightens the paradox. The outward-facing frontiers are still frontiers of defense; the front of decisive action is still the line of the Great Wall. So true is this that it is virtually impossible in any moment of crisis to dispatch the best troops and the best material toward the north. The prestige accruing from success would enable the successful general to turn back with irresistible momentum on Manchuria and China. Armies of the North are armies of defense and forlorn hope. Therefore it is a commonplace in the armies of Manchuria that orders for the North endanger the career of an ambitious man, while orders for the South are welcomed as an opening of the gates of opportunity. [3]

[3] While this passage was written before the Japanese occupation of Manchuria, it may well be allowed to stand. The Japanese are hardly likely to make themselves leaders of the "reservoir" in the old Manchu style, though it is quite likely that, having studied Manchurian history with care, they will attempt it. They are too much alien to the tradition. If they consolidate their position in Manchuria, they are most likely to replace the old style of "reservoir" pressure with a Western style of pressure, exercised through Manchuria and bearing on China proper. If, on the other hand, they should retire to their old position, the rule of China could not be established afresh in Manchuria except by conceding increased power to Manchuria in the affairs of China "within the Wall."

CHAPTER V

THE RUSSIANS TURN TO THE EAST

RUSSIANS AND MANCHUS

IT IS hardly surprising that the modern period of colonization in Manchuria opened with a series of defensive measures;
that these measures failed, and that the first true acceleration
of settlement began with the construction of railways which
were essentially forms of Western aggression.

Although the Manchus are commonly held to have initiated and to have been responsible for a policy of exclusion in
Manchuria, in reality they were highly unoriginal and merely
confirmed a state of affairs which (whatever the people concerned) was usual and traditional. The Chinese Bannermen
in Eastern Liaoning, the Mongols in Western Liaoning and
north of Jehol, the Manchus from Mukden northward to the
junction of the Hurka (Mutan) with the Sungari, each dominated a "sphere of interest" in the "reservoir." Imperial
rulings repeatedly confirmed the autonomy of the Mongols
within their own sphere; an autonomy which included the
right of being tried and punished by their own courts. These
rights were even confirmed where Chinese or Manchu
colonies were planted at strategic points in territory taken
over from the Mongols; and apparently when cases of mixed
jurisdiction arose, affecting both Mongols and Manchus, they
had to pass through two courts. These distinctions are
nothing like so clear as between Manchu and Chinese Bannermen, undoubtedly because of the rapidity with which the
Manchus "turned Chinese."

From the Manchus northward the "reservoir" merged in an undefined way into the "unregenerate," largely unknown and largely *unwanted* regions. Tribes like the Daghurs, the Solons and the Gold, incorporated into the Manchu Banner organization as "New Manchus," mark unmistakably the transition between the people of privilege and the tribes of "outer darkness"; the Gilyak, the Tungus of Siberia, *and, finally, the Russians.* The reluctance to expand northward is clearly borne out by the Treaty of Nerchinsk. The whole of the Amur basin and much of Siberia was, in reality, a no-man's-land. The first Russians began to appear when the Manchus were invading China. This is a fact which has always passed almost unnoticed; yet it is probably of high importance. It is only because the penetration of the Russians to the Amur and the rise of the Manchu power are alike insufficiently documented that the two series of events are usually passed over as if they were merely accidentally contemporary, and had no linked significance. A consideration of the general structure and style of the history of the region, however, makes it practically certain that the advance of the Russians into extreme Eastern Siberia and the emergence of the Manchus on the edge of the Manchurian "reservoir," were both parts of a series of interconnected tribal movements, which originated among the extra-"reservoir" or unregenerate tribes, and are therefore undocumented and cannot be reconstructed.[1] Although the Manchus must have been impelled originally by pressure from beyond the "reservoir,"

---

[1] The first Russian pioneers in this region were Cossacks; and it is not for nothing that the very name Cossack was borrowed by the Russians from the nomadic Qazaqs of Southwestern Siberia. The first Cossacks were adventurers who struck out into the wilderness for various reasons of restlessness and discontent, and borrowed the name to fit their quasi-tribal life. In their later migrations they functioned to an extraordinary degree in a "tribal" manner, and there was therefore every reason, when they first appeared on the Amur, to consider them as merely the latest comers out of the unknown wilderness which had so often bred fierce and incomprehensible tribes.

all we have now, because the middle links have dropped out, are the apparently independent phenomena of the emergence of the Manchus as organizers and leaders of the "reservoir," and the appearance of Cossack adventurers on the Amur. The success of the Manchus in their southward movement allowed an easing off of inter-tribal pressure, and this accounts for the loss of continuity. Yet what was happening, during the lull in tribal movements was (from the point of view of Chinese history) the *assumption by the Russians of the position of latest-arrived tribe among the "unregenerate northern barbarians"*; and, under the thin veil of "modern world history," that is the function the Russians have continued to exercise, and still exercise, on the whole frontier from the Pamirs to the Pacific. The present stratification Siberia–Amur–"Manchurian Reservoir"–North China, which transmits *cumulating* pressures southward, but *diminishing* pressures northward, is the full equivalent of the ancient stratification (which also is not yet out of the picture) definable as Outer Mongolia–Gobi–"Inner Mongolian Reservoir"–Great Wall.

In fact the early Manchu policy toward the Russians must have been characteristically in the "reservoir" historical style. Although the Manchus cannot but have been aware that the Russian raids up to the Amur and the consequent Russian ascendancy among the "unregenerate tribes" corresponded with their own ascendancy in the "reservoir" and their irruption into China, they made no determined effort to clear and define the frontier. They were content with measures of a punitive and preventive order. Finally, after Albazin had changed hands more than once, in an indecisive manner, and before the relative strength of Russia and China had been put to anything like definite proof, frontier relations were adjusted by the Treaty of Nerchinsk (1689) when the Manchus were at the height of their power. The Russians agreed to withdraw north of the Amur watershed; but in spite of the Chinese (Manchu) claims preferred in the treaty, it is clear that there was no desire to expand into and occupy this territory.

In fact the Manchus, thereafter, kept well to the south of the Amur, except for a few outposts. The importance of the great dockyard at Ninguta (later transferred to Kirin city) and the river fleet guarding the Sungari all the way to the Amur was not a function of "empire building" but one of patrol. For the rest, the maintenance of a huge, virtually uninhabited and trackless forested waste between Manchus and Russians minimized frontier incidents. All Northern Manchuria—more than half the area of the three modern provinces—became for the Manchus precisely what Tibet is to the British in India: a buffer region where the encroachment of another power would cause apprehension, but where the responsibility of occupation and government was by all means to be avoided, short of the most imperative necessity. For the Russians, on the other hand, it became what the Dark and Bloody Ground of Kentucky was to the American pioneers: the land of expansion, of adventure and empire-building for the sake of empire-building. Even with a complete lack of population-pressure behind them they were impelled forward. The wilderness, as wilderness, had an *attraction* for them which it has never had for the Chinese pioneer.

All of this confirms what has already been said: that the Manchu laws which hampered emigration to Manchuria, although in the first instance they did maintain "preserves" of the privileged "reservoir" populations, were also congruent with the traditional Chinese statecraft, in maintaining the balance of the Empire by discouraging any pronounced extension of population to the North. It is evident from edicts and imperial pronunciamentos dealing with the "reservoir" that the paramount Manchu principle was not to reserve the waste land for Manchu expansion, but to keep out Chinese because they might contaminate the vigorous Manchu tradition. Even when attempts were made to plant colonies of Peking Manchus in the Nonni-Sungari region (Petuna), the governing idea was not a "forward policy" for the North, but the feeling that there were too many idle Manchus in China, that they were losing the Manchu speech and tradition, and that by moving them back to the "reservoir" they might recover the "reservoir" spirit.

From this point of view the "reservoir" functioned efficiently almost up to the end of the dynasty. It kept up a supply of troops whose loyalty was to the dynasty primarily; who were never used for "opening up" the North, but merely for holding it down, and who were regularly drafted for service in China as well as on the frontier. Thus the Solons were drawn on to garrison Urga, Kobdo and Uliassutai in Outer Mongolia—the stronghold of the "unregenerate"—and Chuguchak and Ili in Chinese Turkestan. They were also employed in campaigns against Tibet, and against the Western Muhammadans in the eighteen hundred and sixties. All of these duties were, strategically, defensive. Manchu Bannermen from Kirin province also served against the Muhammadans, and against the Taiping rebels on the Yangtze. Mongol troops from the Inner Mongolian and Manchurian "reservoir," under a Mongol commander, not only safeguarded the north of China while Ward and after him Gordon trained the Ever-Victorious Army which crushed the Taipings, but were also the most effective of the troops opposed to the French and British advance on Peking in 1860.

Had an energetic expansion of colonists into Manchuria reversed the traditional "reservoir" style which the Manchus did not originate but took over, not only the balance but the orientation of the Empire would have been disturbed (as the balance of the Republic is now disturbed by the vacillation between inward-facing and outward-facing policies), while none of the ancient problems of China would have been any nearer solution. It is perfectly true that if there had been a spontaneous, dynamic urge within the Chinese people, impelling them toward Manchuria, subsequent developments would have been quite different. As far as that goes, there would never have been a Great Wall. Nothing could be more certain than that there was no such overwhelming urge, and it follows that the restrictive measures passed by the Manchus were not felt as monstrous or unduly repressive by the Chinese of China, who were, in fact, still completely satisfied with the grand and final gesture of the Great Wall. It is hard, therefore, to concede total validity to the post-Revolution charges of narrow selfishness that have been preferred against the Manchus, as if they alone were responsible for the character of Chinese northern frontier policy.

THE RUSSIAN ADVANCE DOWN THE AMUR

In effect, then, it was the slackening of the Russian advance after the Treaty of Nerchinsk that allowed the northern frontier regions to become stabilized during the Manchu rule in China. The Manchus themselves were perfectly content so long as the Russians remained out of sight, and in order to help them stay out of sight were willing to refrain from doing more than patrolling the Sungari and keeping a watch on the Amur. They thus forwent in practice the claim advanced in the Treaty of Nerchinsk to a dominion extending up to the northern watershed of the Amur.

It might be possible to draw up an extreme accusation

against Russia of having filched enormous areas of Siberia; but realistically speaking it can only be said that the Russians, although comparatively late arrivals, occupied effectively territories which might have been occupied by China, but never had been. In point of fact most of these territories, up to the Treaty of Nerchinsk, could not validly be assigned to any owners except scattered nomadic tribes which claimed "ownership" in the nomadic sense of freedom to move, not in the elaborate civilized sense of theoretical group ownership superimposed on subdivided individual ownerships. "Tribute," chiefly in the form of sable pelts, found its way from these regions to Peking; but it also, at an early period, was offered to the Tsar.

An historical analysis of the real status of "tributary" tribes would be of the greatest interest. Undoubtedly, many "tributary" offerings were in fact a form of trade, the tribute being purchased by the appointed officials. In extreme instances, the nominal tribute to the suzerain power was actually a form of levy on the suzerain power; the "presents" offered in exchange for the "tribute" greatly exceeding the value of the "tribute" itself. Thus the tribute offered by the Mongol tribes was in large measure a disguise for the subsidies paid to the lords of the "reservoir"; but in the Amur region generally the tribute offerings appear to have been obtained chiefly by trade. The sable-tribute claimed by the Cossacks appears to have been much more in the nature of an oppressive exaction; and it was largely the diminution in the supply of sables, and the consequent extension of Cossack forays into the forests south of the Amur, that brought about the acute political situation leading finally to the Treaty of Nerchinsk.

The lull after the Treaty of Nerchinsk lasted up to the middle of the nineteenth century, when the great modern Russian surge toward the Pacific began to gather way. The ad-

vance of the Russians into Northeastern Asia, although slow
in point of time, was one of extraordinary vigor, considering
the great range of distance and the difficulties overcome. It
has been pointed out that the Cossacks who led the advance
operated largely in a "tribal" manner. As a "mixed group"
they are in some respects comparable to the mixed groups
of the Chinese-Mongol frontier, but with the difference that
they penetrated to a much greater depth and that they never
had the tendency to reverse political action characteristic of
the "reservoir." This all-important difference allowed them
to become to a great extent enlisters and leaders of other
tribes. The heritage of this tendency can be seen even at the
present day; its most important phenomenon being the use
of the Buriat Mongols of Siberia in extending Russian policies
in Mongolia.

Indeed the whole nineteenth-century Russian advance in-
herited a great deal of the Cossack spirit, although in point of
numbers the Cossacks were swamped by peasants, and although the colonizing spirit as a whole was modified strongly
by the convict exiles. One of the striking characteristics of
the Cossack spirit of adventure into the wilderness was that
it operated in spite of governmental policy, and was at its
best when free of official influence. The Russian Government,
like that of China, was not originally oriented toward the
wilderness. From the time of Peter the Great there had been
a strong movement of Europeanization; higher policy condemned commitments in the vast unknown East. Therefore
the regular type of the Russian advance was that government
authority, without having proposed or administered the advance, was more or less dragged after it perforce. In this lies
the great contrast between Russia and China. The Chinese
people as a whole were in accord with the policy which re-
frained from frontier adventures, while the Russians, in de-

spite of policy and apart altogether from such "natural causes" as population pressure, impelled solely by an inward unrest, broke away into the East and drew the government after them into a situation which practically forced the later deliberate policy of Eastern expansion.

The tradition of the roving adventurer goes back clearly at least as far as the mighty Yermak, who conquered "Sibir" as an outlaw, and offered his private conquest to the Tsar as a bribe to recover lawful public standing. In much the same spirit the great Muraviev, on his own initiative, and using the men and resources of Siberia alone and deceiving the home government into the belief that he was only organizing a defense, undertook to reach the Pacific—and succeeded. The home government was then confronted with the alternative of withdrawing, which would not only have damaged its prestige in the eyes of China but, in view of the recent defeat in the Crimea, would have been a confession of weakness to the world at large, or of consolidating the position won. Thus Muraviev was able to conclude the Treaty of Aigun, in 1858, which the home government backed up and amplified in the negotiations at Peking in 1860. Russia then stood on the Pacific, with a port at Vladivostok and a Manchurian border following the course (no longer merely the watershed) of the Amur and Ussuri. The buffer territories established in part through the Treaty of Nerchinsk and in part through subsequent Manchu policy were largely in Russian hands, and a situation had been created which compelled the government to implement the eastward-directed ambition of the pioneers. The crux of the situation, historically, was the moment when Muraviev, acting on his own initiative, confronted the home government with advantageous treaty terms which had either to be accepted or inconveniently disavowed.

The Russians had now emerged as the modern exemplars of

the northern barbarians, threatening the "reservoir" and therefore the whole power of China. As for the tribes of the "unregenerate" region, far from being in a position to stave off the Russians and thus act as the pawns of China, they were obviously incorporated in the Russian advance; witness the enlistment of "Buriat Cossacks" from a comparatively early period. Yet even so, the reluctance of China to face the north was so deep-seated that counter-policies did not develop until Russian railway construction began first to fill up Siberia and then to project railways in Manchuria, which ranked definitely and unmistakably as methods of aggression. It was not until the late eighteen hundred and eighties that the Manchu Government was forced to recognize that the "reservoir" frontier structure, as it stood, was inadequate, and that an active attempt must be made to fill up the northern front in order to make a stand against the northern barbarians; by which time the Russian momentum was too great for the un-aided power of China to divert it.

In default of a flow of raiding, thrusting Chinese pioneers who might have rivaled and forestalled the Russian adventurers, it was necessary to undertake artificial colonization under government encouragement. The method adopted was that of throwing open "public" domains and allotting land grants on terms which might tempt a supply of settlers. Colonies were thus established not only in Manchuria but in Outer Mongolia, and a partial screen of agricultural Chinese was actually settled along the Orkhon river, masking the entry into Outer Mongolia from Kiakhta. So weak were its foundations, however, that it collapsed after the Chinese Revolution in 1911, and it is said that there is now practically no trace of the colonists.

The weakness of the colonization fostered out of policy alone was that it went against the grain of the characteristic

Chinese method of advance. The settlers much preferred to filter up through territory already occupied, and to establish themselves on the fringe, where success would mean early incorporation into the main body. They had never inclined to the "raiding," deep-penetrating Cossack style of advance, which resulted in isolated settlements; though settlements approximating to this type are to be found, notably in the Ussuri region. On the whole, they were shy of getting too far beyond the "spread." The small element which had a tradition of penetrating among the Mongols by means of "going native" to a greater or less extent was already fully occupied. The numbers of such people, rooted in a special tradition, cannot be summarily augmented; and moreover they were not exactly of the Cossack type of combined roving adventurers and land-fast settlements, having been too strongly modified by the Mongol tradition.

In the upshot, the politically encouraged frontier colonies proved to be separated by too great a gap from the main front of the "spread." Nor could the "spread" itself be greatly speeded up, for lack of spontaneous desire for emigration in the people of China proper. The land-grant policy therefore collapsed. Its chief result was that huge tracts passed into the hands of individuals or firms—in which the officials who had handled the grants were, as a group, heavily interested; but thereafter, for lack of colonists and ability to exploit dynamically, they remained undeveloped. The holders resigned themselves to wait patiently while the "spread" approached the regions of political anxiety. The main result was a more general recognition of the importance of the northern frontier (an importance in no way different from that it had assumed in cycle after cycle of assault from the barbarians of the north); but it remained characteristically a defensive frontier. There was no sign of transformation into a frontier of expansion. In the meantime, the Russian expansion developed with increasing power, through railway construction and the comparatively sudden and unpremeditated adoption of a government policy of eastward advance.

FOREIGN AGGRESSION AND CHINESE EXPANSION

The period that followed, that of the wars between Japan and China and Japan and Russia, need hardly be discussed in detail. It is plain enough that they originated in the rivalry between Japan and Russia for strategic command of the Korean-Manchurian region; the stake of Japan being continental security and the stake of Russia an ice-free Pacific port, which alone could energize the vast conquests in Siberia. Not only did the Chinese defensive front in Manchuria break down, but in the second stage, that of the war between Japan and Russia, she was compelled to endure passively the campaigns of alien armies on her territory. The upshot of the period of warfare was the beginning of a period of active exploitation by Japan and Russia, in which China was a partner more in the sense of being exploited than of sharing in the exploitation. It was the construction of the Chinese Eastern and South Manchuria Railways, both enterprises of exploiting "Imperialism," which determined the future of Manchuria as a scene of successful Chinese colonization, for which the Peking-Mukden Railway (itself, from the Chinese point of view, not free from the taint of foreign aggression) was not alone sufficient.

Another result of the wars was the confirmation of the Chinese title to sovereignty in Manchuria, which can thus be regarded as dependent to a certain extent on the adjustment of the policies of Russia and Japan, after failure on the part of China to defend it effectively. The struggle, in fact, veered away from questions of political title and became largely transformed into a rivalry of economic control. Consequently all Chinese measures in Manchuria have continued, ever since, to be strongly influenced by necessities of defense. The modern phase of apparently triumphant Chinese expansion in Manchuria is, in its other aspect, a desperate struggle to maintain control. It is commonly said that the establishment of a successful and growing Chinese population has settled for all time the question of sovereignty in Manchuria. This is true as far as it goes, but it burkes the most vital issue; for the question of sovereignty in Manchuria has to a certain extent (and by virtue of alien policies, not of Chinese policies) become a side-issue; whereas the true crux, the struggle for the initiative in exploitation and real control is a living issue by no means yet decided. Chinese, when an enterprise of far-reaching importance is under discussion in Manchuria, have often to consider not only "What do we want to do?" but "What can we do?" and "What must we do?" This forces the conclusion that the period of "foreign privilege" in China is by no means over, but is merely passing into a new phase, disguised under novel forms, leaving the ultimate antagonism between East and West still uneliminated.

For, from this point of view, Chinese colonization in Manchuria, which is generally regarded as the most important contemporary phenomenon of successful Chinese expansionism, appears as *one of the functions of successful foreign aggression.* All the phenomena of mass colonization are inherent in the very forms of Western-imposed exploiting enterprises in Manchuria; but, until the advent of the West, there was nothing inherent in the Chinese contact with the "reservoir" except a fortuitous and gradual "spread." Therefore one of the capital problems of Manchurian colonization, from the Chinese point of view, is the recovery of the initiative, of the power to determine the degree of Westernization to be aimed at, and of the control of the rate of Westernization. The type and trend of Chinese colonization having been so largely predetermined by Western aggression and exploitation, the influx of Chinese colonists remains, to a great extent, an induced "reaction," and to that extent cannot be considered an original "pioneer" movement.

Chapter VI

LAND AND POWER IN CHINESE MANCHURIA

PUBLIC LAND AND TRIBAL LAND

THE types of land tenure were so well recognized in old Manchuria that, when rapid colonization began, there was no problem of creating new systems. The old land laws and methods of administration could be applied, but on a larger scale, and with gradual adaptation to the accelerating rate of settlement.

Since, in Manchu regions, there had already been an easy transition from a conception of "public" land to a theory of "state" land, no problem arose except the question of administrative processes in allotting state land to private holders. In general, mere "squatter" occupation appears to have been sufficient, in the early period, to establish an option of ownership. Thereafter all that was required was official assessment of the land for taxation. At a later period, when large grants were made from the public domain, the land was, in theory, first assessed by officials and then turned over to colonists. In the case of large grants, it was understood that the owner would himself find and establish cultivators, and that thereafter the tax rate would be adjusted according to the degree of cultivation. If squatters were found already established in nominally empty lands, it was easy for them to make terms with the new owner, because their cultivation of the land had enhanced its value, and they provided a nucleus for new settlement. The development of rent-purchase methods for the transfer of land from large holders to small holders appears to have been early and spontaneous.

This type of colonization naturally affected first such valleys and plains as were most attractive for agricultural occupation. Moreover there seems to be a deep-seated Chinese prejudice which retards the allotment of mountain wilderness to private ownership. It is probably based on the feeling that such "natural" wealth as mines and timber (not man-created, like agricultural wealth) is public property, and should not pass into outright private ownership, though it may be exploited through contracts and concessions leased to private enterprise through official agencies.

"Tribal" questions, largely because of the status of mountain and forest wilderness, have always been comparatively unimportant in the Manchu region and the adjacent "unregenerate" lands of northernmost Kirin and Heilungchiang. The tribesmen were few in numbers and in the main kept to the forested ranges. Where colonization did intrude into their hunting domains, they either withdrew or became corrupted, as savages always are corrupted by civilization, especially by civilized traders; and such remnants as now survive are rapidly being extinguished.

The most interesting question of a "tribal" type, or nearly tribal type, that did develop was perhaps that affecting the Tungusic tribe known to the Russians as Goldi and to the Chinese as one of the group of "Fishskin Tatars." The fate of the Daghur of the Nonni valley, in their transition from tribesmen to Bannermen and later in the inundation of their land by Chinese colonists, is probably a close parallel to the fate of the Goldi or Gold.

The valley habitat of the Gold on the lower Sungari was of a kind to attract Chinese colonists, especially after the opening of steamer traffic, about 1903–04 under Russian influence (a clear case of the determination of Chinese colonization trends by Western enterprise). An arrangement was therefore made which has a certain resemblance to the American Indian "Reservation," with the difference that the American Indians were usually penned into their reservations to get rid of them, while the Gold were given what amounted to an option on the best land. The Gold owed this to the fact that they were auxiliaries of the Manchus, and technically had the status of Manchu Bannermen in the division known as "New Manchus," and to the fact that the project of colonization was inaugurated while the Manchu dynasty still ruled—originally with the intention of frontier defense, although colonization never got under way until steamer traffic was opened and the "aggressors" were, in reality, within the border.

The Gold have long been a non-nomadic people. They live largely by fishing and by hunting; but though the technique of travel and camping used by the hunting parties are reminiscent of an earlier nomadism, and though they travel over great distances and are away from home for long periods, their society is based on fixed village homes. When colonization began, therefore, they were allotted strips of land adjoining their villages, and as these were regularly on the banks of the Sungari, Amur, and Ussuri, they held potentially the most valuable land in centers of future colonization. These block grants were made according to the size of the village, and then distributed to individuals by the clan and village organizations of the tribesmen themselves. The tragedy of the Gold has been that their privileged Banner position had already given them a taste for the benefits of the Chinese type of culture, without a secure enough grounding in it to enable them to meet the incoming Chinese on equal terms. Having already, like the early Manchus, begun the process of turning culturally Chinese, they had no instinct to migrate away from the new pressure. Above all, having learned most of what they knew of the Chinese culture from a position of social privilege and guided by tastes of self-indulgence, they had not acquired the habit of trade. Consequently their lands have passed almost entirely into the hands of the Chinese, and they have become a depressed class, hangers-on of the more able newcomers.

Hunting is now more important to the Gold than fishing; and they also practice a comparatively slovenly agriculture. They bring back from the mountains not only furs, but such valuable ingredients of Chinese medicine as elk-horn in the velvet, and ginseng. These they sell to the Chinese dealers. They spend riotously the money thus earned and remain poor. On account of their fecklessness the Chinese, who are short of women, can outbid the Gold themselves for Gold women as wives, and this has finally determined the extinction of the Gold as a separate people.

Between the time when the Chinese began to enter the lower Sungari valley in large numbers and the time when they unmistakably dominated the Gold, there was a good deal of inter-racial trouble. At first the Gold, holding the privileged status of Bannermen, domineered over the Chinese. Then came a period when the Gold were alarmed by the influx of Chinese. At this time, in spite of the new official sanction granted to Chinese colonization, murders of Chinese were common. All travel was unsafe and all strangers went in danger of their lives in lonely places. The trouble was aggravated by the fact that many of the newcomers were bad characters, that questionable methods were used in trade, and that one of the axioms of trade was the demoralization of the Gold by drink and opium. As for drink and opium, they were inevitable, for the Gold demanded them; but none the less they resented the advantage taken of them through their own vices. Chinese ascendancy grew inevitably, was confirmed with the fall of the Manchu dynasty, and reached the stage when the Gold could be swindled with impunity and no longer dared make reprisals. Thereafter they sank rapidly to their present lamentable condition.

Yet it is remarkable that in spite of the period of lawlessness (now continued in the non-racial form of chronic banditry) the remnant of the Gold are not regarded by the Chinese with anything like that deep-seated hostility which persists between Chinese and Mongols, but on the whole only with a sort of good-humored contempt. This must be very largely due to the fact that they were never numerous enough to threaten to displace the Chinese, once colonization had begun—a contrast with the Mongol regions, where periods of Chinese advance have alternated with temporary Mongol recovery.

It is true that the Gold were associated with the Manchus, who were, like the Mongols, direct conquerors of the Chinese, and therefore, in kind, "oppressors," though they had never handled the Chinese so roughly as the Mongols had. On the other hand the Gold, like the Manchus, had always shown a decided tendency, in spite of Imperial policies which aimed at keeping them "tribal," to admire and adopt Chinese ways of life—though they had begun with the upper strata of privilege, not with the groundwork strata of the peasant, artisan and trader. Their chief interest as a remnant-people is therefore the manner in which they preserved, until very recently, a social transition-stage between the "tribal" and the "reservoir," of a kind which can confidently be labeled "early post-conquest Manchu."

In the comparatively simple land administration of the Manchu "reservoir" and the adjacent "unregenerate" regions, the historical stages can be satisfactorily distinguished. People like the Manchus and Gold, of an original hunting nomad stock (who almost undoubtedly once owned reindeer) became attached to permanent village sites in great river valleys in the wilderness. It may be that one reason for their settling down was the fact that they had ranged south of country suitable for reindeer. While the villages were permanent, hunting was kept up by parties which stayed out in the forest for weeks, and wandered over great distances. A garden-patch agriculture grew up in the villages, with family or individual ownership of the land cultivated. Villages were not restricted to single clans, but members of the same clan lived in different villages. This weakened any idea of clan territory, and all the wilderness remained free to all. Parties from different villages traveled to and hunted in the same forests and mountains. What remained of inter-tribal division was almost obliterated when all the people were united into a military nation; tribal divisions persisted only in distinctions between such groups as the Gold and Daghur, who were outside of the immediate scope of the original Manchu unification.

The similar tribal groups that once existed among the Manchus proper can now be traced only in very faint traditions. A territorial military cadre, that of the Banners (which perhaps derived its numeration in series of eights from some antecedent tribal league, but which retained few tribal functions), was superimposed on the clans and villages. The territorial associations of villages became more important, and the wilderness, which had once been public in the sense that nobody had any more right to it than anybody else, became public in the sense that it was the domain of the sovereign, the lord of land and people alike. Even so, in practice, the custom survived that a clearing in the wilderness and the tilling of fields established private ownership, subject only to the payment of taxes. Efforts were made, however, to restrict the opening of new land to the privileged people, the Manchus and other Bannermen.

In this social structure a new policy of colonization did not require a change of basic social attitudes. All that was required was enlargement of the privilege of settlement, to include non-Banner Chinese. Tracts of the imperial domain were thrown open, allotted to firms or individuals, and developed by attracting settlers. Questions of land measurement, land purchase and land taxation could be dealt with by the existing official organization, assisted by extra land commissioners. As population increased, the administrative problem could be met (as it still is met) by subdividing the areas of government. A "county" of great area, with a population concentrated at a few points, can thus be split into several new counties.

In Mongol-inhabited regions, the tribal concept of land-ownership, and the antipathy felt for individual property in land make the problem radically different—although, superficially, the mechanics of administration, with the allotment of land by special commissioners and the organization of "counties," do not seem to differ greatly. Above all, the permissive expedient of allowing individual ownership to be constituted by occupation and tillage could not work except as an irritant, and could not be practiced at all except at points where Chinese colonists felt that they could choose their own way of doing things in spite of the Mongols—in which case the first operation in clearing the land was likely to be clearing it of Mongols. That "squatter" claims run counter to the Mongol tradition is borne out by the fact that where the Mongols themselves do practice tillage, for the sake of necessary winter supplies, it is common to enforce a rule that the same land may not be permanently cultivated. This practice was additionally encouraged by the fact that Mongol tillage, being crude and slipshod, allowed fields to become overrun with weeds. Moreover the Mongol instinct of the "freedom to move" must be considered, even where, as in the "reservoir," the tribes have long been allotted to defined territorial stations. It is my opinion that, apart altogether from the lesson of experience that Chinese encroachment on unused Mongol lands is followed by encroachment on indispensable pasture, the instinct of the "freedom to move" is an important factor in the Mongol reluctance to allow colonization even on lands that have been unused as pasture for many years.

In order, therefore, to take over even unpopulated Mongol land it is necessary to deal first with a tribe. The land must first be taken over by the state from the tribe, and thus, after having passed through the intermediary status of "public domain," be allotted to private ownership. The concomitant social adjustment that has to be made is thus not, as in the Manchu "reservoir," the abolition of the privilege of a class, or the enlargement of the privilege to include non-Banner immigrants (which comes to the same thing) but the almost complete withdrawal of one people, and the total abolition of their culture, to be replaced by a hostile population and an inimical culture. Hence the *swamping* of the Manchus by a largely contemptuous but at the same time largely tolerant Chinese population, in contrast with the *extrusion* (often amounting to gradual extermination) of the Mongols, accompanied by chronic and unavoidable ill-feeling between Mongols and Chinese.

The two elements of latest growth in the Mongol culture— the development of the princes into a petty territorial feudal aristocracy, and the growth of lamaism, of which the most important phenomenon is the establishment of monasteries— both do violence to the old Mongol instinct for free movement. The monasteries, because they cannot be moved when the Mongols withdraw, often become pawns of Chinese policy. Just as princes frequently sacrifice the interests of the tribe as a whole to their own interest in special privileges and fixed revenues, so monasteries, to preserve their corporate existence and the privileges of the hierarchy, tend to throw their influence on the side of the Chinese when the land passes under Chinese administration. Many lama monasteries, founded in tribal lands, now stand surrounded by a Chinese population. The Mongols continue to come into them on pilgrimage, and pressure is often exercised on the high lamas to secure their aid as intermediaries in negotiating for fresh tracts of land to be taken over for settlement.

As for the princes, their "feudal" status has been badly unsettled by the fall of the Empire. The feudal loyalty felt by a prince for an emperor can hardly be transferred intact to a republic. This point has, in fact, been openly raised in Outer Mongolia, as one of the titles to freedom and independence of the Mongol Republic. There the stand is taken that the Outer Mongolian princes, now succeeded by the Mongol Republic, owed allegiance to the Manchu emperors of China, but not to the Chinese nation. With the abdication of the last emperor, therefore, the Mongols became an autonomous people, as they had been when the Ming emperors ruled in China, and were free to identify their fortunes with China or not, as they chose. The princely families of Outer Mongolia, never so strong as those of Inner Mongolia, because they had not come within the closer organization of the true "reservoir," have now gone under. The princes of Inner Mongolia, therefore, are left in an awkward position. Any move on their part to identify their tribes with those of Outer Mongolia would mean the abolition of their own titles and loss of their hereditary privileges. Every concession made to the suzerainty of China, on the other hand, means a loss of actual power and a fall in status to the position of subsidized figureheads. In this the monastic foundations are practically at one with the princes; and none the less for the fact that the highest lamas are frequently relatives of ruling princes. Under such conditions it has been inevitable that the Inner Mongolian princes and high lama dignitaries should as a class have become tools of Chinese policy; though at times individual princes and lamas have taken the lead in the abortive and hopeless (but also inevitable) Mongol rebellions that intermittently interrupt the modern Chinese advance. The tendency to look out for their own interests at the expense of their people is made stronger by the Chinese method of expropriating land. Not only is the land arbitrarily, and against the main trend of Mongol tradition, treated as the personal domain of the prince; but thereafter, for lack of government funds to pay out cash compensation for expropriated land, the prince is assigned a perpetual rental interest. Temple foundations, in the same way, are assigned a rental compensation to take the place of the previous income from temple herds. At the same time, as the Mongols continue to visit the temple, the trade of Chinese merchants benefits and the temple itself and its lamas become hostages for the good behavior of the Mongols.

When the land has thus been taken over by the Chinese officials, an immediate cash fund to cover administrative expenses is raised by selling it to colonists, or rather to colonizing entrepreneurs. The sale price is very low; it is equivalent to the payment of an option or premium which secures to the investor the future profit on the land when its value has been raised by development. Normally, there is an intermediate stage in colonization, the majority of the land being taken over from the official land-commissioners by individuals or firms with large capital, who redistribute it to the actual farming colonists. A certain proportion of the initial cash fund is passed on by the commissioners to the princes or monasteries; partly to give them an immediate interest in closing the transaction, partly to assist them in moving out the Mongols without untoward incidents of resentment and hostility. In this way some of the cash does find its way to the individual tribesmen who have been dispossessed—or rather, to use a word more suited to Mongol conditions, displaced.

The bulk of the fund raised by the first turnover in land goes to finance the new administration during the period that intervenes before regular revenue can be collected; for the colonists or development agencies, in consideration of their initial cash outlay, are allowed an interval, usually of three years, in which to plow the virgin land, settle tenants and get cultivation started. Thereafter regular land taxes are collected, a percentage of which is paid to the Mongol prince.

It might be thought that after a lapse of time, especially when the Mongols have withdrawn to a comparatively great distance, the payment of such subsidies might be allowed to default. There are three chief reasons why this does not happen. One is the necessity for keeping up the standard of contract so long as any Mongol land remains to be acquired. One is the absence of a popular form of government, under which taxpayers have to be flattered and under which it would be natural for elected representative demagogues to make a campaign issue of the abolition of "unearned and undeserved" revenues paid to a distant and impotent princeling. One— and this is the most important—is that a special bureau, a department of the general administrative system, normally handles the prince's share of revenue. The officials of the bureau have a vested interest in keeping up the collections and payments; the more so as, by immemorial usage, they make a profit on all their transactions which is far more important than their salaries. Thus it is common to find city properties (as in Ch'angch'un and numbers of other places) which to the present day pay revenue to Mongol princes, though the region has long lost any Mongol appearance, or even any special "frontier" associations.

Nor is the profit on the manipulation of funds between collection and payment to the Mongol prince or monastery the only margin of interest in land administration and land transactions. There are many such margins. One, which recurs repeatedly, is the margin of measurement. In the first instance, the land is taken over in great stretches, "Mongol fashion," from landmark to landmark. Thereafter it is distributed by measurement; and the first measurement, granted to large buyers, is more generous than the second measurement, when the extent of cultivation is checked over and land taxation begins. In the course of years, occasional reassessments are made, as the region is filled up and officials multiply. Reassessment commonly requires a tax on the verification of documents, in addition to the fact that the unit of land measurement is more and more strictly narrowed down. A grant originally measured as one hundred *mu* may thus, in time, come to be measured as several hundred *mu;* not to mention the fact that the tax per unit may also gradually increase. In fact, if only it were possible to tabulate the regional ratios between nominal measurement and actual measurement, and relate them to a common standard (a task of enormous difficulty, owing to the play of custom and precedent in each region) it would be both interesting and feasible to estimate the age and stage of colonization of any region by the actual size of the nominally standard unit of measurement.

Owing to the fact that the Mongols, even in retreat, hang

together as a social body, they are not normally swamped by
the Chinese colonists, as the Gold have already been swamped
and as the Manchus have practically been swamped. Race
hostility thus tends to persist, although the Mongols progressively diminish in numbers and power, and are confined to
rapidly shrinking ranges of pasture. Distinctions between
Mongol and Chinese administration also survive, which occasionally amount to a kind of extraterritoriality. There is no
set code or formal agreement between Mongol and Chinese
authorities regulating the extent of this autonomy; in fact it
increases recognizably in proportion to the distance from the
nearest Chinese troops; but it is based to a certain extent on
precedents drawn from imperial edicts and rulings in specific
instances under the Manchu dynasty. Except in times of
tension and heightened feeling there is undoubtedly a tendency for Mongols to get rid of Chinese undesirables simply
by expelling them from the region in which Mongol autonomy is exercised, and a similar, but less general tendency
for the Chinese to hand over Mongol delinquents to the
Mongol authorities; while cases of important dispute between
Mongols and Chinese are frequently settled by a kind of semi-
official arbitration between deputies of the Chinese and Mongol administrations.

Curiously enough, it is probably Mongol autonomy,
especially in regions administered by rapacious under-
lings, the prince having departed to live on his revenues in
Peking or Mukden, that is chiefly responsible for the fact
that a minority of Mongols do remain behind when the
pastures are abandoned, and settle down among the Chinese
to "turn Chinese." Mongols who take up agriculture rarely
feel any "aspiration" for the "higher standards" of the Chinese
culture; they commonly say that they have stayed on in the
sphere of Chinese advance because the exactions on behalf

of the Mongol prince have become unbearable. They look back on the old tradition with melancholy and regret, and regard their new way of life not as the dawn of opportunity, but as the best choice open to a fallen generation in an evil day. When land is first taken over for colonization, settlers are in demand and taxation is light—usually much lighter than Mongol taxation. The Mongol can then take up a holding on excellent terms, or even, under the best-administered modern settlement projects, on nominal terms or entirely free of purchase charges. Even so it is common, and probably general, to find that Mongols who have taken on the Chinese way of life, even after a couple of generations, retain their pride of race and do their best to retain their language, with a vitality which, as has already been pointed out, contrasts strongly with the lack of vitality in the Manchu language— though it is true that the oldest settled groups, like the Tumet, both those north of Jehol and those of the Suiyüan-Kueihua plain, after probably two centuries of settlement, have almost or completely lost their language.

OFFICIALS AS EXPLOITERS

While these methods of allotting lands to colonists, thus briefly and schematically described, may seem as simple as any in the world, it is impossible to understand them in operation properly without some insight into the manner in which officials work and authority is exercised in China. The question of the part played by officials becomes of even greater importance in the consideration of the development of the land after allotment.

An adequate analysis of official methods in China is not easy. For one thing, newly established, "model" administrations interlock, in practice, with remnants of the old ad-

ministrative order. The new influences affect, to a certain extent, even the old-model administrations; while the spirit and
point of view of the old officialdom also affect, very powerfully, officials who are making a career in new-model administrations. Nor is it easy to isolate characteristics which are
peculiar to Chinese society—which belong to the culture as
distinguished from other cultures—from characteristics which
are only relatively different—which belong, that is, to the
age of the culture and the stage of development reached,
and which are therefore not to be distinguished from, but
to be compared with, the stage of development of other
cultures.

For instance, there is a decentralization, a diffusion of responsibility and a style in the handling of local affairs, allowing an enormous scope for the indirect exercise of individual
policy, which is probably essentially Chinese. There is also
a style of family linkage, and an idea of the personal career
worked out through family connections, which may, perhaps,
be called Chinese. On the other hand the prevalence of
nepotism, involving the use of state information and public
machinery for private and family benefit, which is often called
a "Chinese" characteristic, is not by any means peculiar to
China. Such things are becoming more and more potent in
contemporary Western societies, and probably, by the time
any Western society has reached the same relative stage of
development as that of China, will be equally significant.
"Reform" and "progress" are terms too loosely used. Economic conditions can, to a certain extent, be affected by social action; but the type of social action itself is, on the whole,
a matter of growth, age and decay. Even the ideals of "reform" and "progress" current in a given society are on the
whole predetermined less by the direct force of "environment"
than by the period of growth and age of the living society.

No society can fully control its future, because it cannot alter its past.

Partly because of the lack of government funds to administer "from above" the development of colonization lands, but ultimately because of the Chinese type of decentralized official administration, officials as individuals are inseparably associated with colonizing exploitation. Thus, in default of budgeted and audited colonization funds, the colonization and the officials administering it pay their own way from the beginning. Officials appointed to distribute land allot themselves, as a matter of course, large private holdings; and thereafter they are concerned in the development of the region both as individuals and as officials. Moreover, because of the instinctive feeling for diffused responsibility, official approval, even official control is not enough for any enterprise with a powerful effect on society. Officials must also be implicated as individuals with a personal interest at stake. The power of the official, and his methods in action, are not closely regulated functions, but mutable indices. In the West, official policy reveals a "scheme," a "system"; in China, what has to be apprehended is the "feel" of the characteristically obscure trend of development and center of gravity. Consequently the actual functions and social value of the official cannot be elucidated by reference to definite regulations, but must be artistically felt out and manipulated.

In fact Western "systems" of government are assertive, and informed both with theory and purpose. The commonest cause of abuse and confusion in action is the over-multiplication of principles, which conflict in practice. Moreover "corruption" often proceeds from deliberately engineered social principles which, once launched as laws, favor particular classes, groups, or individuals. The tendency characteristic of China appears to be a preference for "schemes"

of authority which are largely neutral. They indicate a manner of action, but they do not prescribe a course of action.
Therefore the things which actually happen and actually are
done, within the non-prescriptive framework, are mainly
determined by fluctuating individual adjustment and manipulation.

The facts of "corruption" in America as discussed in books
by enthusiasts of "reform," are no more peculiar to America
than they are to China; but the style of working is different.
Again, in China, as in other countries where railways are
State enterprises, it is a frequent occurrence of fact that officials of the railway use their official knowledge for private
speculation in land; but, here again, the style of working is
different. The whole history of foreign railway enterprise in
China is, for instance, a struggle to insure to the investing
bondholders a kind of railway familiar to them; a self-
defined unit with functions that are specified in every respect
—an ambition which is inevitably suspect to the national
feeling, which requires enterprises of which every function
is variable, in spite of definition, and in which Central Government interests, Provincial Government interests, local interests and the personal interests of the officials representing
these groups of authorities, can all have room for manœuver.
According to this counter-feeling the bondholder, by infer-
ence, cannot rely on his "rights," but must work through his
alliances of interest. The condition aimed at is one in which
the identity and affiliations of the investor are more important
than the fact that he holds bonds—a condition seen also in
the West, but for different reasons, arising from principles
and precepts which have been enforced by a given group in
its own interests.

Purely Chinese enterprises are operated as a matter of
course by linking the interests of the backers with the private

interest of officials. It would be quite absurd for an individual to buy a large tract of land, bring in tenants, pay his taxes and set out independently to become a land magnate of the pioneer colonizing frontier, with only a copy of the official regulations as a guide to his relations with officials. The lonely responsibility of such a career would be insupportable to the individual, and the bald assertiveness of it would be abhorrent to society. Even if he could refer to regulations of the most elaborate kind, he would feel uneasy about dealing with the definition of *an* official; he would seek to find touch with, and accommodate himself to, *the* officials. The office, as an abstraction, is not negotiable; the officials, on the other hand, as human beings, are variable and therefore understandable indices to the tendencies current in the official world. To this group, as it feels its way in action, the individual can make functional but undefined adjustments, which satisfy his instinct for keeping up a play of policy, which potentially may last for an indefinite time into the future, without committing himself to a scheme of action assertively projected into the future. Thus he can remain, so to speak, "in balance" with his society, without having to strike a balance that would commit him individually, and can remain one of a nexus of individuals without isolated responsibilities.

Consequently, it is axiomatic that in any enterprise of large scope, officials will be found as implicated participants, but not as declared participants with fully limited functions. It will never be possible to strike a balance between the office and the official, the person as public official and the person as private agent, the individual as manager of a large enterprise and the individual as nephew of a general. That is why what we call the "abuses" of nepotism, "squeeze," private participation in public affairs, the use of state information for private ends, and so forth, exhibit parallels of fact between

East and West, but cannot be called parallels of style in action, and why it is a gross misundertanding to call them all, without further consideration, "defects" of the Chinese system which have crept in through decay. They are defects in the Western system, and they indicate the age of any given society to the extent that the older the society, the more likely they are to be both prevalent and, in a way of their own, discreet.

In all Western societies, however, such "abuses" are both felt and defined as defects. We recognize their existence, but the public conscience, through repeated redefinition, works incessantly (however hopelessly) to eliminate them. In the Chinese society, the stigma of "abuse" does not automatically attach. "Abuse" is not "abuse" in kind, but in degree. Too much nepotism is considered reprehensible, and in due course brings retribution; but it is characteristic that the degree is not defined; reproof and correction work themselves out through a gradual play of forces, without reference to a rigid scheme. As for the "system" itself (so to call it) not only does it provide the most obvious, but the most necessary and practical channels of action. If these channels were abruptly cut off, all the processes of society would be paralyzed. There is an effort to do away with them in modern times; it is this effort which produces many of the discords of contemporary society, and the chief motive power of the effort itself does not come spontaneously from within the society, but from the growing necessity of adaptation to alien standards—it is one of the reactions to foreign aggression.

These considerations are of the greater importance in that colonization enterprises are preponderantly carried on by "big interests." The low standard of living of the colonists themselves has apparently led to a general assumption that the whole phenomenon of colonization is a primitive, spontaneous surge of migration. It is nothing of the sort, and the style of operation of the "big interests" proves beyond a doubt that as a social phenomenon the colonization of Manchuria belongs to a highly elaborated, highly self-conscious, highly artificial, very "late" stage of civilization. In southeastern and central Manchuria, it is true, the natural pressure of increasing population is responsible for a certain amount of spontaneous enterprise in adjacent undeveloped lands, and the same is true of the "oldest" parts of the Mongol "reservoir." Even here, however, all new industry and manufacture is dominated by "big interests." In the open, typical "pioneer" lands, not only such industry as exists, but the actual settlement of the land is an affair of the "big interests."

The two most typical kinds of large enterprise are the land company and the grain company; and these often interlock. The bigger they are, the more certain it is that officials are implicated in them. The norm of operation is as follows: either an official has taken up an allotment of land and needs to have it run for him, or a group interested in land exploitation need to have official connections in order to work smoothly. A combination is accordingly formed in which interest and influence have a capital value; the consequence being that the cash returns on the capital actually invested cannot be mechanically distributed as calculable dividends, but must be apportioned by mutual agreement according to all kinds of incalculable categories. Even a manager drawing by agreement a stipulated percentage of profits would never expect to draw a sum exactly calculated on a fixed basis. Both real basis and real sum may vary from year to year, and moreover the exactness of the sum finally entered in the accounts is shaded off either by delays in payment or by presents and perquisites. Indeed, the value of the position itself is not an exact quantity, for it depends in part on the facilities it affords for the occupant to use the advantages of his nominal position for other activities.

It is not surprising that such alliances of capital investment and official interest are often reinforced by intermarriage; with the result that a marriage settlement often has the effect of a business merger, or a tariff agreement. Thus the activities, profits and liabilities of every participant become subject to perpetual concession and manipulation. When credit or fresh capital are needed, they are acquired by comparably unregulated methods. Each investment that comes in has its own terms; it comes in on nominal terms that vary with the status and ramifying relations of the investor, and remains at work on actual terms that are subject to perpetual rediscussion and readjustment.

In enterprises thus constituted, it is obvious that even when a scheme of operation has been drawn up, it must be worded as non-committally as possible, and be largely meaningless in practice. No step that has to be decided on and carried out falls within the prescribed sphere of an executive with defined duties and responsibilities, but is on its merits a matter for complicated delegation and combined execution. Thus all responsibility for performance is diffused; all are involved in a drift of action stimulated by merging interests and accommodated by pliant adaptation to circumstances, with the result that personal initiative and assertiveness have to be discounted as dubious qualities in business and society. On the other hand negative responsibility, though equally undefined, must always be met. If anything happens, responsibility must be adjudged; and normally it is adjudged, not by discriminating the person whose positive position, duties or actions point him out as the responsible agent, but primarily by ascribing it to the person who happened to be nearest in position when the event occurred, and secondarily by making a scapegoat of the person whose relative position makes it better for him to bear it than anybody else.

In such involved operations the official serves as the link giving an adaptability of relation between the nominal functions of private enterprise and the nominal functions of governing authority. From the very beginning there is manipulation of the measurement and allotment of the land. There is a nominal division into "first," "second" and "third"-class land; but this is merely a concession to the "natural" factors, which have thereafter to be brought into relation with the "human" factors. The practical problems which have to be met are:

On the part of the land. Is it, while falling within the general "first-class" category, good, extra good, and so on? What are its possibilities in the way of development, transport, bandits and so on, and is there anybody who is "on the inside" with regard to any of these questions?

On the part of the purchaser. Who is he? What are his other interests and activities? What are his relations with other buyers, officials and those whose interests converge on the land, whether in matters of development, transport, banditry or anything else?

All of these factors may be called potentials of policy, rather than principles of action. They invade the future with no too definite assertion, but rather provide a neutral standard of manner in action, which may as well continue perpetually if nothing happens; consequently, when anything does happen, it can be adjusted without loss of principle, so long as the manner of doing things is not affected. As for practical function, all these factors must be taken into account when land devolves from the government to the individual. The land measure may be expanded or contracted and the price may be shaded off by terms of cash, credit, installments and so on.

Obviously such adjustments cannot be made unless officials are involved as understanding participants; for, from the very beginning, an official personally interested in a tract of land can make arrangements for not collecting his own taxes from himself.

With a central government that is weak in authority and lacks funds for the impartial development of distant lands by strict bureaucratic methods, there is often no alternative to this expedient of localizing the capitalization and development of each region, and allowing the officials of the administration to become heavily interested in the projects they administer.[1] If accidents of situation and auxiliary facilities encourage the officials to develop the interests they have staked out, the expedient often works well. On the other hand there is often a tendency on the part of those interested to let the investment wait until the facilities arrive. It is general, at least in the modern period, to insert a clause in the regulations of land grants to the effect that if the investor does not begin development within a specified time, the grant reverts to the government. When, however, the officials themselves are heavily interested, this clause becomes a dead letter. There are huge tracts of apparent wilderness, especially in the north, which actually have been allotted to private ownership under land-grant projects, with title deeds dating back twenty or thirty years, which have never been developed. Occasionally

---

[1] While this type of unassertive central government and the unofficial expedient of allowing inadequately paid officials to enrich themselves by lending the aid of their official positions to personal and extra-official undertakings were inherent in the Chinese system as taken over by the Manchus, the extra-official activities of officials at least were further promoted by the Manchu law that Manchus might not engage in trade. The Manchu official and his relatives had therefore to engage in trade and other activities indirectly, through agents, in order to invest their funds. Such proceedings could hardly be put on a contract basis, because they were in the nature of things extra-legal. Obviously it was both effective and discreet for the official to operate as an unseen angel in the affairs of business concerns with which he had an understanding.

smaller holders have begun development and then been forced out, because the rules of taxation were enforced against them, but not against the "big interests" about them, with the result that, failing to make a profit because of the lack of development in the region as a whole, they have abandoned their farms—either selling them at a sacrifice to the "big interests" or allowing their titles to lapse and be redistributed, thus also passing, eventually, into the hands of the "big interests."

When a big exploiting enterprise begins to operate, linked with the interests of officials and with its balances of capital, management, executive responsibility and so forth delicately but vaguely disposed about an obscure, undeterminable, mobile center, all of its functions have to be adjusted in terms of policy, in preference to principle. None of the terms of tenantship, rental, taxation, "assisted colonization," loans, provision of livestock, are rigid. When taxation is to be levied, the governing standard is not a rigid assessment, but the standard of "how much is enough?" So long as the higher authorities get "enough" the lower authorities are given scope to make their own adjustments, and so on down to the actual taxpayer. When rental is to be collected, if it is in kind, as is most general, there is an agreed ratio for the division of crops; but this has to be recurrently readjusted. How good is the crop? What is the current relative value of different crops? What is the state of money, transport rates, loan quotations? If a tenant's crop has failed, has he really got nothing, or a little something? What are his other resources? Who are his relatives and friends? Nor are the accommodations arrived at by the bald calculation of a profit and loss account, but the terms are shaded off by granting a somewhat smaller measure, or by giving a new plow or by counting two donkeys as a horse, or by not counting the number of young pigs, or by helping a boy through school, or transferring a family to different land, or urging that the value of services rendered in making a marriage settlement be considered, or any one of a countless number of expedients.

In marketing a crop, such a thing as a "straight deal," written up, balanced off and closed out, must be very rare, if not practically impossible. Transport rates, terms of delivery, quality, are all subject to rediscussion at any moment. Foreigners trading in China are only beginning to appreciate this lack of clarity in Chinese business as they are being forced gradually to meet Chinese terms in order to do any business at all. The saying that "the word of a Chinese is as good as his bond" dates back to the trading conditions of the eighteenth and nineteenth centuries, when amidst a maze of perplexities it was the only basis on which business could be done between Chinese and foreigners; it was the minimum condition dictated by foreigners. In Chinese business proper, neither time, price nor quality is the essence of a contract; bondsmen have to be associated with every contract in order to diffuse responsibility during the almost inevitable negotiations for adjustment and readjustment. Nor is the foreigner, demanding payment on the nail for goods delivered, or delivery on the dot for goods contracted for and paid for in advance, regarded as a sound, practical, hard-headed business man, but as a stupid, violent, simple fellow who does not understand the secrets of keeping a business running, but must always close his deals with uncivilized plunging and bounding.

In the marketing of agricultural produce there is a mixture of tenant's transport, landlord's transport, and outside professional transport; and the initial cart transport must be carefully adjusted to rail transport. There are questions of taxation in transit, and the relations of those engaged in transport to those engaged in tax collection. For this reason transport men of all kinds avoid working off a beaten route which they have made their own; to encounter tax officials with whom they have no acquaintance is as bad as encountering robbers.[2] Moreover, taxation being farmed out to concessionaires, there is a fluctuating margin between the receipts estimated and the amount the traffic can bear; not to mention the margin between the amount the concessionaire has agreed by contract to pay the authorities above him, and the amount he may be called on to pay, or the amount that he thinks ought to be enough for him to pay. Finally, woven through many types of commercial activity, there are the interests of officials associated with land companies, with grain companies, with transport companies, and so on.

The introduction of new types of activity, like railways, alien to the traditional complex, immediately forces an important issue; there is a tendency for the kind of strict control and schematic planning associated with railways to crystallize the loose organization of the older activities into closely defined units, in order to facilitate the work of the railway. This is one of the effects of the impact of Western aggression. There is also an opposite tendency for the rigid, self-inclusive organization originally associated with the railway to break up into the vague associations which characterize the economic structure of the region in which it operates; this is the effect of the reaction of the traditional society, endeavoring not to be dominated by the alien method, but to adapt the alien utility to its own methods. Generally speaking, the more obviously a railway is the tool of "Western aggression," the more Western it remains. Unless it was financed by a foreign loan, with a certain amount of foreign control over accounts

---

[2] For a tax collector, conversely, the question "Whose goods are you carrying?" is almost as important—sometimes more important—than the question "What goods are you carrying?"

to guarantee the service of the loan, there is an almost overwhelming tendency for the actual functions of the railway to
diverge from its planned functions; and the most obvious
sign of this is the margin between the freight carried and the
freight charges collected. Thus it is characteristic that a region of new colonization may be booming, with rising land
values, an expanding outward trade in grain and a compensating inward trade in general merchandise; and yet be
served by a railway which is badly in arrears in payments on
interest and capital. The railway serves the community, in
a manner of speaking, very efficiently; all benefit by it; but
the benefits, instead of being made manifest in a definable and
accountable sum marked "railway profits," are dispensed
through the community by a multitude of indirect and invisible channels. All railways run through the spheres of
operation of a number of officials; and as all railways are
State railways, there is a perpetual flux of adjustment between
central authority and regional authority, and between the officials who are primarily interested in the railway and those
whose local interests impinge on the railway.

It is easier to understand the structure of a region that is being developed by rapid colonization than to summarize it.
The briefest summary possible is to say that the land com-
missioner takes up good holdings for himself in the land he
distributes, and delegates his interest in development to a
land company. The land company delegates a part of its interest to a grain company. The grain company delegates a
part of its interest to a distillery (for grain that is too far from
a market can be turned to profit by distilling alcohol on the
spot and transporting the alcohol); and another part of its
interest to a transport company. Each sphere of operation
pays for itself, but each depends on intimate understanding
with all the others. The land company turns over part of its

profit to the official, who needs it because failing a strict bureaucratic organization and a career based on a definite schedule he must pay most of his own salary and all of his own pension. The grain company turns over part of its profit to the land company; the distillery and the transport company turn over part of their profits to the parent grain company. Finally, at the base of the whole structure, the tenant peasant, who may hold his land either from the official, the land company, the grain company or the distillery, turns over part of his crop to his landlord, and keeps the rest for himself. What he does not need for food he turns in to the grain company, partly for money but mostly for utensils. The peasant has only a minimum hold on the money, the cash, which in the highly developed civilization of China, as in that of the West, is the one universally and rapidly negotiable agent of power. The peasant therefore has only a minimum scope of ambition and enterprise. It is almost impossible for him to escape bondage to the land he tills and the grain he harvests, except by cutting loose from the land and turning to the towns and cities. It is almost impossible for him to win through money an economic independence in the use of land; for money values are determined by paper currencies which, with the banks that issue them, are overwhelmingly dominated by the private interests of various officials.

Under modern conditions in the settlement of new land, the independent small holder is inevitably swamped by tenant farmers whose entire economic life is dominated by the big interests. It might appear that the great supply of land, matched by a great supply of colonists impelled to migrate from China by famine conditions, would stimulate a free-for-all colonization favoring individual enterprise. Actually, because the big interests have a priority of choice in taking up land, and can recruit tenants who, being economically des-

perate, are willing to accept almost any terms, the majority
of the new land is settled by people who do not go where they
want, but are put where they are wanted. The new colonists
arriving by the ever-expanding new railways, transported
either free of charge or at special minimum rates, and either
taking up land at a minimum capital outlay or land on which
they may begin work without any capital at all, and with
housing, plows and livestock provided by the landlord, have
a minimum economic initiative. The new land company and
the new grain company have their representatives in the new
chamber of commerce, and their interests interlock with the
interests which direct railway policy. Therefore they are able
to plan in advance the number of new tenants they can settle
in a given season, and by representations in the right quarter
to secure the required supply at a minimum cost. In other
words the allotment of land and the transport and settlement
of colonists are not directed by impersonal agencies; nor are
impartially administered state funds available for financing
settlers without capital. On the contrary, the distribution of
the land itself is manipulated largely in favor of the interests
of people in privileged positions, and these interests develop
into "big interests" of a thoroughly sophisticated type, which
thereafter interpenetrate and influence the whole mechanism
of settlement and development.

It is in consequence misleading even to attempt to discuss
colonization in terms of bureaucratically administered, self-
contained "schemes," isolated region by region. The best that
can be done is to attempt to interpret the manner of working
of an intricately patterned drift of personal and public action.
One of the most characteristic phenomena of the merging of
the private person and the official is the fact that invariably
the official is dealt with as individual rather than as func-
tionary. Therefore every time an official is promoted or trans-

ferred, a ripple of adjustment spreads over the former sphere of his activity, followed by a corresponding ripple as his successor works into place. For this reason in every province, every county, every tax-office, every military district and innumerable industrial, commercial and agricultural enterprises, there can be detected not only the growing influence of new interests, but the waning influence of old "connections." Because of the diffusion of his interests, the individual cannot wind them up, write out a profit and loss account, realize in cash and boldly invest his capital elsewhere. He cannot abruptly form new connections any more than he can abruptly sever old ones. He must make countless exchanges, concessions, delegations of interest; and while his diminishing influence is being sloughed off in one group and region, he is fostering its introduction and tentative growth elsewhere.

CHAPTER VII

EXPLOITATION AND WESTERNIZATION

WESTERNIZATION AND THE STRUGGLE AGAINST THE WEST

HOWEVER important the "style" of operation in land settlement and agricultural development, it remains evident that there are strong parallels between modern Chinese colonization and colonization under a Western government. The results achieved—above all, the importance of large corporate activities which can bring pressure to bear on the activities of government are in many ways more obvious than the manner of operation. In other words it appears to be more significant that the civilization of China is mature and "late," and that Western civilization is beginning to show the same phenomena of age, than that the styles of the two civilizations are different. Perhaps the most obvious distinction that appears is that in the West "big interests" tend to control individuals in official positions, in order to increase their scope of operation, while in Manchuria officials tend to increase their influence and power by taking a hand in and controlling the enterprises of "big interests"; so that under one system the public pays a toll to private enterprise, while under the other the officials take a toll from the public through the manipulation of private enterprise.

When, however, we consider industry and manufacture, finance on a large scale and all activities that require the use of machinery—in short, all activities in which it is necessary to cope with Western standards, Western competition and

Western pressure—the cleavage between East and West becomes more obvious. The cleavage is not one which the Western mind readily appreciates. We are too much accustomed to think of Western civilization as a force in itself, which spreads over the world with the imperative converting effect of a new religion, imposing a unity of creed and social life. We are therefore impatient of differences in attitude toward our style of civilization. We are prone to assume that a bank is a bank, a factory a factory, a railway a railway and a mine a mine, all the world over; that there may be differences in nationality but none in the essential structure of civilization, wherever the civilization of which these are the visible portents has been established. Yet the truth of the matter is that differences of culture and the feeling of what life and civilization ought to be do continue potent in operation. In Northeastern Asia may be seen the phenomena of three great processes in the life, death and transformation of civilizations. Japan has taken to itself the whole of Western civilization and attempted to master it, and has become, with differences of national culture and tradition, but not of essential economy and civilization, as nearly as possible a Western nation. Russia, which was never a Western nation of the genuine Western tradition, is now apparently succeeding in taking over the powers of the Western civilization and transforming them, and at the same time the Russian nation, with results which point to the emergence of a new style of civilization, with social, economic and intellectual values peculiar to itself. In China, the struggle has not yet swung finally in one direction or the other. There is no overwhelming national ambition to discipline the nation in Western modes and make the Western civilization its own, as in Japan. Nor is there any overwhelming ambition to adopt the Russian method, that of disintegrating both old and new, the indigenous and the alien, in order to create, by inspiration from within, something fresh and unheard of in the world. The majority of the vigor available in the nation appears to be working toward a stalemate decision; namely, a maximum objective use of the new means available, with a minimum adoption of new subjective values.

One of the pronounced characteristics of the new Russian civilization is the decided assertion of national taste in the choice of borrowings from the Western civilization, particularly the Western industrialism. In spite of what appear to be failures—abortive experiments and uncompleted programs—the Russians on the whole would seem to know both what they want from the West and how they intend to use it. In such a momentous creative experiment as the Russian revolution, the failure to carry out a few details of the program is immaterial, in face of the lively assertion of likes and dislikes which testifies to a living national inspiration at work. It is as though the Russians always know inwardly what they want, even though they cannot always define and execute completely what they want.

Herein lies the great difference between modernization in Russia and Westernization in Japan. The Russians are highly critical and selective, and do not hesitate to remodel what they are not prepared to take over in its European-American form. The Japanese, carried away by the desire to be Western, have always tended to swallow everything whole. Selection has gone chiefly by countries—the navy being modeled on that of one country, the army on that of another, and so on. Hence the charge of imitation without imagination that is almost a catchword in criticism of Japan. There is, however, evidence in history that the Japanese have a power of digestion equal to their boa-constrictor method of acquisition. The Chinese civilization brought over to Japan a thousand years and more ago, and reinforced at intervals later, became in time a genuine Japanese growth, with a national cast in literature, art, religion and society, and a vitality which in many respects has outlasted that of China itself. There have already been reactions in Japan against indiscriminate Westernization, and the final achievement of a new Japan, developed out of the present nation with its characteristics of over-Westernization in some respects and incomplete Westernization in others, depends chiefly on the ability of Japan to stand the economic strain. When the Western culture, already adopted, has been finally assimilated, the Western origins of the new Japanese culture will be as obvious as the Chinese origins of the older culture; but, like the older culture, it will have an unmistakable Japanese cast and a life of its own.

In contrast with this sense of certitude and inspiration, one of the major phenomena produced by the impact of the West on China appears to be a feeling of doubt and indecision. The crucial question "What do we want?" which was the touchstone of Westernization in Japan, and is, though differently applied, the touchstone of the creation of a new Russia, is replaced by the question "What do we have to have?" The New China is not at all impressed with any inward, moral or spiritual superiority inherent in the West. There is none of that urgent desire to assume the standards of the West, to measure up to the standards of the West and to pass proudly as "first class" by the standards of the West which made the Westernization of Japan as passionate as a crusade—although Westerners commonly enough, with gross lack of appreciation, deplore that crusade as nothing but a drab process destructive of a picturesque old culture.[1]

Nor is there any of that instinctive feeling for what is to be

---

[1] It is true that China also passionately desires to be recognized as a "first-class" nation with a "first-class" culture; but the essence of the Chinese demand is that the Western standard ought to be modified to admit China, without the antecedent remodeling of China to suit the Western standard.

chosen and what rejected, and how that which is chosen is to be used, which characterizes the Russia of to-day, and which often confounds and disgusts Western enthusiasts, reformers and idealists who think they know what Russia ought to want. The arrival of Perry's squadron had, in Japan, the effect of the revelation of a new dispensation. The war in Europe, which destroyed the superficial strata of Westernism in Russia, released the dormant energy of the autochthonous Russian inspiration. In China, the different assaults of Western nations led only to defensive measures and a conviction of the essential savagery of Western civilization; and the war in Europe, and its sequelæ, put an end to any hope that China might accept the civilization of the West as admirable in itself, and gave strength to the instinct that China ought to bide her time, in the hope eventually of sloughing off the West and its barbarisms. Hence a strong intellectual tendency, in the China of to-day, to accord to considerations of the possible decay and collapse of Western civilization an importance at least equal to considerations of the desirability of Westernizing China.

There is, indeed, in the processes of Westernization in China, a play of fashion which often appears irresponsible to Westerners, because random and unconvinced. Western standards, far from being considered admirable in themselves, are all suspect and feared as "soulless," because inimical to the spirit of China. Accordingly there appears to be, very often, in the course of adaptation to Western standards, a difficulty in distinguishing between the mechanics of any given process and the spirit that informs the process. In this way attempts are often made to take over a method, without adopting the spirit of the society in which the method was originally developed, and of which it was the natural fruit. Perhaps the most striking illustration of this type of contradiction is to be found in the adoption on a large scale of Western armaments, with the minimum adoption of the Western style in warfare. In the same way, when there is a question of handing over to Chinese control any enterprise originally developed by foreigners, the least of the difficulties is that of training a technical staff. The true crisis comes when, with the full assertion of Chinese control, a standard of enterprise and responsible direction based on adaptation is substituted for one based on assertion.

The pronounced tendency toward State monopolies and State activities of different kinds is a part of the feeling of uncertainty in face of the alien spirit which lingers about all kinds of alien activities. This tendency is the stronger for being based on a preëxistent attitude toward mines, forests and all such natural wealth as men do not create but find: it accounts for an effort to treat many Westernisms, particularly those which are bound up with machinery and industrialism, as if they were, by analogy, not phenomena that men choose, invent or construct in the pursuit of individual ambition and self-fulfillment, but phenomena which men encounter, phenomena which they find it necessary to deal with as if they were complete in themselves.

It is therefore not surprising that the greatest danger to the independent strength and freedom of initiative of a nation like China (or Turkey) which is making an effort to adapt itself to the standards of the West is that it thereby admits, at least by implication, the superior authority of the West; with the result that, by the time it has mastered Westernization as a thing complete in itself, the West proper, whose Westernism is a living force informed with growth and activity, has progressed spontaneously to a further point —with the result that the nation striving for adaptation, having once admitted the authority of the alien standard, finds itself still chronologically in arrears and accordingly restricted in the faculty of initiative. Even in a nation like Japan, where the process of Westernizing was less an adaptation than a transformation, a genuine phenomenon of rebirth, the effects of this chronological handicap can very definitely be traced.

In China, the old conception of state rights of possession in respect of natural wealth ("wealth in itself," like gold) is increasingly being extended to all kinds of activities ("wealth created by work") notably rail transport, and many industrial and exploitational enterprises, and even the distribution of commodities. There is, for instance, a strong and recurrent tendency to assert regional-monopoly control of trade in oil products, tobacco and matches—all of which are dominated by foreign interests. The type of state monopoly that works out in practice is different both from the Russian conception, which aims at doing better than individual enterprise, and the normal Western type of state control which aims as a rule at prevention of abuse by private enterprise; in the Chinese type, apart altogether from the perennial question of revenue, which often superficially appears to be the main question, the problem of the relation between the State and the individual is secondary to the profound problem of safeguarding Chinese standards, during the period of adaptation, from coming too far under the authority of Western standards. Manœuvers of defense are constantly in evidence.

Although Russian state enterprises differ in inspiration from those of typically Western nations, yet in Russia and the West alike the type of action is the use of state machinery to express the policy, the will, of individuals who have mastered the state and use it for the assertion of their own ideas of what should be done and how it should be done. The State is the *spear* of the individual. At the core of the system the individual is always to be found; the system itself is one of pyramided individual wills and responsibilities. The state machinery in China, although fitfully and opportunistically exploited by the individual, functions above all as a *shield* for the individual. The state and its organizations, in the modern phase, play a part of vital importance in deadening the impact on society of aggressive Western activity; they diffuse responsibility where the Western instinct focuses it. At the core of the system the group can always be found; the individual is hard to define. The individual shelters within and behind the group, in order to work out his own position; though this does not impair the importance of the individual, whose personality has always been of high importance in China, and never more than at the present time.

This can be felt in all negotiations with the State, not only international but domestic. The individual is responsible when responsibility for what has happened can be pinned on him; but when responsibility must be assumed in advance for what is going to be done, for what is willed and projected, it is diffused as widely as possible over the group. In the West, both in domestic crises within the State and in international negotiations, the individual with convictions steps out to make a claim for leadership; the strongest claim he can make for himself is the number and loyalty of the group that follow him; he works by persuading the group to follow his lead. In China, when something must be decided, the individual works from behind the group, pushing it before him to the best of his ability. The strongest case he can make for himself is that he has followed the most important group.

It is not for nothing that, in the West, all important treaties, of the kind that mark epochs, turning points in history, are associated naturally, and as it were unthinkingly, with the names of great men who dominated the decisions and terms of the treaties. There is never any doubt about the figurehead and the representative, the spokesman. In treaties between China and Western nations, owing largely to the series of treaties brought about by Western insistence, there has always been a disconcerting vagueness about the relation of the signatories of China to the feeling of the Chinese nation. The comparative unimportance of the individual name has persisted remarkably even into the modern phase where China is manœuvering energetically to hold the initiative in foreign treaties. Able and brilliant as is the Foreign Minister who has conducted, under foreign eyes, the foreign policy of the Nationalist Government, it cannot be doubted that in Chinese eyes the treaties he has signed are not his treaties but the treaties of the Kuomintang, the Nationalist Party. Probably the man who was most conspicuously a leader and an individualist in Chinese negotiations with a foreign power was Eugene Chen, the man who conducted and dominated the negotiations for the rendition of the British Concession at Hankow—and he was an overseas Chinese, educated abroad, who first came to China as a man grown, rose to high power under the influence of a Russian military advisor, and shortly after his most brilliant achievements was eliminated from Chinese political life and forced into exile.[2] Much of the bitterness in China over past foreign treaties arises from the fact that the West habitually enforced the Western interpretation of treaties, the terms of which carried neither intellectual nor instinctive conviction to the China with which they were concluded. In the same way much of the friction between China and Western nations during the revolutionary period has been due to the stubborn Western persistence in trying to find a "strong man" with whom to deal—a type of "strong man" abhorrent to Chinese statesmanship; not exactly the Yüan Shih-k'ai type, but the type that the Powers tried to prod

[2] He returned again in 1931 to join the anti-Nanking Canton faction.

Yüan Shih-k'ai into becoming—ignoring the fact that the nearer a Chinese statesman approaches to this type, the nearer he is to downfall through being rejected and disowned by the group-feeling of the nation.

In Manchuria, easily accessible regions of great geographical extent lie open to development by either new methods or old. It is therefore of extraordinary interest to consider the interaction of the groups and the individual, and the old Chinese tradition proper, the regional tradition of the "reservoir" and the pressure from without of a civilization of totally different style. To begin with, modern banking operations, modeled on Western lines, tend very strongly to become official monopolies—especially provincial monopolies. There is probably not a provincial bank in China that is not closely linked with the personal credit of the members of the provincial governing group. The tendency is to identify personalities of the governing group with the impersonal entity, "the province," and also to identify the financial prosperity of the province with the personal careers of the governor and his group of supporters. It is a tribute to the national skill in negotiation that when a provincial administration falls, the currency and credit of the province do not necessarily collapse altogether. In fact the common procedure, when a governor is removed, whether by death, defeat or transfer, is not to repudiate the provincial currency but to discount it. The new controlling interests agree, in effect, to redeem a proportion of the currency and to confirm a proportion of the province's credit. This form of compromise represents a personal investment by the new official in the region he has undertaken to govern, and the process of identifying the personal interests of the official with the public interests of the sphere of office being thus repeated, a continuity of routine and procedure is assured. Thereafter, if the official is of the type that develops and exploits his interests as investments, the value of the provincial currency begins to improve; but if he is of the plundering type, it remains depreciated.

The great value of the system is that, during a period of transition such as that of modern China, the political affiliations of an official, and the extent to which he is involved in civil wars, do not prevent all the economic interests within the region he governs from supporting him, so long as he endeavors to promote economic development. The great disadvantage, in a region like Manchuria where the general economic condition is of necessity sympathetic to the development of great untouched lands, is that colonization cannot be developed uniformly under an impartial administration, but must proceed locally and to a certain extent spasmodically, being always under the influence of a great number of individual careers. Moreover, though an official may be just toward individuals and encourage every kind of immediate development, he is hardly able to take a long view of the development of natural resources, being inevitably inclined to forms of exploitation which offer the greatest immediate profit, regardless of waste and rapid exhaustion.

Obviously, in the financing of colonization projects, provincial banks are of the greatest importance. Their operations interpenetrate all land development, the grain trade and the foundation of new industries; and there is an obvious tendency for those who exercise authority to take as much as possible of their own profit in cash, and to pass on to the public as much as possible of its share in the form of credit—largely in the form of paper currency. Thus it frequently happens in a new center of the grain trade, for instance, that the men who direct the local banks—private banks as well as the provincial bank, for the larger a private bank the more likely it is to be identified with the interests of some official—exploit their bank positions in order to foster their own activities in the grain trade, thus throwing a certain burden on the grain trade as a whole. Nor is this to be condemned as malpractice; the imputation of malpractice only attaches if it goes too far. If the general development of the region begins to be impeded by such preferred interests, the converging pressure of the majority interest eventually results in a change of bank directors; whereupon the process is renewed on a more reasonable scale.

Under such a system it is evident that in negotiating for a mortgage on land, for instance, the economic soundness of the transaction itself must be secondary to the question of the identity of the owner of the land, the identity of the bank director, and their relation to each other and to various officials. Thus different landowners, grain companies, flour mills, promoters of new industries and so on not only secure different terms according to their personal affiliations, but the original terms are, by tacit recognition, subject to revision, in spite of written terms, as the result of changes in the bank, or changes in the personnel (not necessarily connected with commercial profit or loss) of the enterprise which the bank is financing. By corollary, the importance of any given person in any given corporate enterprise is likely to be determined by the question "Who is he?" in preference to the question "What can he do?" Even the amount of actual cash investment which he represents may well be less important than his political and family associations. The advantages of the system have been pointed out, particularly the tendency to make those participating in government sensitive to the economic life of the community: but its weakness (from the Western point of view) must again be pointed out; particularly the phenomenon, obvious everywhere in Manchuria, of enterprises of industry and exploitation dominated by men who, far from having "grown up with the business," are limited in the extent of their interests by the degree of official power held by relatives and friends, and in the duration of their interests by the tenure of office held by those same relatives and friends. This accounts for a comparative paucity of large-scale undertakings developed slowly over a long period of years and the existence of numbers of enterprises which, however large in scale, are operated fitfully, governed by circumstances of opportunity, and characterized by phenomena of heavy investment risk, quick turnover and large profits when successful.

Associated with this type of enterprise is the phenomenon of industries and activities of all kinds which "run down"; the more mechanical and technical the undertaking, the more likely being the phenomenon of running down. Flour mills, for instance, very commonly pay for their capital cost by the end of the second year; sometimes in one year. Thereafter, every cent of intake is regarded as profit, and there is a pronounced reluctance to reinvest any serious proportion of the profits in maintenance and adequate care of the machinery. There is no prevalent feeling that the directors of such a mill are under any moral obligation to hand over the mill in perfect running order to their hypothetical successors; and indeed the average director is more likely to advise investing profits in a totally new mill than to urge the reinvestment of a smaller sum in keeping up and looking after the original mill. The fact that many prosperous regions are conspicuous for factories and other enterprises that have been "sucked dry" and abandoned is not, in Manchuria, an anomaly. Manchuria, indeed, owes its continued and comparatively rapid increase of prosperity to two circumstances which do not depend on the national style of culture and political economy at all. One of these is the fact that no prolonged, and only one serious campaign in any of the civil wars in which Manchuria has been concerned since the foundation of the Republic has been fought out on Manchurian territory. The other is the fact that political and factional continuity has been unbroken, allowing a much greater continuity in social and economic development than has been possible in most parts of China proper. These factors are probably at least as important as the great reserves of surplus land and untouched resources in Manchuria; for other Chinese frontier regions, analogous to Manchuria in natural wealth and social structure have not enjoyed an analogous prosperity, but have suffered the same cultural, social and economic disintegration that characterizes the main regions of contemporary China.

Given the circumstances which have made for prosperity in Manchuria, the indigenous economic methods work happily enough, geared as they are to the structure of society. They are readily adjusted to margins of risk, scales of profit and terms of family organization which are all matters of common understanding. It is when Western pressure appears, in the form of foreign investment—through railway loans, for example, or through construction undertaken or machinery supplied on credit—that friction becomes inevitable. Western interests are not so adjusted, financially, that they can easily compromise on the original terms of a contract, or pursue their enterprises by fits and starts. Consequently, in periods of political and financial readjustment, when Chinese interests philosophically compromise in the traditional manner, or resign themselves to a period of coma, foreign interests try to hold out for their "rights" to the limit of their ability —and, in so doing, make it impossible to escape the imputation of foreign arrogance and ruthless exploitation.

Again, it is increasingly difficult to sell foreign imports, especially machinery, on a large scale and on credit, without first inflating the price in order to allow commissions to the middlemen without whom the business could not be done. In the case of official or semi-official business, only too often, a large part of these commissions is taken by men who do not actively further the enterprise, but who are entitled to a percentage simply as their price for not obstructing the deal. The degree of inflation, in turn, increases in proportion to the wealth and credit of the buyer, in accordance with the principle that the man who has more money ought to pay more than the man with less money would pay for the same article —this being yet another difference in point of view between the East and the West, where normally the buyer with good credit can purchase more cheaply than the buyer with limited credit. Since this type of inflation is a concession to Chinese methods, it is easy to accuse foreign entrepreneurs of collecting profits on the Chinese scale, while taking advantage of foreign "special privileges" to insure a Western standard of protection from risk, thus evading the Chinese remedy of readjustment of contracts and terms of payment. With the decrease of actual foreign control in China, it is not surprising that there is not only a tendency to default on payments to foreign enterprises, but to justify the defalcation as a form of resistance to outrageous exploitation.

One of the expedients now being tried as a remedy for the bad condition of credit in China is the use of guaranteed funds for enterprises of Westernization. The recent allotment of portions of the remitted British Boxer Indemnity for railway construction and other enterprises is an example, and an example of the highest interest. For, while the British manufacturers who are thus guaranteed payment for the materials they supply can hardly be accused of "imperialistic" designs, it is impossible to deny that the arrangement necessarily increases the interest and responsibility of an alien government in the internal affairs of China. Nor can it be doubted that leaders of the Chinese Government would avoid the arrangement if any other were open to them. Indeed the whole experiment, while intended and described as a gesture of amity, cannot but be considered as an important instance of that change in the form of Western pressure on China to which I have already referred.

The tendency, on the one hand, to regard Western products and methods either as necessary for China (and chiefly "necessary" in the sense not of what is wanted but of what has to be had) or merely as profitable to the individual Chinese who are concerned with them, but on the other hand to manipulate foreign activities concerned in the Westernization of China as if they were dangerous and inherently hostile, is given a special emphasis by the fact that officials are so generally interposed between the foreign activity and the Chinese public which it affects. Not only direct attempts to introduce Western capital, but many kinds of commercial and industrial activity, especially those leading to the installation and increased use of machinery, and the employment of foreign technical supervisors, come in touch at once either with official bodies or with the private interests of officials. Thus not only the State, but officials as a class are assigned an important part in distributing through society the impact of the West on the old order. The larger the enterprise, the more likely it is that officials who are developing their private interests as well as those of the State will interpose the organization of the State between themselves and the actual enterprise, in order to diffuse and minimize their personal responsibility. This, in turn, not only reinforces the trend toward State monopolies and semi-official corporations, but casts about every important activity of Westernization an atmosphere of State concern, of the public interest and of international affairs. It is hardly surprising that, in the popular estimation, any important activity in which any foreign interest can be detected is regarded as a form of contest, in which with varying fortune either the officials succeed in exploiting the foreigners, or the foreigner succeeds in exploiting China: thus relegating to a secondary importance the question of the desirability of assimilating, subjectively, Western technique and the Western point of view; and perpetuating the popular feeling of an immanent hostility between the Chinese way of doing things and the foreign way of doing things.

THE TECHNICIAN—MASTER OR SERVANT?

The function of the machine itself, as an instrument through which the people of a particular society express the aims of their culture, is worth a special study. There is an obvious tendency, in the West, to elevate the machine and its technicians to a dominant position in society, and an increasing tendency to regard specialized mastery of some one technique as the highest qualification for an important position in society at large; and a tendency to subordinate the living organisms of society and culture to the dead, inorganic structure of machines, industries and other creations of technique. The term "engineer" is a powerful catchword in government and many kinds of social administration, and it is a characteristic Americanism of the mind, only to be expected in the most advanced and mechanized state of the West, that multiplying millions of Westerners undoubtedly accept, without any sense of the ridiculous, formulæ of the general category: "Henry Ford's opinions on history must be of first-class importance, because look at the Ford car." The specialist, the technician, is the true dictator of culture and society, and far more important than the man who has great wealth only.

In China, on the other hand, in spite of the vital importance to the nation and its culture of all questions bearing on the acceptance or rejection of Western technique *and its accompanying mentality,* the technician has not progressed beyond a comparatively servile status. In view of the importance of "big interests" as a gear for connecting the machinery of authority with the enterprise of personal interests, which points obviously to an advanced and sophisticated civilization, it is extremely significant that the "big men" of the "big interests" are normally *not* the technicians. Given a social and cultural order as highly developed as that of China, the crucial factor in the modification of the economic order is the factor already emphasized, of the strong objective operation of Western technical appliances, associated with a poor subjective assimilation of Western technique. Thus we have the paradox that the recent rapid progress of Chinese colonization in Manchuria is directly proportionate to the spread of Western methods of transport and exploitation; while these activities themselves continue to be generally valued only as sources of profit, not as providing opportunities for admirable careers. The normal ambition, in respect of such activities of alien type, is to be able to control them, in preference to being able to do them. Socially, it is more admirable to be a mine owner or mine-concessionaire than a mining engineer. This throws into relief once more the fact that very few technicians of Western training are to be found in positions of control. Trained railwaymen do their best to administer railways under the control of men who have no understanding of, and still worse, no *feeling* for the technical needs and professional standards of railway administration. In spite of numbers of men available who have thoroughly mastered different techniques of industry, manufacture and all kinds of mechanical exploitation, only a very few can be found working with a free hand in positions of real control. Normally, they remain subordinate to men and interests whose whole instinct is to avoid fusing West and East organically; who endeavor to take what profit they can out of Western machines, but are unwilling to subordinate their own way of doing things to the demands of the Western technique that goes with machinery. The machine is welcome so long as it is obedient to orders; but it is not regarded—as it was in Japan—as the symbol of an epoch, a turning point, and the revelation of a new way of life.

The machine was a natural product of the Western mind, whose latent mechanical instinct woke with full vigor at the very moment that adequate motive power became available, and made inevitable the domination of the Western world by a civilization grounded on machinery. Yet, inevitable though the transformation was, the strain on the whole structure of society caused agonies in the process of adjustment, until a generation matured which had been bred in the living tradition of machines, mechanical technique and mechanized industries. The mastery of technique now so dominates all our society that every type of activity is increasingly restricted by the demands of specialization; and there can be no doubt that much of the discontent that disturbs the Western world today springs from the fact that we have so thoroughly worked out the major implications of the mechanical age that little remains for the youthful and ambitious but the subdivision and re-subdivision of specialized techniques.

Considering the pains of transformation in the West, where the new order was generated in and grew out of the old, the transvaluation effected in Japan approaches the miraculous, and the convulsions of Russia and China are no matter for surprise. Russia, however, was a formless barbarism overlaid by an aristocratic crust which gave a misleading impression of identity with the West. When the crust was destroyed the barbarians below began to construct a civilization of their own. Crude though their barbarism yet remains, it is so strong and individual that it disdains mere imitation of the West, and holds obstinately to its own vision of the construction of a new industrialism and a new mechanized civilization, which is to be something new in all history. China also instinctively rejects the idea of straightforward adoption of Western standards; but for the totally different reason that its most genuine idealism lies in the past. Nor is this past a primitive Golden Age falsified in the manner of Rousseau. A certain loose type of thinking describes the social and economic conditions of China as "medieval," because they are not galvanized by the instinct for machinery which germinated and began to flourish in the West after the close of the Middle Ages, and was only delayed in its full development by the lack of suitable fuel power. For no better reason than this, Westerners are instinctively prone to compare any non-mechanized culture with their own pre-machine past as "primitive." The past to which China turns for its ideal of civilization is neither one of medievalism nor one of oversimplified "natural simplicity," but one of great spiritual richness, creative achievement and elaborate structure, so indubitably noble that it is not unreasonable to argue a case attributing the misfortunes of China to a decline from its ancient standard, instead of to failure to assume an alien standard.

The fact that gunpowder, the compass, printing and other inventions which played an enormous part in the development of the West from medievalism to civilization were previously known in China proves much more than the flat statement usually offered that China was already civilized when the West had not emerged from barbarism. The fact that these inventions were never developed in China in the dynamic style which characterized their effect on the culture of the West ought to be recognized as proof that the genius of Chinese civilization chose not to develop in the channels which appeared obvious to the West, but sought by preference other media for the highest expression of the powers of man. The true point at issue in the conflict caused by the impact of Westernism on China, including the reintroduction of original Chinese inventions metamorphosed by Western use, is therefore not one of "progress" from medievalism to civilization, but one of the substitution of one civilization for another. Hence the long struggle, not yet decided, to master the West and hold in check its inventions, rather than offer up the proud heritage of the true Chinese civilization to the Moloch of the West and its machines. In manufacture, in mechanized agriculture, in motor and rail transport, in all the range of Western activities, the old proud instinct holds with the obstinacy of a fine tradition to the judgment that it may be expedient, for the sake of cash profit, to have the thing done, but that there is not necessarily any virtue, any moral superiority in understanding how the thing is done; far less in undertaking a career in the doing of it for the sake of satisfying the personal instinct for a noble and superior life.

The man of technical training, unless he has political connections or family connections of a first-class order, approximates in social status to the mechanic; and the mechanic, far from being the aristocrat of the artisans, is one of the most dangerously discordant social elements in modern China. Nor is the reason far to seek; for while Westernization has proceeded as far as the adoption of the machine for the sake of profit, the processes of the machine, technique itself for its own sake, have not been naturalized. Failing high control and direction, the machine is therefore exploited by manipulation, by negotiation with the machine-men. While the engineers, the masters of machines, have never risen as a class to the direction of policy and the control of power, the mechanics, the servants of machines, form a jealously self-conscious class whose power depends on guarding the "secrets," the "mysteries of the craft," of their mechanism, and who can by no means be flatly ordered about. I have seen a major, in command of a party traveling by military motor transport in a region under direct military administration, where effective military control was based in theory on a system of motor patrol-routes, unable to proceed at his own discretion because his mechanics had reached a place where they preferred to stop. The major shrugged his shoulders. "You can't get in wrong with mechanics," he said; "if you do, they monkey with the works."

Nor does this machine-servant even approach machine-mastery, as might be expected. Strictly speaking, he is not artisan but artist; if one goes far enough back it is not too much to say that he is comparable, art for art, with the inspired alchemist who stands in the background of the origins of true Western science, or with the magician or shaman, of whom it may be said that he does not "control" the powers with which he works; the powers manifest themselves through him and control is negotiated in terms of art and adaptation. Much has been said of the remarkable versatility which a Chinese with no advantages of education or training can achieve in the working of an engine; the knack of driving a car with a motor "tied together with string" is a constant source of humorous admiration. What is invariably missed is that this knack of improvisation is a quality, not of trained skill, but of adaptive ingenuity. The car is persuaded to run in spite of the violence done to the principles of the engine. It remains essentially an unmastered, alien group of forces, which are not analyzed but taken as a whole and manipulated.

The art or knack, not the science, the magic, not the technique of engines forms the craft-knowledge of the mechanics as a class. There is a difference in kind between this cajoling of engines and the flair often demonstrated in the West, where also many instances can be seen of machinery used beyond its proper power. The commonest difference is that in the West the "type" of such performances is either the tinkering of decrepit engines to work when they ought to be scrapped, or the coaxing of normal engines to do more than their designed work, this being accomplished by a quasi-instinctive feeling for machinery, a mechanical second-nature now bred into the fiber of the Western nature; whereas by contrast the gasping bus (for instance) that still miraculously achieves its daily run over Manchurian roads has been allowed to decay to its distressing condition within a few months after purchase, and is kept running not by the best tinkering possible in the circumstances, but by some fortuitous, hit-and-miss "inspiration" that "does just as well."

Many of the dominant men in China to-day, socially and economically, the exploiters, the men of the "big interests," would very likely prefer to be able to use foreign mechanics with the foreign engines, thus putting themselves in a position to deal with the alien but profitable force as a unit; but this is precluded by the danger of the foreigner as an assertive, aggressive personality. In Manchuria, however, where non-Soviet Russians with no "rights" are available, and too strong trade-union organization of Chinese mechanics (who would tend to agitate against the employment of Russians) is officially discouraged, it is common to see Russians in charge of machinery operating under the control of Chinese interests. Nor are these man-and-machine "units," though admitted to be more efficient than the one-sided combination of Chinese mechanic and foreign machine, placed under the control of one man who is given a free hand. Indeed, such men regularly complain that they cannot bring their employers to adopt a method of running and operation that is really economic; that really meets, in fact, the requirements of the machine. The Chinese employers, at the same time, complain that foreign technicians are a cranky lot to put up with; "they are so unbusinesslike."

There is, in fact, a constant, shifting, and to the blind foreigner incomprehensible, futile and wasteful process of negotiation, adaptation and compromise between the man-machine-unit and its owners or employers. Yet this is nothing, after all, but the instinctive effort to subordinate the foreign means to the Chinese method. It is the same struggle as that (usually disguised by greater amenities) which takes place in the working of every railway in which foreign investments are protected by a partly foreign personnel whose duty is to maintain the foreign standard of values of operating-costs, profits, interest-payment and so forth; to do which it is necessary not merely to "train a Chinese staff," which is easily enough done, candidates of excellent quality being in good supply, but to protect all the Western concepts implicated in a railway from being transposed into Chinese terms. In proportion as control of a railway is foreign, it is unsatisfactory to Chinese; in proportion as it is Chinese, it is unsatisfactory to foreigners. Yet, apart from the obvious passion-engendering resentment of a sensitive, proud nationalism, how little the inner meaning of this truism is dealt with by either Chinese or foreign publicists, who perennially essay to convince each other with claims for reasonable justice, disregarding fundamental cleavages of instinct and point of view—owing largely, of course, to the lip-service now universally rendered to the Western theorem that all true culture and civilization are one.

An enormous proportion of the technical terms that are currently being incorporated into the Chinese language is not directly created; they are either artificially translated, or taken over through the Japanese. The fact that such terms are written in the Chinese character tones down the fact that they are none the less in a foreign language, and a language far more foreign to the existing body of Chinese thought than are, for instance, the technical terms created from Latin and Greek roots that are commonly used throughout the West. It is difficult for foreigners to appreciate that such terms have a sort of unreality which keeps them alien from the body of the language, and that the processes of thought behind these terms are so alien to the language itself that many of them cannot be expressed in terms naturally evolved from the language, but must be dealt with in a language within the language.

Nor is this a true parallel to the use of Græco-Latin technical-scientific jargon in Europe and America. The swift development of technique in different nations of the West was pursued on parallel courses; but a genuine unity of culture throughout the nations demanded a universal technical phraseology. Nevertheless, the major part of the jargon of medicine, of engineering, even of chemistry and physics, can also be expressed clearly, without loss of scientific clarity, in the vernacular of each nation, for the antecedent processes of thought are native in each nation. In this lies the great handicap of Chinese technical phraseology; for many terms either cannot be expressed in locutions understandable by the people, or have to be expressed with such a burden of circumlocution that the thought which it is intended to convey is borne down and smothered, becoming in the end meaningless and absurd; for the thought inherent in the processes which it is desired to express is alien to the modes of thought inherent in the language itself. Consequently a terminology which is thought of in the West as merely a *specialized* language remains in China a *foreign* language, though written in the Chinese character. The final proof of this is in the fact that it is better for a Chinese to learn a foreign language as a means to the mastery of advanced technique than to attempt to study it in Chinese. The equivalent is true to a certain extent of Japanese; but it would be absurd to say that an American chemist or physicist needs to be proficient in Latin and Greek.

This truth is perhaps more evident in Manchuria than elsewhere; for throughout the North, where the alien machine is frequently operated by an alien mechanic, the use of Chinese neologisms is foregone, whether or not they are borrowed through the Japanese. In Northern Manchuria especially the language of technique, of technical appliances, of technical occupations is Russian, used as such not only between Chinese and Russians but among Chinese themselves. The operating language of the Chinese Eastern Railway has from the very beginning been Russian, and this of necessity, not because of political domination only. Recently, as a matter of politics, it has been declared in principle that in railway affairs Chinese must have an equal status with the Russian language. Presumably a Chinese vocabulary, with its burden of neologisms and its quota of terms borrowed through the Japanese, will be introduced accordingly; but neither Chinese nor Russians concerned with the railway feel this to be anything but a gesture.

It is not only the higher ranges of the technical vocabulary that are affected, however. On a Sungari river steamer all the officers and crew may be Chinese, but the whole process of operation and navigation is carried on in Russian. Nor are the captain, helmsman, pilot, engineer, greaser and deckhand by any means necessarily men who have grown up under Russian influence in Harbin or along the Sungari. A very large proportion of them come from Taku (near Tientsin) or from one of the Shantung ports, and therefore had an inclination to work for their living on boats; but on reaching the Sungari as grown men they found that the "trade-union" language of the profession was Russian; and Russian they learned. If this language were not a class-language it would not be used, as it is, even for such elementary terms as "left" and "right" and even in calling out the depths (in Russian feet!) when sounding at the bows. Yet, at the same time, this initiate language is not adopted out of pure admiration for the superior virtues of Russian civilization; as is abundantly proved by the way in which numerous Russian words, used in occupational jargon and in all kinds of slang, are adopted by shifting the pronunciation into Chinese phonetic equivalents, to which at the same time a twist is given that imparts a sort of humorous contempt to the whole. *Sao Ta-tze*, "smelly Tatar," for *soldat* is a good example. I remember also an occasion on a Sungari steamer when a dinghy came away from one of the davits and trailed precariously awash. A sailor rushed forward crying *Hsiao ch'uan lao-ma-i-la!*—an expression which puzzled me, since it meant literally "the small boat is old ants," which might be rendered, perhaps, "the small boat is full of ants." After inquiry I found that the phrase was perfectly intelligible to the whole crew, *lao-ma-i* being the Chinese pidgin-Russian for *slomat*, "the small boat has broken loose." In the same way *ma-shen*, "horse's body," is used for "machine" —thus conveying also the idea of "horsepower"— and *ma-shen lao-ma-i-la*, "the horse's body is old ants," means "the machinery has broken down." *Liu-ti*, from the Russian *lyudei*, means "people," especially in the sense of "passengers." Here the syllable *liu* means "to wander," "to travel." *Ke-lu-t'i* or *ku-lu-t'i*, from the Russian *krutit*, means "to wind up," "to crank a motor." Here the association is with the Chinese word *ku-lu,* "a wheel." *Lao-po-tei,* "a workman," is from the Russian *rabot,* "work," incorrectly used for *rabotnik,* "a workman." Here the syllable *lao,* "old," conveys a sense of familiarity toward the person spoken to and of superiority on the part of the person speaking. Many terms in this category are used not only by the uneducated, but even by educated people who do not happen to have studied Russian.

In other words, it is just as easy to learn a foreign language and be done with it as to learn an awkward vocabulary of terms that are none the less foreign for having been rendered into Chinese. The learning of a foreign language, however, in no way implies admiration for any inherent superiority in foreign civilization or any of its mores. On the contrary, the most illiterate unskilled workman who speaks a garbled Russian, and for that reason rates himself high among his fellows, none the less looks down with moral superiority on all Russians as uncouth creatures entangled in barbaric misconceptions of all the true values of life and culture. Even such innocent Russianisms as the wearing of Russian costume are felt to be, at the best, amusing self-indulgences, while such mores as dancing and free-and-easy public association with women are definitely felt to be vices—vices that may be forgiven in the young, perhaps, but that are considered rather serious if not shaken off when the time comes for a young man to settle down.

The older generation regard with a good deal of alarm the spread of Russian standards of courtship and marriage among Chinese students. "They married of their own accord" (that is, without previous arrangement through the parents) is a common equivalent for "he keeps a mistress"; while "he married a Russian" is the exact equivalent for "he keeps a native woman." Foreign standards of morality, and even the structure of the family, are not generally admitted to be worth the name of "standard." The common verdict is, "They

mate and part like beasts, and have no notion of filial piety"
—much as the colonial Westerner might say, "The position
of women among the natives is inferior, and family life may
be said hardly to exist."

In a society in which affairs of machinery tend thus to fall
into the hands of an artisan-class, with a jargon of their own
and a social outlook of their own, who keep their quasi-occult
knowledge to themselves and endeavor consistently to uphold
the privilege of being negotiated with as a group before effective orders can be given to set the machinery in motion,
the effect of Western impact is more sharply focused than
ever. This isolation is all the more obvious because the men
of genuine expert technical training, having little real control
in the direction of affairs, unless they use a political approach,
are handicapped in undertaking enterprises in such a manner as to make them more truly expressive of novel but genuinely Chinese ambitions.

From this lack of integration in the national life springs
a great danger of class-isolation identified with cultural hostility, growing with the increase of activities that require
machinery, and increasing instead of diminishing the sense
of conflict and social disintegration already associated with
Westernization. Artisans, as a class, are men who by neglect
have lost a great deal of what is finest and soundest in the old
culture, especially that inarticulate but vigorous tradition
which makes the yeoman-peasant, for instance, a bulwark of
the old social morality, but have not acquired enough genuine
Western training to make them intelligent agents of Westernization. Consequently Westernization is felt to be a bru-
talizing agency among the lower orders, while educated men
of superior technical qualification find that if they are truly
ambitious the best use they can make of their Western
degrees is to use them as a gambit for entering a political
career.

Chapter VIII

SOLDIERS, OPIUM AND COLONIZATION

MILITARY FRONTIER COLONIZATION

IN THE history of the "reservoir" military colonization for the specific purpose of garrisoning areas of strategic importance must always have been of great consequence. This type of colonization might even be employed as a measure for holding in check the power of the "reservoir," in the interests of a dynasty whose authority was largely based on strategic use of the "reservoir." Thus under the Manchu dynasty one part of the "reservoir" was played off against another. Mongol troops were used in China, but at an early date measures were taken to prevent actual control by the Mongols of the passes from Inner Mongolia into North China. In spite of the fact that Inner Mongolian levies proved their loyalty during the Taiping Rebellion and against the French and British in 1860-61, strategic control of the frontier was extended by increased colonization in such regions as Jehol and Suiyüan.

Later attempts to plant colonies along the frontiers in the areas of Russian pressure were also made chiefly through the military organization. It may be said that under the Manchus the colonization of remote regions was primarily a question of strategy; and this applies especially to the Amur frontier, the North Mongolia-Siberia frontier and Chinese Turkestan. Granted the fact that there was no urge toward colonization except as a matter of government policy, and that all colonization was dominated by government officials, the garrison method of settlement was probably better suited than any other to the conditions of the time. The garrisons were regarded, not as cantonments of professional troops permanently under arms, but as groups of land-owning, self-supporting yeoman farmers with a military tradition. The able-bodied men were not permanently in service, but were liable to be called on for service at need. They reported regularly for drill and archery training, and instead of drawing fixed pay they received subsidies in accordance with the degree of qualification. Settlement was initiated by moving Bannermen and their families to the chosen region, whereupon the able-bodied men at once and automatically formed a military reserve of land-fast, self-supporting yeomanry— a much better method than the maintenance of regiments in barrack-garrisons. Successive imperial edicts make it plain that the "reservoir" was in truth a "reservoir," for there is little reference to military units, but repeated reference to the reliance of the State on a good sound Banner tradition—conservative social ideas, a yeoman-farmer economy and a martial spirit.

A curious and typically Manchu blend of Chinese and tribal ideals is apparent in imperial references to a model manner of life combining agricultural work in season and hunting in the forests in autumn after the harvest. Any tendency to revert to the tribal life entirely was deplored. Efforts were made at intervals to clear the mountains and forests of wandering hunters, ginseng-gatherers, gold-washers and men who cut down timber without authority. Nominally these men were guilty of trespass on imperial preserves and suspected of banditry; but there are also repeated references to the fact that they were men "without registry." Evidently there was an underlying feeling that all good subjects ought to be identified with places and settlements, for while the profession of the wandering forest hunter was forbidden on principle, the settled farming population was not only permitted but exhorted to ride and hunt, and it was even considered permissible for such farmers to penetrate, in season, into the imperial domains. The people who had taken to the Chinese ideal of a settled farming life were urged again and again not to forget the manly practices of horsemanship and archery and, later, musketry.

When settlements of this type succeeded at all, especially in Northern Manchuria, it is obvious that the area brought within reach and under control must have been far greater than the area actually opened to cultivation. The progress of settlement also benefited by the use of slaves, especially when city Manchus were given land grants which they lacked the experience to farm themselves. Slave-cultivators must undoubtedly have increased the area under cultivation, but the system had its disadvantages. It encouraged the wealthy, especially those who had become successful in official careers, to become absentee landlords. It is a matter of common knowledge that at the present time a great deal of land in Manchuria is held by the descendants of slaves and stewards who usurped in time the estates of their proprietors.

On the whole this type of military colonization, relying on the establishment of a population of martial spirit, from which good recruits could be raised at need, appears to have been satisfactory. The greater number of the colonists were yeomen who had not been dissociated by permanent professional military service from the life of the prosperous and self-reliant small-holder. In the age in which it was devised, no better method could have been found for holding down a frontier and maintaining the essential spirit of the "reservoir." It had, it is true, the inherent weakness of the "reservoir"—the able and ambitious men, instead of turning their energy to frontier expansion, were attracted irresistibly to the south, to the quest of power and preferment in official careers, in which they could turn to profit the great initial advantage of belonging to the dominant regional faction. It suffered also from the clumsy economics of the age. Poor communications and distance from markets excluded the idea of exploitation, which is an essential element of pioneering colonization as understood by the pioneering nations bred up in the Western civilization. The chief growth of population was effected by the natural increase and gradual spread of agricultural communities economically self-contained. In fact, only the particular social and political spirit of the "reservoir" distinguished Manchu Manchuria from the general polity of China. Even military colonization was analogous to colonization generally, and to the influx of Chinese into the "reservoir," in that the expansion achieved can best be expressed in terms of the characteristic Chinese "spread," as against the terms of "drive" in which Western colonizing is typically worked out.

Military colonization at the present time shows very clearly the continuance of the old tradition. Its aim is still a combination of providing a population and providing a defense. Its function is still analogous, in a striking degree, to the function of the military colonies of the "reservoir"; for the Manchurian provinces which are heirs to the old "reservoir" continue to exercise on China proper a pressure greater than the pressure on Manchuria exerted by China. This may be concisely expressed in the formula that the northern foreign frontier policy of China remains secondary to the China policy of the Manchurian provinces. Nor is this by any means to be construed as a bias toward Manchurian autonomy or independence as Western societies understand those terms. Important moves toward political autonomy there have been in Manchuria, and they may recur; but they are altogether different from any independence movement of any colony of any Western nation. This again cannot be identified with the geographical fact that most outer dominions of Western nations are separated by oceans from the colonizing nation, while the outer dominions of China are contiguous with China. As far as that goes, California cares less for the old United States than they do for California, while conversely the sea-divided Chinese communities of Malaysia have more influence on China than China has on them.

The fact is that Western movements of independence are centrifugal and uni-directional. When the American Colonies established their independence they did no more than define schematically the fact that England had become a historic focus of minor validity, the new future foci of imperative validity being the Continental Divide and the shores of the Pacific. When an outlying Western community divides politically from the parent nation, influences of all kinds continue to flow vigorously from the old community to the new; but when received they are not reflected back —or at least the reflex action is of minor importance. They are taken up, informed with new vigor and projected onward and outward. The Pacific Ocean and South American future of the United States entirely dwarfs its European future. The contemporary importance of the United States in the affairs of Europe is a chance effect of the unity of Western civilization, and is as much distrusted and resented by the people of the United States as it is by the peoples of Europe.

Conversely, in the affairs of China, a different organic style is to be discerned. No matter how effective the political autonomy of Manchuria at any given moment, China itself remains the major focus of the life of the community, eclipsing the importance of the Korean-Siberian-Mongolian frontiers.

The influences received from China are reflected back on China with a fresh and intensified vigor, and what is radiated toward the periphery is passed on with diminished force. It is not exactly that the frontier provinces of China are centripetal, for "centrifugal" and "centripetal" are Western terms that lose the edge of their exactitude when applied in China. Rather, the autonomy-tendencies of Chinese provinces reveal an omni-directional capacity, in contrast with the unidirectional force of Western political action. The autonomy of provinces, avoiding the stemming-off process of Western independence movements, works itself out in a coagulation of groups disposed with the lack of declared form of a "Chinese puzzle" about a center pulsing with life, and strongly felt but weakly defined. Unity of civilization, in spite of regional politics, reveals the strongly felt center, but it is a center without schematic definition, a "center" that may be said to vacillate, perhaps, in the huge region of the Yangtze basin, from the ramparts of Tibet to the Yellow Sea. In no nation is the site of the capital city so revealing, and so superficial in importance, as in China.

Military colonization at the present time illustrates the importance of new factors. The terms of land grants are a modification of the old system, and the governing ideas are largely the same; but they are hampered in fulfillment by the prime change of military organization from a system of regional levies engaged in soldiering only when called out to a system of mercenary professional armies. This in itself is an effect of Western influence, and consequently the armies, in spite of their inefficiency from a Western professional point of view, are a dreadfully efficient factor in the threatened destruction of the old Chinese way of life, and the old values of civilization.

Because there is at present a superfluity of soldiers, modern schemes of military colonization are normally drawn up with a view to the desirability of disbanding troops; whereas under the Manchus there was no over-supply, and the main problem was the safeguarding of the potential supply. The most obvious impediment to the successful disbandment and settlement on the land of professional mercenary soldiers is that they make very poor colonists. It is true that the majority of the men are country-bred and have either worked on farms or know something of farm life; but the overwhelming majority are men who have long been dissevered from their families, and in their years of military service have lost the taste for the monotonous drudgery of farm labor. It is true that the soldier, like the peasant, lives on the coarsest of food and rarely has money to spend; but at least he has more opportunities for the diversions of city life, besides which he is usually thoroughly infected with that spirit of the reckless adventurer which always pervades a nation torn by revolution and civil war, when every illiterate trooper stands an equal chance of thrusting his way to rank and power. The average ranker in a military colonization area makes no bones about his distrust of the project into which he has been drafted, considering that he has lost status.

The social background of the soldier-colonist is thus as different as can be from that of the yeoman type available in Manchu days. Although, under the Manchus, efforts were made to provide land and opportunities for Peking Manchus and other city Bannermen who had lost touch with the life of their forbears, a good stiffening was always available, of Manchuria-born, farm-bred men, Chinese and Manchu, of admirable stock. Under modern conditions a great many, if not most of the soldiers in the Manchurian armies are recruited from Shantung and Chihli, who may be of peasant stock, and may have been in Manchuria for some years, but were certainly not bred to the pioneer colonizing tradition. The Manchuria-born farm lad, if he is making good money, is not

likely to join the army; if he has joined the army, he is un-
likely to welcome the idea of being put back on the land.

Not only do the troops themselves tend to distrust the
whole business of colonization, but they do not mix well with
civilian settlers. I remember asking a tenant farmer, who was
working on the land of a great official on a forty per cent crop-
share rental, why he did not move up a few miles and take
land of his own under the good terms offered to colonists
who were needed to supplement a military colonization enterprise. "With *them!*" he said. "That's likely! What with
the beating and the cursing!" In fact the Manchurian farmer is
comparatively independent and self-reliant, and likes to make
his own terms. He is willing to work in association with officials, but is exceedingly suspicious of official "schemes."
Since, however, civilian colonists, preferably men with families, are needed to round out a project for disbandment-
colonization, they are generally gathered from among refugees
from China proper. The refugee, unfortunately, is comparatively shiftless and unadaptable. Once he has received
subsidy, he tends to demand further subsidy. Soldier and
civilian colonists together therefore tend to form a somewhat
unassimilable *bloc* on the outskirts of older "natural" pioneer
settlements.

In the upshot it is not surprising to find that military colonization tends to run a course of compromise. A minority of
soldiers do take up land, often in association with officers.
The majority of the land actually taken up on special military
terms is acquired by officers who have enough capital to bring
in civilian tenants and proceed in the manner of ordinary
capitalists engaged in land development. The rate of civilian
settlement gradually increases and becomes normal, while
the bulk of the troops for whom the project was nominally intended remain in garrison cantonments, occupied from time
to time with patrolling the country against bandits. The

fringe of settlement in any country is likely to pass through a period of lawlessness—until, in fact, it is no longer the fringe. In Manchuria they have, besides, a saying that "the more soldiers the more bandits." In a period of recurrent civil wars, troops naturally prefer campaigns on a large scale, with chances for loot and promotion, to the equal risks and smaller rewards of frontier patrol. Consequently, when troops are scattered out over a wild country in small detachments, desertion is common, the men turning bandit and increasing the general disorder. Conversely, when bandits are really hard pressed, they often come to terms by enlisting as units in the army; whereupon they come within the law but all too commonly do not lose the habits of violence and indiscipline.

If the region prospers, passing beyond the first period of lawlessness, the importance of the group of officials concerned in its administration and exploitation increases accordingly. This importance in turn demands an increased military establishment, in order that the new regional-political group may make itself felt. From this derives the paradox that it is a usual procedure to send out recruiting agents to Shantung and Chihli to find farmers to be turned into soldiers to garrison a region that is ostensibly being developed as a measure for disbanding surplus troops; at the same time that refugees are also being gathered to colonize the region to produce revenue to finance the troops.

In this respect there is a marked contrast between conditions under the Manchu dynasty and at the present time. Under the Manchus, one of the normal abuses of official life (frequently referred to in, for instance, the satiric and picaresque novels which were often under official ban and had to be surreptitiously circulated) was the practice of reporting a nominal payroll of troops far in excess of the actual establishment. At that time military officials were allotted revenue, but only exceptionally had the power of controlling or directly levying it. At the present time, all real power resides with military groups, regionally based and masking their territorial identity under the name of political factions, who monopolize practically the whole of the inland revenue of the nation. The ambitious official, therefore, *of necessity* maintains a military establishment in excess of the numbers to which he is nominally entitled, holding the surplus in reserve to make a bid for increased power when opportunity offers. He draws what pay he can for these troops from whatever central organization nominally claims his allegiance, and pays the rest what he can, when he can, from the revenues which he raises himself or derives privately from enterprises of exploitation in which he engages through agents.

Considering the strong continuity between the history and present situation of Manchuria, which is bound up with the necessity of upholding a strong military position in relation to China proper, any measure that promotes colonization, expands the exploitable area and increases the revenue-producing population, is a good measure, including military colonization. At the same time military colonization, whether or not undertaken with the intention of disbandment, is strictly conditioned by the fact that the very structure and mode of function of contemporary political life forbid any real reduction in armed strength. In the near future therefore it is likely that the total military establishment will have to be increased at least in proportion to the general increase of population, if not at an even higher rate.

THE OPIUM PIONEERS

Of all forms of unassisted colonization in Manchuria, especially of adventurous colonization, the most creative, fruitful and beneficial, with the single exception of the remarkable Shantung style of migration, has undoubtedly been opium colonization. Opium has played in Manchuria the part played by gold in California, Australia and elsewhere. The fact is plain, and ought to be frankly recognized, that hundreds of square miles in frontier regions of Manchuria, now inhabited by an industrious and prosperous population, could never have been opened up and settled so early, rapidly and thoroughly without the lure of opium.

Unfortunately it is impossible to obtain the figures of opium production and trade, and difficult to approach the study of the real importance of opium in the economic and social life of the community. This is chiefly because, in all public discussion of opium, conventional attitudes have become obligatory. It is hardly considered respectable even to discuss the opium problems of China as if they were, in the main, like the prohibition problem of the United States, problems of national legislation and social morality; convention demands that they be discussed as if they were governed by standards of universal validity. This attitude is essentially unreal and certainly not Chinese in origin, but is subscribed to by Chinese who enter the debate because the association of opium with political events of international significance has artificially attached to all opium questions a quasi-political value of international importance. Not since the implication of opium in the issues of the War of 1840, issues which basically had nothing to do with opium and in which opium was only fortuitously involved, has it been customary to deal with the non-moral aspects of poppy growing, the opium trade and opium smoking.

To make matters worse the British apologists for opium in the nineteenth century, by pushing to absurd lengths arguments intended to vindicate on moral grounds a trade that in its origins had nothing to do with morality one way or the other, succeeded in permanently discrediting the one real argument, reasonable in itself, that the use of opium is not necessarily a degrading vice. Since that time, and largely on that account, as well as because opium and its derivatives are rarely used *in Europe and America* except by people already on the verge of degeneracy, there has been a practically universal acceptance of the canon that opium must, *a priori,* always and everywhere be an overwhelming evil for Asiatics, whether under self-government or under the imperial government of a Western power. It is now hardly possible for a serious student, except at the risk of having his motives impugned, to air the fact that Chinese can, and often do, consume a great deal of opium without becoming addicts or suffering any harm whatever, any more than the Westerner who has a drink when he feels like it but is not a drunkard; and that probably men of any other race could do the same, under equal conditions. It is, indeed, impossible to discuss reasonably the opium trade in China, as a trade, comparable, but for the letter of legality, with the brewery trade in Great Britain as "the trade," and open, like the purveying of alcoholic drinks, to grave abuse if not regulated on practical and social rather than moral grounds. It is quite in keeping with the associations of "guilt" now attached to all trade in opium that, in order to press home the moral claim against foreigners who profit from opium and, latterly, other narcotics, the Chinese profits from the same trade should be habitually obscured.

On examining the actual business of growing poppies and distributing opium in China at the present time, it at once becomes apparent that the most serious abuse, creating a social danger far greater than the tax on society of unproductive drug addicts, is forced cultivation of the poppy. The normal form of overproduction is that found in territories where land taxation is enforced at a rate which can only be met by poppy growing; the revenue usually being spent in the maintenance of armies. Production on such a large scale brings down the price and increases the consumption; but, more than that, it weakens the economic structure by reducing the area under food crops. In heavily populated agricultural communities in China this is very serious, for the average farmer, even in normal times, not only lives poorly and eats poorly but is unable to hold more than a very small food reserve. Lack of railways, bad roads and the slowness and cumbrousness of road transport have always made it difficult to transport food supplies even over comparatively short distances. Under the stronger unity of an imperial government, supplies were brought to Peking by the Grand Canal, and State granaries in the provinces protected the greater part of the country in seasons of bad harvest. Since the fall of the Manchus, the regional storage of grain by officials has been generally discontinued. One of the consequences of this loss of grain reserves is a decided weakening of rural economy. Opium, in loads of small bulk and high value, can be sent out much more easily than grain consignments, of great bulk and lower value, can be brought in; and this applies not only to hilly regions but to any region distant by more than a cart-haul of two or three days from a railway. In a region, therefore, in which the land tax has enforced poppy growing widely enough to reduce food crops to a bare subsistence level, one bad season can precipitate a famine, even when other parts of the country have an ample reserve.

As for the abuse of opium in consumption, the chief danger is not that men smoke opium, but that they do not know of anything else more worth doing. The chief social danger of drunkenness in the countries of the West is among the lower strata of the population, where the individual, sunk in the crowd and losing hope and ambition in an apparently soul-less economic situation, may be reduced to spending what he cannot afford in the only way of alleviation and temporary release that he knows. In the same way in China, in an era of social change, of strife without end, lack of economic security and hopelessness all too often seemingly without horizon, it is in the lower strata, the foundations on which society ought to be based, that the greatest damage is done. If people of the leisured classes destroy their own usefulness by dissipation, whether they prefer drink or drugs, they can always be replaced. They make a sensational topic for dis-cussion, but they are not nearly so great a tax on the nation, nor so great a danger to society, as a degraded producing class. The men who are most harmed by opium, and who do the most harm to society, are not those who can afford to pay for their pleasures, but those who buy opium to-day because the inadequate money they have is pitifully insufficient to buy hope of security or real betterment for the morrow. Even superficial observation shows that there are noticeably more hopeless addicts in a region where poppy growing is en-forced by high taxation than in a region where it is volun-tarily but illegally grown, and locally consumed to a certain extent but chiefly exported at a high profit.

On almost every frontier of settlement in Manchuria the evil features of the picture are altered in a most remarkable way. The pioneer settler can often make out of opium a profit offered by no other crop. Agricultural districts in China, generally speaking, are self-sufficient to a degree unknown in Western countries with highly developed transport systems. They export comparatively little, and transport that little over comparatively short distances, the agricultural communities being grouped about market towns which provide most of the needed trade and traffic. In Manchuria, the figures of railway mileage per square mile of territory are higher than in China. The real figures; that is, the railway mileage per square mile of inhabited and productive territory, must obviously be very much higher. Agricultural Manchuria, in strong contrast with China proper, lives by the export of its produce in great bulk over comparatively long distances. The producing areas nearest to the service of railways and river steamers have so great an advantage that the new settler, moving out to the fringe of cultivation, faces a difficulty in getting his grain to market at a profit; and this difficulty increases rapidly with the ratio of distance. If, however, he produces opium, his problems are solved. High price for small bulk covers the cost of transportation and gives a handsome profit. Money brings in traders, and encourages the growth of villages and small-town communities. These in turn create a demand for cheap locally produced food, and result in the settlement of normal agricultural communities.

The settlement of the Lower Sungari, from Sanhsing to the Amur, was due chiefly to opium cultivation; much more, by universal local testimony, than it was to the river steamers. First the opium made it profitable to increase the steamer transport, and then the increased transport made it profitable to increase the production of grain and soy beans. It is also said that the extended service from the Sungari to the Ussuri would not yet be profitable were it not for the opium, but that the existence of the service will rapidly increase traffic to a point where opium becomes of minor importance. A great proportion of the settlers now moving by steamer down the Sungari to the Amur, and thence along the Chinese bank of the Amur and up the Ussuri, are attracted by the prospects of opium growing. Fuchin, the largest town on the Sungari below Sanhsing, grew from a village of Fishskin Tatars to a town of probably well over one hundred thousand population, in a few years, chiefly because it was the center of a great poppy-growing region. From farmers and traders alike can be heard the tale of the boom years and easy money when opium was the paying crop. Opium has been driven out now toward the farther fringes, but that does not mean that Fuchin suffers from depression. It has several flour mills which are credited with profits equal to the total invested capital, every normal working year. In spite of the long up-river haul to Harbin it does a flourishing trade in agricultural produce; and if trade on the much shorter and easier down-river haul to Russian territory across the Amur were freed of legal restrictions, it would increase enormously.

A comparable region is that which will be traversed by the Solun Railway, now under construction. Here, on the western frontier of Manchuria, all Chinese colonization in advance of the railway was based either on the supply of grain to the Mongols, or of opium to the Chinese market. With the introduction of an official program of colonization in that region, poppy growing has been forbidden, and many of the original colonists, discontented with the law, have moved on beyond its reach. In this and many another region just coming within the scope of rapid settlement and development the complaint can be heard, "If only we were allowed to raise opium, you'd see how this place would boom"; but as a matter of fact the mere transfer from poppy growing to normal agriculture is a standard indication that transport and other facilities have been developed to a point which eliminates the importance of opium.

Luckily, the administrative authorities of Manchuria do not have to rely on moral conviction alone for the formulation of a policy in dealing with opium. It cannot be denied that officials are sometimes involved in the opium traffic. A late governor of Heilungchiang, now deceased, was reputed to draw a large income from opium grown on his wilderness holdings; or at least, minor officials under him profited by the trade. On the other hand, the more powerful an official is, the more likely he is to be interested in land development, grain companies, flour mills, railways and steamers. All of these require normal agricultural production to furnish trade and cargo; for which reason the overwhelming tendency, as a frontier region is settled up and comes under the same general administrative system as the older Chinese-populated regions of Manchuria, is to clear out the poppy farmers, forcing them on to a still farther frontier. It is the enormous reserve of unpopulated land that saves Manchuria from being seriously menaced, economically, by poppy growing.

Opium has been cultivated openly, under official license and land tax, in the oldest settled regions of Manchuria, in years when the large revenue thus available was imperatively needed for the financing of Manchurian armies participating in civil war in China. In ordinary years, however, this is not necessary. A sufficient supply can be raised in outlying regions, beyond the scope of fully established and fully staffed civil administration, satisfying the public demand without endangering the economic structure of ordinary society or reducing the food supply and the tonnage demanded by trade and transport. The highly practical attitude toward the laws against opium is well illustrated by the progressive laxity of enforcement as one moves outward toward the frontiers. The steamers and carts that feed the trade of Harbin by water and road are searched for opium on arrival at Harbin; but aboard the same steamers, and at the inns used by the same carts, on the radii outward from Harbin, opium is bought, sold and smoked without concealment.

The communities whose chief occupation is poppy growing provide some of the finest frontiersmen in Manchuria— men of adventure and enterprise who year by year expand the frontiers of effective Chinese occupation. This the gold prospectors have never been able to do to anything like the same extent, because of the enduring social and administrative prejudice against the private exploitation of minerals. The gold prospector, once his "strike" is known, and authority arrives, cannot stay to share in the benefits of his discovery. The gold is placed under official or semi-official monopoly, and he has no choice but to become a laborer on the site of his own discovery, or to vanish and seek for himself some new site for furtive exploitation. The opium grower, on the other hand, knows that he may be able to stay for years, until the whole economic aspect of the region changes. He founds a community and a village, which grows its own food and gradually develops a trade, which is attracted by the comparatively high buying power of the village.

A frontier opium-producing region is, on first acquaintance, lawless and bandit infested; but in reality there is far more peril for the stranger than for the people of the region. Banditry is ruled by strict convention. Many of the bandits are themselves poppy growers in season. A great number of them are recruited from outside adventurers, but others are drawn from among the unmarried men of the poppy-cultivating villages. The men with families live in villages, and often the bandits are chiefly financed by subsidies from opium villages which they protect from the law. Inter-bandit and inter-village feuds arise, but on the whole the man who knows his way about the region need not find trouble unless he looks for it. Outlying detachments of troops or police may demand a share in the profits, and occasionally one gang will jump the opium convoy of another; but the average tendency is to break new ground rather than challenge a community already established.

When in the course of time the frontier of normal settlement is pushed forward to include the fringe of outlying opium villages, it is quite common for a number of the villagers to stay on, using their local knowledge to advantage in the expansion of trade and the rise of land values; just as it is quite common for local bandits to make terms with the newcomers and turn themselves into police or troops. These elements that remain provide a continuity between the old days and the new. On the other hand a large proportion of these outlying frontiersmen, who have never known any law but that of their own gangs and resent the imposition of outside control, move on still farther into the wilderness, carrying on the vigorous tradition of founding fresh communities. There are, by common report, "outlaw" opium villages on the Chinese side of the Ussuri that are virtually autonomous. They defend their valley approaches, govern themselves and hold themselves independent of ordinary civil administration, admitting no officials and paying no taxes.

Yet these outlaws are valuable defenders of the frontier. Were it not for the poppy, Chinese colonization in force would not reach the Ussuri for a good many years to come. Although it can be reached by steamer, the distance from markets and the expanse of unsettled wilderness to be overpassed before the Ussuri is reached are factors that as yet forbid an agricultural boom. Were it not for the lure of opium the Chinese on the Chinese side of the Ussuri would find themselves in danger of being outnumbered, in a region difficult of access, where adequate policing is as yet impossible, by Russians who have migrated across the frontier because of dissatisfaction with Soviet rule, and Koreans who, after migrating from Korea to Primorsk because of discontent under Japanese rule, have later moved again from Russian into Chinese territory. As it is, however, every steamer that runs from the Sungari down into the Amur and then up again into the Ussuri carries its complement of Chinese colonists, and the Chinese population is growing at a yearly accelerated pace. It can only be a question of a few years before the increase of numbers will demand other kinds of exploitation and a greater development of normal administration. If these demands can be met by an expansion of transport, both by river and land, the Ussuri valley will automatically be brought within the scope of "regular" colonization.

THE SHANTUNG TRADITION

The long-established practice of migrating to Manchuria to work for a season, in order to get funds for going back to China to stay, is one of the evidences of the negative style of Chinese migration, and illustrates its characteristic form of drift. On the other hand, it has played a large part in the establishment of the Shantung element in the Chinese population of Manchuria, and is also responsible for the fact— which might at first seem paradoxical—that the Shantung settlers are, by general recognition, the soundest and most successful of all immigrants. There is no adequate explanation other than the fact that the settler who derives from the old system of seasonal migration has behind him a solid tradition. To him Manchuria means something definite before he ever goes there, and when he sets out he has before him a known course of action. This, more than any question of facility of transport, similarity of agricultural methods, or any other factor whatever, explains the extraordinary predominance of Shantung men in Manchuria. A living social tradition has more validity than the most pressing economic necessity.

The association of Shantung with Manchuria is very old, having in all probability been established in prehistoric times, and appears to be connected primarily with the ease of sea-communication between the Shantung peninsula and the Liaotung peninsula. Even at the time of the rise of the Manchus there seems to have been a conspicuously strong proportion of Shantung men and men of Shantung descent among the Chinese enlisted as Chinese Bannermen. Certainly they have been regarded, ever since Manchu times, as a special class in the community. In everyday speech, in Manchuria, Shantung men are referred to simply as Shantung men; people from that part of Chihli province adjacent to the Great Wall at Shanhaikuan by a slang name which refers to their accent, and men from the rest of North China (except for Shansi, which is almost exclusively associated with pawnbroking) under the inclusive term "people from within the Wall"; while Southerners are specifically called Southerners, with the implication that they are, comparatively speaking, outsiders.

The facility of sea communication first made it possible for men to migrate from a thickly populated region, without passing through intermediate territory in which there was no room or need for them, to a thinly populated region in which there was a demand for their labor. They could embark in Shantung at a number of convenient ports and disembark also at a choice of ports; while the valley of the lower Liao gave a direct route for penetration into the hinterland. The land approach was through the bottle-neck passage at Shanhaikuan, west and northwest of which penetration was limited physically by hilly country and politically by the comparatively unreceptive attitude of the Mongols. Moreover this region was more or less monopolized by the early established frontier Chinese, whose great center was at Chinchou. This population, while itself expanding as opportunity offered, and exploiting the Mongol trade in particular, impeded the advance of non-frontier Chihli men from behind, who neither shared their traditions nor understood their methods. Thus the land migration depended largely on the increase of the actual frontier population and was in the main characterized by "spread" without "drive." It is true that poor men from remoter Chihli and Shantung have always been able to find their way by land to Manchuria. Their numbers, however, until the railway was built, were kept down by difficulties of time and expense, and the inert resistance of an intervening population which had no particular interest in supplying work or food to poor migrants.

The shorter time and expense of the sea passage, together with direct access to regions where work could be found, encouraged the practice of seasonal migration and return. This was further encouraged by the fact that the great land holders of the "reservoir" had no particular need of tenants, but benefited by extra "hands" during the short plowing, planting, cultivating and harvest season. With the extra labor they could produce a surplus of grain, a great part of which was also exported by sea. There is, however, no doubt that a certain number of the seasonal migrants remained, after perhaps one or two trips, as permanent settlers, and that a far greater number could have remained, in spite of the Manchu laws of land tenure, if they had been impelled by a true quest for new lands and opportunities, and elbow-room for new growth and self-expression. Indeed, the seasonal migrants to Manchuria often prolonged their stay to several years, without entertaining the idea of permanent settlement; and this type of long-term temporary immigrant is still very common. The land laws alone cannot account for the strong tendency to return to China after working in Manchuria for a season. The provincial records frequently refer to the need for keeping the *liu min,* the wandering people, from settling without authority; but whenever they did settle and establish a hold, the offense was repeatedly condoned. The desire not to leave China permanently must therefore have had a deciding importance; it manifested itself in the feeling that definite settlement in Manchuria was an expedient only for those destitute of other resources, a mark of exile, failure and defeat. To my mind, this pull toward China is proof of the orientation of the true Chinese tradition; while the Manchu land laws themselves are a proof of the assumption of this tradition by the Manchus. The desire to safeguard the Manchu dominance in the "reservoir," far from being a measure solely designed to repress the Chinese, was congruent with the immemorial Chinese formula, long before expressed in the Great Wall frontier system, that a northward shift of Chinese population must never be put forward as a desideratum, and never effected save as an expedient. The most successful emigrant, and socially the most respected, was the man who went out, made his money, and came back.

When, however, railways and modern exploitation increased the demand for men in Manchuria, and the cumulative disasters of disintegration within China began to force up the supply of emigrants, the Shantung type of seasonal migration provided a transition-period link of inestimable value. Numbers of "old hands" were available, men who had been to Manchuria several times, knew the conditions and were able to guide contingents from their old home villages to the places where they could find work or land. Other "old hands" who had already settled in the new country provided nuclei for further settlement, gathering about them friends and neighbors from their old homes and giving news in advance of the number who could be accommodated. The services of these old hands are curiously similar to those of the Russian peasants described by Stephen Graham,[1] who used to travel through Siberia to select in advance a site for colonization, returning after they had made their choice to fetch a contingent from west of the Urals.

Even so, the supply of permanent settlers never satisfied the potential demand, and seasonal migrants continued to outnumber permanent settlers until the situation in Shantung made it increasingly unsafe to return there with money. The period of maximum disorder in Shantung, when famine augmented the effects of military demands and bandit depredations, coincided roughly with a period of minimum assertion in Manchuria on the part of both Russia and Japan. In this period the whole population of Manchuria took heart of grace; a spirit of increased confidence and optimism was abroad, and there was a feeling that Russia at last was in retreat and Japan on the verge of yielding. The years of spectacular migration, in which the yearly immigration first showed a preponderance of settlers over seasonal laborers, and the figures mounted to something like a million a year, with half a million permanent settlers, were 1926, 1927, 1928, with an abrupt check in 1929 when Russia at last jibbed at the pressure that was being put upon her, and the Japanese attitude hardened in sympathy with Russia.

The years of rapid expansion are curiously interesting. Settlers who might never have been drawn into Manchuria by the power of attraction were forced to go there, and in enormous numbers, by the conditions within China. At the same time Russia, feeling for a new and stronger position in the Far East, was diplomatically conciliating Japan and en-

[1] Stephen Graham, *Through Russian Central Asia*. London, Cassell, 1916.

deavoring to secure an orthodox diplomatic recognition in North China, as a basis for more definite procedure. For these reasons Russian activities in Manchuria were greatly curtailed and directed instead toward suitable parties in China itself, especially in the South. Instead of bearing directly on Manchuria an effort was made to increase the Russian influence throughout all China, thus eventually bearing on Manchuria also. It appears that Chinese opinion misjudged the Russian policy as a confession of weakness in Manchuria and an attempt to effect a lodgment elsewhere instead. In the meantime Japan, attempting to improve the tone of its relations with all the Powers interested in the Pacific, and making extraordinary efforts to show its adherence to the spirit of the Washington Conference, was doing its best to conciliate China both in Manchuria and elsewhere. The main object of Japan was to show that while nothing would be yielded to China as a concession to forceful measures, sympathetic attention would be given to a number of old points of dispute if they were approached through friendly negotiation.[2] The rapprochement between Japan and Russia al-

---

[2] The Japanese "policy of conciliation and coöperation" broke down calamitously in 1931. It can hardly be doubted that the Chinese considered this policy to be no better than a velvet glove intended to make more decorous the dreaded mailed fist. The Japanese, for their part, considered that a fair (in Japanese eyes a generous) offer had not been received in the spirit in which it had been made; that the Chinese, instead of meeting the offer of coöperation, were construing it as a sign of weakness and endeavoring to take advantage of the supposed weakness. The whole Japanese "overseas" community in Manchuria—the military in the lead, but with the agreement of probably the majority of the civilians—began to agitate for the abandonment of the "policy of conciliation and coöperation" and the revival of a "positive" policy. Tension between Chinese and Japanese increased, and the "Nakamura incident"—the killing of a Japanese officer traveling in the hinterland—gave the Manchurian Japanese material for renewed agitation in Japan. Up to this point there was a certain similarity with the conditions preceding the break between Chinese and Russians in 1929, with the difference that the Chinese had been obstructive rather than aggressive and the Japanese more resistant than the Russians.

After this point had been reached, the Chinese began to yield over the Nakamura incident—but too late. Feeling in Japan had already been worked up to the point of genuine public clamor that "something be done," in spite of the fact

lowed a better understanding in regard to Manchuria, where the quiescence of Russian policy gave Japan a margin for conciliating China. Thus the old Japanese policy of opposing the construction of Chinese railways which might impair the commanding position of the South Manchuria Railway was very considerably modified. The Chinese were actually assisted in the building of some of these lines, with Japanese capital and material, while Japan acquiesced in the construction of others.

The apparent recession of both Japan and Russia was followed up with great eagerness, but the real strength of the foreign nations was misjudged. The pressure of Chinese expansion was lacking in coördinated policy; opportunism was allowed to go too far, and the enthusiasts overreached themselves, forcing Russia to take a firmer stand. In the upshot, the Chinese "forward policy" collapsed, in a manner hardly to be understood except in the light of the inherent negative characteristics of Chinese expansionism that have already been discussed. It is at least open to argument that the three years in which the forward policy reached a peak in Manchuria represented an aberration from the historically rooted main trend of Manchurian colonization; for a comparatively trifling display of determination on the part of Russia was enough to check the Chinese forward policy with startling effectiveness. Not only did the forward policy fail alarmingly, but a strong reaction set in at once, with a return to the old emphasis on the "inward-facing" characteristics of the old "reservoir." The immediate result of the revelation of real danger on the northern frontier was a strong assertion of the importance

that the Government wished to settle this affair—and other questions outstanding—with as much decorum as possible. Consequently, on the occurrence of an excuse —an "outrage" on the Japanese railway which the Chinese accuse the Japanese of having manufactured—the Japanese military forces in Manchuria struck, without waiting for authority from Japan, and with paralyzing effect.

of the southern frontier; and at the moment the chief concern of Manchuria is no longer the outer frontiers, but once more the important option of authority which it holds in the affairs of China.[3]

Even at the height of the boom, when every form of immigration was modified as far as possible in favor of speed and general expansion, the Shantung tradition retained to a notable degree its own character and quality. It is extraordinary how many Shantung families, even the most destitute, forced out of Shantung by disastrous necessity, without the possibility of making definite plans, have yet a knowledge of where they want to go and what they can expect when they get there. Inevitably, while opportunities of individual choice were smothered by the rush of numbers, they became increasingly at the disposal of the "big interests"; but even when submitting to the manipulations of the great land agencies the Shantung family retains enough individual purpose to edge its way persistently toward a place where "neighbors" of the old home are already established. Time and again the same story can be heard from a Shantung family, starving and dependent on charity, but working toward a known goal: "If we can reach such-and-such a place, we have people we know."

One of the most exclusive fields of Shantung settlement is along the lower Sungari, from below Sanhsing to the Amur. In this region there is not only an overwhelming general preponderance of Shantung people, on the land and in the towns; but in district after district there is to be found a remarkable proportion of people from the same county in Shantung.

---

[3] This remained true up to the moment when the Japanese forced the issue of the Manchurian policy toward Japan. On the whole the Chinese in Manchuria were much more obstructive and non-coöperative in their Japanese policy than aggressive; the active attention of the Manchurian Government being preoccupied with affairs in China proper.

This holds for merchants and exploiting groups as well as for peasants. It indicates that the local "big men" shared in manipulating the flood of migration, guiding toward the interests in which they participated a supply of settlers in whom they had also an interest.

The adventurer and the forerunner, the single men coming without their families, are as dependent on this linkage as are the family groups. The commonest explanation given by the solitary immigrant is *chao jen,* "looking for a man." The man may be a relative, or somebody linked by old group obligations to the impoverished newcomer. Whatever the linkage, the raw immigrant knows not only the name and connections of the man he is seeking, but the place where he is established or was last known to be. Even if he has moved, and both men are illiterate and unable to communicate, the newcomer is certain of finding his man so long as he works through the reticulation of Shantung men and Shantung interests. When the man is found, the procedure exemplifies the whole method of graduated manœuver. The established man seeks out someone with whom he has a connection, and finds work for the newcomer, and the three then form a minute complex of triple interdependence and obligation. The newcomer, finding his feet and gradually establishing fresh connections, may work away from the original point of lodgment; but the web of mutual dependence and diffused responsibility—not each for himself, but each as a member of his group—is never wholly broken. It is the same indefinite but tensile web that links not only peasant with townsman and artisan with capitalist, but merchant with official and bandit with soldier, and even limits, according to time and occasion, the sphere within which the bandit works and, sometimes, his choice of victim.

Even when the Shantung man has arrived with a mob of refugees, and finds himself placed willy-nilly on a land holding under the control of some large enterprise, he struggles to escape the absolute authority of the "interests." A man may give up one holding and move to another, with no evident difference in status or real economic freedom, and for no reason whatever, except that he had been *put* on one holding, but was able to *negotiate* the second. It frequently happens, not only with Shantung men but even with the comparatively helpless men from other provinces, that the settler absconds from the holding allotted to him in a scheme, and sets up for himself as a squatter—on land not occupied, but already privately owned. He does not know the owner, and to all appearances has wantonly put himself at a disadvantage.

In practice, however, he has improved his standing. The uninvited squatter has a social position of tacitly recognized social value. It is not that he has any legal "squatter's rights," for he is an intruder on land already owned and registered; but public opinion is against the landlord who would summarily evict a man already established, on the strength of a mere legal theory. He must compromise with the practical fact that the man is there. In the Chinese conception of responsibility a fact that has happened is of more importance than the motives or actions that led up to it. Moreover, he has improved the land, not only by farming it, but because his mere presence has enhanced the value of neighboring land, since the average "pioneer" abhors the wilderness but is comforted by the presence of people who are already established. The squatter, then, has the strong advantage of simply being there, and the supplementary advantage of having contributed to the value of the land; while the owner for his part has the advantage—for this also is an advantage, and no small one—of not being responsible for having put him there. Consequently, it is easy to come to terms.

One major fact relating to the importance of the Shantung element in Manchuria is probably not generally recognized; the part played by Shantung men in military affairs. The soldiers, like the settlers, are linked by an unbroken tradition with the earliest Manchu days, when Shantung men filled the Chinese Banners of the Manchu army. It is a commonplace remark in Peking at periods when the old capital is occupied by Manchurian troops, that they "are just like the Manchus when they first came in"—that is, like the early Manchu and Chinese Bannermen of traditional memory. Yet a very large proportion of these troops have acquired their "Manchurian" manners and character in only a few years in Manchuria; for in the Manchurian armies the Manchuria-born men are at least equaled and probably outnumbered by non-Manchurian-born Chinese, among whom the Shantung men are the most important. The recruiting of Shantung troops is a parallel to the recruiting of Shantung settlers. Just as the "old hand," seasonal laborer or settler, returns to Shantung to bring back men that he knows to a country that he has learned to know, so the trusted old soldier or noncommissioned officer returns to Shantung, with money furnished by his commander, to find recruits. He pays a bounty for each recruit, and this method is frankly called "buying soldiers." The new men are placed in the ranks with seasoned troops, among whom they find many from their own district in Shantung, and in a year or two are thoroughly "Manchurian" in attitude.

This association with the army is of great importance, for in an era of civil war promotion from the ranks is rapid and common. Similarly, the ultimate measure of an official's importance is the measure of his military connections and backing. There is thus inevitably a large proportion of men of Shantung birth or extraction among important civil and military officials, and these men, when looking for opportunities of investment and exploitation, naturally turn to Shantung land holders, merchants and industrialists. The army, the administration and the great moneyed interests being, to a great extent, different spheres of activity of the same controlling group, it is common to find that the different subgroups are closely linked by exchanges of appointments and influence among the leaders; and that these private alliances are confirmed by intermarriage among the controlling families. Thus the Shantung element ramifies through the whole economy and social structure of Manchuria. The Shantung town merchant or industrialist of importance will be found to have an elaborate reticulation of alliances, extending to civil and military officials, holders of great estates tenanted by Shantung farmers, and so on—all Shantung men or local men associated by marriage with the Shantung group.

Moreover, in spite of the sufferings that Shantung province has gone through, every comparatively safe place in Shantung has its prosperous homes of leisured people who live on the income of fortunes made in Manchuria, or on incomes remitted by relatives in Manchuria. If conditions in Shantung improve, the numbers of successful Shantung men returning from Manchuria will increase. In the meantime, not a little of the money made in Manchuria is reinvested by buying up land at cheap prices during famines in Shantung.

Chapter IX

REFUGEES, FRONTIERSMEN AND BANDITS

REFUGEE COLONIZATION

THE colonization of waste land in Manchuria by refugees from famine regions and overpopulated regions in China is almost entirely a phenomenon of railway exploitation. So far as the natural pressure of population within China had an effect in promoting emigration before the period of Western impact, it worked through the old Shantung type of migration, and the spreading expansion of border communities along the fringe of the age-old "reservoir." In the first place, there was the difficulty of escaping on foot or with animal transport only from a famine region, and of passing through regions poor in cash and food reserves and unable to support refugees on their way to territories suitable for colonization. In the second place, there was the extreme traditional repugnance toward migration and the stigma of despair and defeat attached to the permanent abandonment of the ancient home. In the third place, there was the special fear and dislike of all the "barbarian" country north of the Great Wall—the region of defense and fear, not of advance and hope. Thus along the whole land frontier it was exceptional to find any spread of Chinese colonists except such as was effected by specific order, as at strategic points like Jehol and Suiyüan.

The border population itself did tend to expand northward. The men of this population had a tradition and method of their own; but even so their expansion was a "spread" in character, lacking drive and the ambition of conquest. They were prepared to sacrifice Chinese characteristics and standards by "turning Mongol" whenever it was expedient. They moved forward tentatively when conscious of a strong China behind them, but withdrew hastily or "turned Mongol" completely when the government weakened and the old forces of the "reservoir" reasserted themselves. For comparatively large numbers, bringing a strong, definitely Chinese impact to bear on a comparatively short front, we have to look to the Shantung type of migration, where the direct sea passage and the possibility of quick return broke down to a certain extent the "irrevocable sentence of exile" associations of emigration from non-frontier China.

The development of railways modified the old conditions in a remarkable way. Refugees could be transported over great distances in a very short time, and brought direct to regions that needed colonists. Rail transport disposed altogether of the inert resistance to the passage of emigrants that had been offered by intervening territory thickly populated and not adapted to accommodate even a temporary influx of migrating strangers. Railways, moreover, quite as much as the acquisitions of Western armament, destroyed the old military ascendancy of such "reservoir" people as the Mongols. Under the immemorial conditions when there was no appreciable difference in armament between Chinese and barbarians, it needed a very large military effort on the part of the Chinese to confirm the conquest of very narrow strips of territory. The barbarians, on the other hand, could raid into and "hold down" comparatively wide settled Chinese regions; though they could not convert these regions entirely to their own social code. Manchus, Mongols and the Central Asian tribes, traditionally able to campaign without fixed bases and heavy transport (especially transport of food) and accustomed to warfare in terms of rapid mobility over great distances, and to quick apprehension of the topography even of unknown country, offered a military problem as difficult and expensive to deal with as that which confronts the British on the Northwest Frontier of India. The Chinese military tradition, that of a land-fast peasantry, demanded a solid front in battle and the use of large numbers of men who could see and hear one another all the time; together with food and transport supplied from the rear—in other words, the basic requirements of infantry warfare throughout history. Even at the present time, Chinese troops with superior arms cannot operate effectively against Mongols, in Mongol country, without very great superiority in numbers; because there is no fixed population to conquer, and no opportunity to assert their superiority in pitched battles. In times past, the most effective method of counteracting the Mongol strategy of raiding attacks and quick movement over long distances was the encouragement of lamaism and lama monasteries. The great, wealthy monasteries did to a certain extent tend to make the Mongols land fast, or at least vulnerable at fixed points, and to impair their essential tradition.

Railways clinched the decision. A line of railway is equivalent to a fixed base. It gives to troops the comfort of a fixed line to fall back on, and it makes possible the rapid concentration of forces, thus tending to restore the balance of mobility. Wherever a region of frontier colonization is served by a railway, there is no longer any doubt of the ascendancy of Chinese over tribesmen. Road transport by motor, the most modern development in Manchuria (aviation not yet having reached the practical stage), enormously increases the range of operation from a railway base, and has been used with great effectiveness in the Hsingan Colonization Project, in Western Fengtien (Liaoning) province, where a great stretch of land is being taken over from the Mongols and settled by civilians and troops together. In this region, the Mongols are held down by military outposts, linked by motor transport, while a railway is being built which will permanently decide the matter.

The "reservoir" tradition has thus been so far modified that it is no longer imperative for the frontiersman, if he is within reach of a railway, to acquire a special technique of frontier life, or to "turn Mongol" in any important degree. The continuance of the "reservoir" tradition now depends essentially on the fact that the expanding Chinese population, in spite of its new advantages, still maintains the social outlook and regional orientation bred under the old conditions. Given, therefore, the wealth of a boom of colonization in the "reservoir" and the tradition of the superiority of success in China over success on the frontier, it is just as easy for the railways to bring the increasing power of the frontier to bear on China as it is for them to transport fresh colonists to the frontier.

The true frontier tradition in Manchuria was always confined to a comparatively small and socially specialized population, as it was also in America: and the advent of the railway is killing the true frontier tradition, as it killed it also in America. There is a pious fiction in America that the great post-Civil War railway and industrial "reconstruction," and the westward spread of population, carried on the old pioneer tradition and that we all have a pioneer heritage in our blood. That fiction performs a certain service, in that it transvalues otherwise non-American values in our society; the manipulation of herds of immigrants, as a form of big business, we call by convention a triumphal march, in order to preserve the spirit of "onward and upward" which animates the expansionist drive in the American tradition. In reality, the later expansion in America was a secondary phenomenon, distinct from the original expansion of the wilderness pioneers. It was controlled in the main by "big interests" which satisfied the demands of the new industrialism and at the same time provided traffic for the vast new transport systems which, in America then as in Manchuria now, were the hinge on which turned the change to a new era.

The present colonization of Manchuria equally represents a secondary stage, which both supersedes and destroys the primary stage. It is equally dominated by "big interests," and is equally dependent on a cheap supply of docile immigrants. The primary stage differed from the early period of the great colonizing movements of Western nations in that it provided no outlet for discontented minorities. In China also there are discontented minorities; but coming as they do within the orbit of Chinese civilization, in spite of being dissenters, they tend to work out their differences on the spot, not to migrate for the purpose of setting up a new dispensation in the wilderness. The secondary stage is closer to that of the West; for the migration settles no fundamental issues within the civilization itself, and the migrants are anything but arbiters, or even champions of their own destiny: and certainly migration to Manchuria, however great the numbers involved, no more solves the problems of population pressure in China than the transport of immigrants to America solved the population problems of Europe. Nor has the refugee colonist in Manchuria any more option of pursuing the "pioneer tradition" than had the gangs of Italians laboring on railways to cross the Rockies and open America's "last frontier," or the Poles and Bohemians fed into America's coal mines and steel mills. The fact that the expansion into Manchuria is as yet predominantly agricultural gives a certain pioneering color to the present great population movement; but the fact that practically all the land open to colonization is already privately owned by the "big interests," who dominate the economics of the country as effectively as the "big interests" in the days of unrestricted immigration into America, determines the major colonization phenomena of Manchuria.

The typical refugee colonist is a man who leaves his home in despair and unwillingly, for a destination which he does not choose but which is appointed for him by a relief organization or the recruiting agent of a landholder in Manchuria. He is carried by rail from his old home all the way through and past the old frontier territory to his destination, at a speed which precludes his learning anything of the old frontier spirit or methods. When he reaches the destination, he is put on the land on terms in which he himself has the minimum of choice. This usually means rental terms as high as forty to sixty per cent of the yearly crop. Even if the terms make rental purchase possible, the interest charged for equipment and initial financing during the settlement years makes it extremely difficult for him to succeed in becoming the owner of land with a clear title: and even if he does succeed in becoming a farmer with land of his own, he has to deal with a grain market and a transport system which are thoroughly under the control of great vested interests.[1]

In the outlying districts, in order to hold the colonists on the land at all, and keep them from drifting back to China or beyond the reach of organized control to become squatters, terms are granted which mean that for at least a generation the farmer will eat more and live better than he did in China. Basically, however, the economic and social system is not one built up in Manchuria—the time is past for that; the

---

[1] Compare the situation of the great numbers of "crop-sharers" or tenant-farmers in America, whose fundamental economic impotence is revealed in any time of general agricultural depression.

pace is too fast, and such societies can only be found in the heart of the old "reservoir" country—but one imported from China. This means that, apart from the political bias imparted by the regional feeling, and the disruptive effect of Westernization, the new population, as it grows, tends to reproduce in full the situation as it is in China, with the same problems of over-population, pauperization, economic bondage to the land and landholders and insufficient margins of food reserve and financial security.

The most favorable terms of all are offered in regions which are at the same time the frontier of Chinese settlement, and adjacent to an international frontier—that is, to Russia. Where the Mongols are still powerful, settlement on the edge of Mongol territory is also encouraged on specially favorable terms. The setback suffered by the Chinese as a result of the Chinese Eastern Railway dispute, and the facile military successes of the Russians, caused a feeling of the greatest uncertainty all along the frontier. As a result, this is the last region in which colonists are anxious to settle of their own accord. Obviously, however, from the official point of view, the settlement of at least a screen of Chinese colonists all along the Amur frontier is a measure of imperative importance; while the great landholders are willing to give good terms in order to get their land opened at all. The favorable terms offered in this region are roughly as follows, and they are arrived at by coöperation between the provincial authorities and the landowners—it being understood that the greatest land holders are likely to be officials themselves, or related by blood or marriage to officials. The terms differ a good deal in Kirin and Heilungchiang, the Kirin Government being more liberal and progressive, on the whole.

Villages are marked out at convenient distances in absolutely virgin, uninhabited country, usually from three to six in a day's journey of twenty-five to thirty miles. Building timber is transported to these sites, in advance. This is likely to be done or supervised by a special Agricultural Bureau, centered in the nearest county town, and linked by organization both with the local chamber of commerce and the provincial authorities. Colonists are recruited either by agents of the land holders themselves, or by "old-timers" (usually Shantung men) who, having gained experience as laborers, market gardeners or small tenant farmers, are prepared to take up land on permanent tenure, and have gone back to Shantung to fetch relatives, friends and neighbors in order to form a congenial village nucleus. When the settlers arrive, they build their own houses, using the timber provided, and for bricks digging out earth themselves, pressing it in wooden frames and drying it in the sun to make adobe.

Settling down, and perhaps the breaking of a little soil, takes up the first short season. Then they hibernate for the first winter, living on provisions supplied under the settlement scheme. With the next thaw and the first full plowing season—using draught cattle and plows provided for them—each head of a family selects what land he likes, near the village, and all plow as much as they can. They may not even know whose is the soil they plow. Virgin soil is often simply plowed and harrowed, to break up the sod, without planting; but sometimes a rough crop of beans is planted. I believe that the slowness of getting cultivation started is partly due to the poor quality of the plows, which do not bite deep. The top sod has first to be turned over, harrowed and left to disintegrate. A second plowing, in the following year, then gives the required depth. Cultivation is based on a system of deep furrows and high ridges, which are maintained year after year. They are renewed in the spring by light plowing in the same old furrows, while the ridges are kept up during the season by hand cultivation with hoes.

In any case the third season (the second of plowing) produces a crop; and at the same time extra land can be broken. By this time, usually, the country has been "opened" enough for a reckoning. The actual landowners or their agents then arrive. The land is all remeasured, and owner and settler negotiate a partition, on the basis of six parts to the farmer (without purchase price) and four parts to the owner (without charge for plowing). It may happen that a farmer finds he has been plowing for several owners; but most of the original land grants were so large that he will find he has only one owner to deal with. The site of the village itself is deducted from the reckoning, the landowners among themselves contributing its value. The title deeds for the farmer's land are then made over to him; and as for the four parts which revert to the original owner, he may rent or sell them as he pleases.

This method contrasts well with the standard in more developed regions, where from the beginning the settler is likely to find himself a tenant, paying a rental of from forty to sixty per cent of the crop, with little chance of acquiring ownership. Under these special terms the settler becomes a landowner on a scale that would require a generation of toil, and a lot of good luck as well, in his native province. The original owner is left with forty per cent of his land; but this forty per cent, by virtue of having been opened, is worth the whole of the original undeveloped holding. Often the original landowner remains the largest individual land holder of the region, and its most important capitalist.

The new peasant-proprietor is not subject to land tax until the seventh year. From the fourth year to the seventh year, inclusive, he pays off by installments the capital cost of the building material, equipment, livestock, food supplies and so forth, with which he had been supplied in advance. Thereafter he pays ordinary land tax, police dues and so forth. "You are well off here," I said to one such man; "enough people to open the land, but plenty of land for expansion. Not too many people and too little land, like Shantung." "Ha!" he replied, contentedly; "you wait a couple of generations! We'll be running around like ants!" And indeed, judging from the visible rate of development in many regions where settlement has once taken hold, I think that in two generations many of the new settlements of to-day will be approximating to agricultural districts generally in North China, in size of farms and ratio of land tax to capital value. A Liaoning province man, whom I met in Heilungchiang, told me that in districts of Heilungchiang developed within the last thirty years, taxation was much lighter than in Liaoning, the "oldest" province. Taxation of undeveloped land in Heilungchiang, he said, was even lighter; not only is the tax light in itself, but it is assessed on only an estimated percentage of the land. The tax is made lighter yet by the fact that a larger, more generous measure is used for undeveloped land. In the "oldest" parts of Liaoning, he said, not only is the tax higher and the measure smaller, but the measurement is made to include even ponds and rough patches of irreclaimable land, which in Heilungchiang are simply "thrown in," without being measured.

Incidentally, the power of the big interests is illustrated by the custom of taxing undeveloped land very lightly. Thus there is no pressure on the great land holders, forcing them to sell or develop; only when, at their convenience, they have found settlers, is the tax increased, and it can then be taken out of the value developed by the settlers.

The refugee colonists, who are now numerically the most important, and whose importance has forced down the old standards of the Shantung migrants, owing to the fact that Shantung in recent years has suffered as heavily as any other province, illustrate all the most "negative" characteristics of so-called "pioneer" colonization when undertaken by a society of advanced civilization. Being quite unable to fend for themselves, they are poor material to begin with. Being emigrants by necessity only, they have not the mental attitude which facilitates adaptation. Indeed, they are inclined to resent everything in food, climate, housing and so forth that is not "like home"; even though, with properly directed energy, the environment might be made better than home. Moreover—ironic though this may seem—the relief projects and colonization projects which are most efficiently run and treat the refugees best have the most trouble with them. This is largely because of the peasant's interpretation of "responsibility"—"you have saved me, therefore you are responsible for my being alive *and for my future;* and now, what are you going to do about it?" Relief of the old type was purely defensive. Grain was issued from the local state granaries, and taxes were remitted; if the grain gave out, the people died. That type of relief has gone. The new, "dynamic" type, with its overtones of expansion and the creation of new wealth, is essentially a new concept, and the reaction of the conservative, simple-minded peasant tends to be: "You must be getting more out of this than I am. Anyhow, this is not my idea. I am not responsible for being saved. You are responsible for bringing me here. Now you ought to do something more for me."

Consequently the losses by desertion from relief-colonization projects are very high. The landowners consider that the settlers are ungrateful, and are on the whole glad to get rid of those who are not docile, although the rate of development is slowed down. The settlers very soon find out that they have in fact been brought out largely for the benefit of vested interests in need of cheap labor. Consequently, the most capable of them are the most likely to desert. From this it might appear that the only people who stay on the land are the least enterprising and energetic. This is not wholly true; for some of those who abscond do in fact settle on the land, often as squatters, in regions not yet being systematically colonized, where later they can make their own terms with the landowners.

In order to minimize this type of defection, organized colonization projects endeavor to secure a high proportion of married settlers with children. Even this admirable measure, however, does not wholly obviate the loss. Only too often, the family which is able to hang together at all is one which has enough resources of its own, or ability among its members, to support itself and eventually find its way home again, without going to the dreaded extreme of migrating to Manchuria. On the other hand, many desperate people, in order to secure cheap transport to Manchuria, band themselves hastily into fictitious families—a man and a woman who are not married, gathering up several children not their own and applying for relief as a family. When such a group is placed on the land, very little discontent is enough to make the man abandon his adventitious family; especially if he has endeavored to turn them back on the authorities, and been refused. He may well abandon them; he has reached Manchuria, there is work to be had, or he can at a pinch join the army or turn bandit. If he wants to work his way back to his native province, he can do so more easily without his following. Losses from this kind of defection, and similar causes, may run very high in the first year or two of a colonization project; sometimes, I believe, as high as forty per cent. I have heard higher figures quoted locally in such regions; but of course, no accurate statistics are available.

When women are thus deserted, they do not necessarily starve. Owing to the great shortage of women, particularly on the fringes of settlement, the ordinarily strict Chinese standards are relaxed during the settling-down years of a new population, and almost any woman who has any qualities to recommend her can form a fresh alliance—often with a man who has already begun to prosper. Girl children even are popular, and can find homes, because when they grow up their marriage-settlements will be profitable. In China proper a son is more valuable; girls are in such plenty that, unless a family is already well-to-do, it is hard to marry off a daughter advantageously. The son stays in the family and his earnings contribute to it, while a daughter, at marriage, "goes out of the family." In Manchuria, on the other hand, women are so scarce that if a daughter is at all personable there will be many bids for her hand, and the parents can choose a son-in-law on terms advantageous to themselves.

Nor is the case of a young boy, when a refugee family or pseudo-family has broken up, too desperate. Once a boy is past his infancy he can earn a living. Perhaps the greatest difficulty, in practice, is that an adopted son tends to desert his adoptive parents if they do not prosper, so soon as he is able to fend for himself.

COLONISTS BY BIRTH AND TRADITION

One other important type of frontier settlement has yet to be considered—that of the secondary migrants. These are men with families; men whose forebears have been in Manchuria for several generations and who derive from the old pre-railway times of the drifting spread into Manchuria. They form a special class among the old frontier or "reservoir" population, functioning as developers of agricultural land, in close touch with the exploitation undertaken by officials. They are chiefly to be found in lands taken over from the Mongols, but they differ from the first-line frontiersmen of the old Mongol "reservoir" in that they are definitely not a "mixed class"; they rarely have Mongol blood, and rarely speak Mongol. At the same time they have a strong "reservoir" color; they are not land fast; they tend always to move forward, and their special knowledge is the knowledge of how to break and develop raw land. Naturally, they are of the greatest value in extending the frontiers of Chinese occupation, and are looked on with high favor by the officials concerned with border expansion. They form an admirable core for any project of new colonization; the pity is that owing to the pace of modern colonization brought about by railway construction their numbers cannot be multiplied fast enough to keep up with the opening of suitable new territories.

They are the only settlers who, as a class, have capital, which they raise by selling out the land which they have previously developed and enhanced in value, in order to move on to new land. Their careers are thus worked out in terms of continuous generations, not of a single lifetime. The land which their fathers or grandfathers took up on the edge of Mongol territory has doubled and trebled in value through the arrival of later colonists and the growth of communications and markets. They themselves have a personal or family background of "raw" land. Therefore they capitalize their old holdings and move on. They know the working of frontier methods and the ways of frontier officials; and they know that as they prosper they increase their prospects of having sons graduate into the ranks of the real controlling classes—the officials and the "big interests." Indeed, patriarchs of such groups often have a semi-official standing and are frequently consulted by the officials.

Settlers of this type tend to move as communities, and will

be found in groups all of whom lived in the same old villages and benefited by their loose group and class association in bargaining for the new lands and founding the new villages. They continue to benefit by this group organization, forming a subsection of the new community as a whole. They act in conjunction in matters of policy, and among themselves they have their own gradations of leaders and followers. Their land operations are often complicated, owing to differences in value between old lands and new. Often they will even settle for a generation and more on comparatively poor land, waiting until better regions are expropriated from the Mongols. Thus there is a long stretch of land between Ssup'ingkai and T'aonan in Western Fengtien (Liaoning), filled with abandoned villages, whose inhabitants have moved on west of T'aonan or southwest toward K'ailu. West and northwest of T'aonan can also be found contingents of secondary migrants from the Petuna region who, with the weakening and withdrawal of the Mongols have overpassed the inferior lands between their old homes and their new settlements; although actually their new lands are often not so rich as the fields they formerly owned. They have sold out good land, moved across poor land, and settled in land of medium grade, having nicely calculated the profits to be made by selling out developed land, buying at least three times the acreage of undeveloped land, and opening it to cultivation in order to clear a further profit.

This type of settler is far less conspicuous in non-Mongol regions, because there, the land not being "Mongol" but "public," the settler was able in the past to settle as a squatter on land chosen for a permanent home, and to arrange terms of tenantry or purchase when the land was eventually released for settlement and passed into private ownership.

The "reservoir"-bred, secondary migrant and the semi-outlaw opium-growing settler are probably the nearest in tradition and feeling to the old-style Western pioneer; at least to the early, pre-railway American pioneer—and, like the early Western pioneers, they are the survivors of an older order. They cannot stand the pace of a machine-grounded economy; their style of life demands a training too long drawn-out, and too close a linkage of tradition-informed generations.

It is noteworthy, however, that the "pioneer" in one of the oldest and most typical Western senses of the word—the "lonely settler"—is almost unheard-of. This is of significant interest because it means that the quest for loneliness, the hunger for an empty land in which a man can express his own starkest individuality, are psychological characteristics of an individualism that is not congruent with the Chinese tradition and the Chinese civilization. The farthest-outlying frontiersman forms for himself a group-connection by attaching himself to Mongols, Manchus or other non-Chinese tribes; the second-line frontiersman moves forward as part of a group; the squatter is always found as an extension of the group never wholly removed.

The general instinct running through society is not to get away from the old order, nor to found any new order, but merely to extend the old order, and to reproduce it as fast as possible. Although there are outlaw communities, there are no communities of revolt; no rebellious minorities that have migrated from the old home in order to get away from an unsympathetic majority, and founded new communities in order to be independent.

THE BANDIT AS FRONTIERSMAN

Banditry is one of the great plagues of modern China, and is commonly said to be chiefly due to civil war, famine and desperation. Yet in Manchuria also banditry is endemic. If, then, banditry has not been eliminated in Manchuria, where food and work are plentiful and where the population is practically free from the effects of civil war, how is it ever to be eliminated? The answer is that the banditry of Manchuria is essentially a "frontier" banditry, organically different from the banditry of social disintegration and despair which characterizes so much of China proper.

The axiom that "the more soldiers the more bandits," though heard all over Manchuria, does not indicate a peculiarity of Manchurian conditions. On the contrary, it points to a condition of over-militarization, from which Manchuria does not suffer so badly as any equivalent area of China proper, under which the soldier, becoming the master, not the protector of society, takes to banditry and soldiering alternately, according to the current chances of profit and promotion. This type of downright destructiveness is much more "sophisticated" than the old Manchurian banditry, is not so local in its connections, and is as modern as the phenomena of mass-colonization. Like modern colonization, it tends to obliterate antecedent conditions, while occasionally preserving certain elements of the antecedent tradition.

The Manchurian bandit tends very strongly to adhere to a group; and to a group which is identified with a particular region. There are no more solitary bandits than there are solitary settlers; there are bands of robbers and occasional footpads, who hardly count as bandits. Single desperadoes, or very small bands of two or three wandering outlaws, of the kind that, in the history of the American frontier, are far more typical than the group, are almost non-existent. In fact the bandit not only seeks the comfort of plurality; he likes to belong to an organic body, with a recognizable place in the community. His chief comfort is that, through various affiliations, there is always a degree of communication between the outlaw community and the law-abiding community. This explains the fact that when a countryside is rid of bandits, the cleaning-up is normally accomplished by negotiation, only exceptionally by the shock of conflict.

Bandits are most commonly disposed of by enlisting them in the troops or police, or, not uncommonly, by betrayal and massacre; but even betrayal and massacre are essentially the results of negotiation, not of outright warfare. Violence, it is true, is common—in fact, general—all over Manchuria; but it is sporadic, spontaneous and undirected. The collective organized violence of the vigilante is, in my experience, unknown. Village and regional self-defense corps are quite frequently formed, and maintain on the whole better protection than ordinary police or regular troops; but this is because the self-defense corps and the bandits are very well known to each other. They almost never fight it out to a finish; on the contrary, a stalemate arises and the bandits avoid the organized villages, while the defense corps refrain from pursuing the bandits. Unfortunately for the villages thus defended, the more efficient their local volunteer corps, the more likely it is to be brought within the wider organization of regular troops; whereupon outsiders break in to the "racket," the local interest is handicapped, and the plague of banditry begins again, because of the easy interchange of profession as between bandits and soldiers.

The older Manchurian banditry is not only regional, but is obviously a phenomenon of the old "reservoir," and like all "reservoir" activities has a recognizable historical derivation. It was originally a by-product of the restrictions on Chinese penetration into the "reservoir"; and this explains why numerically there are always more Chinese among bandits than Manchus or Mongols, and why, to the present day, China-born Chinese (especially Shantung men) are rather more common than Manchuria-born Chinese.

It has already been pointed out that "illegal" Chinese settlers, under the Manchu rule, were in fact commonly allowed to remain if they had really succeeded in establishing themselves before being officially noticed. If, however, the settlement could not be said to have taken root, and especially if it encroached on the forest preserves, the Imperial Hunting Grounds or the fringes of the sacred Ch'ang-pai-shan, it was likely to be broken up, with the result that the evicted settlers turned to banditry. Thus to the fringe of tolerated settlers and the outer fringe of nominally illegal squatters, there was added an outermost fringe of bandits, commonly based on hidden villages as well as on camps. Obviously this bandit fringe, and its representatives of the present day, must often be indistinguishable from the lawless fringe of opium-growing villages.

The bandits also drew recruits, and still draw them, from gold prospectors, lumbermen, hunters and ginseng gatherers. Owing to the ancient prejudice against private exploitation of such natural resources as mines and forests, those who exploited them without a license granting a semi-official monopoly (which required a certain amount of capital and a social standing high enough to allow familiarity with official circles) were always outside the law. Hunters and ginseng gatherers were also perpetually on the outer edge of the law. Ginseng was under a kind of imperial patronage, its collection and distribution being under official supervision. Indeed, at one time it became so scarce that an effort was made to conserve the supply by restricting collection. Naturally, the resulting high prices tempted men to venture into the forests without license. In much the same way sable hunters continually attempted to evade the *yamen* or collecting stations, in order to dispose of their catch not as articles of tribute but by sale, sables having become very scarce throughout Siberia and Manchuria because they were demanded in tribute both by the Russian Tsar and the Emperor in Peking.

Such pursuits as these were originally Manchu; but as the Manchus became accustomed to living comfortably in their villages, enjoying government subsidy and concerned with securing official employment for their sons, more and more *liu min* or unauthorized Chinese immigrants, disappointed in the attempt to settle on the land, turned to the profitable occupations of the wilderness. The knowledge thus gained of topography, routes and hiding places naturally aided them when they took to banditry. Much of their way of life and point of view has been passed on to the bandits of the present day. It might seem strange, for instance, that a large proportion of the modern bandits of the Kirin and Liaoning forest belt are Shantung men, with no experience of forests prior to their emigration to Manchuria. The explanation is that through working at different lumber camps they have gained a special knowledge of the region, and scraped an acquaintance with the semi-lawless, practically ungoverned outermost settlers, squatters and hunters. After a season of hard work, lumbermen frequently gamble away and spend in dissipation the whole of their pay, at the first little town reached. Unable to return to Shantung, or to find congenial work in the off-season, such men bolt back into the hills they have learned to know so well, and from the wilderness make bandit raids on highways and villages.

The significance of Manchurian banditry cannot be appreciated without bearing in mind that very few men take to the life of the outlaw for the sake of adventure and excitement, though some do. There are more men of the naturally wild and adventurous type in Manchuria than in any non-

frontier province of China, because the frontier tradition tends
to produce them, in spite of the peaceful counter-tradition of
the steady-going Chinese stock. Their numbers also are
augmented by escaped criminals and desperate characters.
Nevertheless a surprising proportion of them are men who
would naturally settle down to cultivate land or follow a
trade were it not for the difficulties in the way of private exploitation of the wilderness, the laws against the highly
profitable opium business and the difficulty of acquiring a
holding in the untenanted but privately owned wilderness,
without capital.

The result is that Manchurian bandits found more villages
probably than any outlaws in the world, and though lawless
are an effective advance-guard of normal settlement and exploitation. Almost no bandits are truly independent of bases
either in villages founded by themselves or dominated by
them because of their isolated position. Thus there is always
a certain amount of communication between bandit villages
and law-abiding villages, and it is almost always possible to
"reclaim" most of the population of a bandit region, as
normal administration is pushed forward into previously un-
administered country. The negotiations for "reclaiming"
bandits are often marred by subsequent treacherous massacre;
nevertheless, as has been said, negotiation and not outright
warfare is the normal method of reducing a bandit region
to order. It is as a result of such negotiations that so many
bandit leaders become transformed into military officers.
From the military career many of them achieve administrative
power; and thus it comes about quite naturally that some
of the ablest and most powerful officials in Manchuria are
men who got their first schooling in the ranks of the bandits.
When I was dining once with a general in whose territory the
bandits were an important initial problem, obstructing the

beginnings of peaceful development, one of his staff, a man of the new school of national patriotism, referred to the bandits as a pest that must be destroyed outright. The general —himself not by any means a man of bandit antecedents—corrected him, saying that bandits were by no means all "bad." "It depends on how you treat them and use them," he said. After a good deal of frontier experience, I understand perfectly well what he meant; for the bandit, properly understood, is in some respects a valuable frontiersman and pathfinder.

The old banditry of Manchuria is recognizably divided into several regional types. There is the opium banditry that has already been discussed. There is the banditry of the central region of Kirin and Liaoning. There is the banditry of the Mongol frontier of Western Liaoning and Western Heilungchiang, and there is the banditry of the previously uninhabited wildernesses of Northern Heilungchiang, which has a somewhat milder counterpart in northernmost Kirin.

The banditry of the forested and hilly country of the central region of Kirin and Liaoning is strongly colored by "reservoir" traditions, and has an unbroken connection with the old days when most of the bandits were Chinese who had not succeeded in establishing tolerated settlements in the Manchu "reservoir." Many of these bandits are still lumbermen, hunters and ginseng gatherers by turns. With the increased settlement and development of the region, however, the days of the really big troops of bandits in this region are passing.

The banditry of the Mongol frontier is peculiar in that many Mongols are among the bandits. In strictly Mongol territory, bandits are so rare that they may be said not to exist at all. The Mongol population, is as mobile as the bandits themselves could be, and knows the country as well. Bandits are far more afraid of Mongol levies than they are of Chinese regular troops. Mongol banditry only breaks out on the fringe of Chinese colonization, where numbers of Mongols, whose pastures have been taken and who have not been properly provided for either by the colonization officials or their own princes, turn their hands against all men.

Pastoral Mongols do not like to live within less than a day's ride of Chinese villages, partly because they are afraid of being governed and taxed, but chiefly because their livestock, trespassing on fields, might be the cause of quarreling. It is in this gap that the bandits range. They are recruited not only from discontented Mongols, but from Chinese—some of them men who have given up trying to get land for themselves, some of them deserting soldiers, others young men who have got on the wrong side of the law through quarreling or gambling. In addition to these, the most outlying settlements frequently contribute a man each to the bandits, in order to secure themselves from attack. The mere fact that so many of the bandits are malcontents means that among them are some of the most independent, able and vigorous men of the region. Such men frequently see a quicker, though more dangerous way to power and position through rising to the command of bandits than through ordinary industry or even ordinary enlistment in the army. If they can make themselves formidable enough, there is always a price at which they can negotiate a position on the right side of the law. An ambition of this kind is, however, far more dangerous for Mongols than for Chinese as, being outsiders, they are much more likely to be treacherously killed in the process of negotiation. A Mongol bandit is therefore a man who expects no other end than a violent death; consequently he is a much more determined and dangerous fighter than the ordinary bandit.

Such mixed groups of bandits attack only the Chinese, unless they are desperate. The Chinese clannishness enables them to play off one group against another—getting information or supplies from one village, and attacking others— whereas if they attacked one Mongol encampment, all the others within reach would send out men against them; and, not content with driving them off, they would push them until it came to a fight.

While the Mongol element in these bands contributes mobility, the Chinese element requires touch with fixed communities. Thus they use the unoccupied no-man's-land to give them freedom for manœuver, and from it raid in among the thinly scattered outer villages. They frequently descend on one outlying farm or settlement after another, for food and shelter, and the general rule is that from the poorest people they demand food and shelter but nothing else. The commonest end of such a band is that they are either enticed into negotiation and killed, or else enlisted as a part of the regional military establishment—often with the title of anti-bandit patrol. This comes about as their sphere of activity is narrowed down by increasingly close settlement. They are rarely driven out permanently while the country is not yet thoroughly settled. It not infrequently happens that those who have relations among the respectable succeed in making terms, and even betray the outsiders who have no connections, so that the "biggest" men are taken over while the others are trapped and killed.

Where there is practically no clash of populations to foment banditry, as in vast stretches of Northern Heilungchiang and Kirin, banditry is largely a winter avocation of settlers in thinly populated regions. The bandits of Heilungchiang have a special reputation for savagery, and I should not be at all surprised if this were the result of influences imparted in earlier days when Heilungchiang was a place of exile for criminals and political offenders, many of whom subsequently escaped and took up banditry. In such regions, the farmers themselves are often bandits, and prey on one another's base-villages; though the highways provide most of their victims. The winter season is long, and while numbers of people then engage in the carting trade, hauling grain to market, others are idle, for lack of subsidiary occupations like stock-raising or home industries. Moreover winter is the season of travel, the roads of packed snow being at their best. Banditry in Heilungchiang, until recently at least, had the reputation of being often a kind of "racket," engaged in by people who had relatives among the troops or petty officials, who could protect them from being too seriously pursued. At any rate it is certain that where the Sungari forms the boundary between the provinces of Heilungchiang and Kirin (it being possible to cross on the ice in winter) the common people consider that the bandits of their own side are a nuisance, but part of the natural social order and usually amenable to diplomacy and reasonable arrangement; while the bandits from the other side of the river they loathe and dread.

The banditry of this region has one characteristic in common with that of the Mongol border; it is at its worst near the fringes of settlement. Colonization has followed the main lines of travel, leaving wide uninhabited stretches on either side, which give the bandits room for dodging and hiding.

It is commonly held that banditry slows down the rate of colonization.[2] This is perfectly true; but I do not think that it is altogether an evil. While the bandits are themselves in a

---

[2] One of the important economic effects of banditry is that over wide regions transport by ox-cart is common, where horses would be more efficient, and would be used, were it not that bandits leave oxen alone, but are in perpetual need of horses as remounts. The introduction of motor transport is tending to solve this problem.

sense active frontiersmen, continually pushing forward into the wilderness, they do delay the period of intensive colonization that comes after them. Banditry often expresses the feeling of resentment that the true frontiersmen have against the powerful interests which own great stretches of wilderness land. The more they can make themselves feared, the better chance they have, when the eventual period of negotiation comes, of securing good terms from the great landholders on whose land grants they have founded villages. While the bandits themselves are taken into the army, their relatives get a chance to take up land on much more favorable terms than could be secured by refugees. Thus while they slow down the rate of colonization, they tend to add to the quality of the community, offsetting the poor "tone" of purely refugee colonization, which tends to be too helpless and too much at the mercy of a limited and over-powerful class, and can well benefit by the tradition of independence and self-sufficiency which the bandit element contributes.

The greatest danger of banditry in Manchuria, in fact, is that the old indigenous banditry, with its occasional flashes of the Robin Hood instinct, may be entirely overwhelmed by the savagely destructive soldier-banditry that harries so many thousand square miles of China proper. It is already true that the common soldier has no great stomach for fighting bandits. He would far rather come to a sensible arrangement by which the bandits withdraw when the patrols come around, and the patrols, as they make their rounds, do not look over their shoulders at the bandits coming back. Even when, under orders from above, it is necessary for the troops to make a definite effort to clear a given territory, the private soldier will often give the game away. He will have one signal by groups of rifleshots which means "We are on patrol, but nothing serious," and another which means "Look out! We'll fight you if we find you!" This is because, in a generation of unscrupulous violence, the soldier is far from regarding the bandit as his natural enemy. The soldier, like the bandit, is a professional. The bandit wants to take villages and loot them; the soldier waits for his chance in a civil war to take towns and get either loot or promotion and power. Neither sees any point in a stand-up fight, when the prisoners and the dead are not likely to have anything on them but arms. Moreover the bandit may some day be a soldier and the soldier a bandit. Consequently they regard themselves as colleagues with a certain professional rivalry, but not enemies unless personal quarrels arise.

The great wealth of Manchuria and the necessity of maintaining a good army in view of the civil-war phase of politics in China account for a higher average and greater regularity of pay than in the armies of North China generally, while the prospects of recognition of merit and quick promotion on active service are also very good. Consequently the soldier-bandit, bandit-soldier menace is not nearly so great as in China proper. It is at its worst in the province of Jehol, which now forms an extra fourth added to the three nuclear provinces of Manchuria. Where it does occur, however, it tends, as has been said, to overwhelm and supersede the older banditry. While it often perpetuates some of the methods of the older tradition, it has none of the same quasi-constructive, pioneering qualities. The elimination of the typical Manchurian banditry, indeed, is largely a question of the passing of the frontier phase, and the extension of normal administration. The elimination or increase of soldier-banditry and the banditry that accompanies social collapse, on the other hand, depends largely on the quality of that supervening administration, and on the soundness of the new society. It is not a specifically Manchurian problem but a question of victory over or defeat by the major problems of society and civilization that confront China as a whole.

CHAPTER X

ALIENS AND THE LAND

JAPANESE AND KOREAN IMMIGRATION

IT HAS frequently been stated that the idea of a great Japanese colonizing migration into Manchuria, once dreamed of, has now gone by the board because the Chinese have everywhere proved that they can underlive the Japanese as farmers and farm-laborers. To my mind, however, the simple opposition of the standards of living of farmers and laborers is not the whole of the question. The example of Korea ought to have demonstrated this—Japan introducing Western technique for the development and exploitation of Korea, and Korean peasant-laborers migrating to Japan. It is, to my mind, more important that the Japanese have reached a stage of social, economic and above all historical development where settlement on the land, out of Japan, even under urgent economic pressure, no longer appeals to them. The land-hunger has gone out of their blood just as effectively as it has gone out of the blood of the Americans who, in spite of their constantly cited pioneer traditions, and long before the pressure of population has become anything like as severe as that of Europe—not to mention Japan—are now turning from the land to the cities; and, when they go abroad, go only as exploiters, never as settlers. In both nations the historical phase is the imperative factor; economic pressure and economic opportunity are only contributory and permissive factors.

The Japanese have now developed the instinct for exploitation as capitalists, industrialists, technicians—entrepreneurs, in fact. The average peasant would far rather move to a town and become a factory worker than go abroad to take up land. The average townsman will move gladly to a bigger town, but not to the country. The colonization problems of Japan are somewhat similar to those of Great Britain, which finds it easy to export technicians and traders, but difficult, even with severe unemployment at home and ample lands for colonization within the Empire, to export colonists. Not only are the unemployed unwilling to emigrate even under severe economic pressure, but when they do emigrate, even on favorable terms of settlement, they make such poor settlers that they are less and less in demand in the dominions.[1] The chief difference in the case of the Japanese is that Japan has not the same reserve of lands within the Empire, nor the same supply of raw products, to keep the swarming towns in food and work. The type of agricultural colonization for which the British are now best suited is that of the plantation —which, historically considered, is late and decadent—in which they can act as overseers and directors. Hence the great modern British interest in Africa. Much the same is true of the Japanese; but with the additional handicap of lack of suitable territory under their own flag.

Failing such territory, the land which potentially could offer them the best scope is Manchuria, which offers obvious opportunities for capital and skilled training. Even this, however, raises intricate questions of treaty relations, treaty privileges and treaty restrictions. Japan, besides being one of the nations which, by treaty, holds concessions in certain of the Treaty Ports, and extraterritorial jurisdiction over its own

---

[1] At the present time, the British Dominions tend increasingly to legislate against all immigration. This, however, does not alter the fact that even before the days of such legislation, encouraged emigration from Great Britain had more and more obviously become a failure.

nationals in Chinese territory, also holds on lease the area adjacent to Port Arthur and Dairen known as the Kuantung Leased Territory, of over thirteen hundred square miles, together with the one hundred square miles occupied by the South Manchuria Railway right of way and settlements adjacent to railway stations. Like other aliens, however, the Japanese do not in practice have the right to buy or lease land in China outside of the concessions [2]—a restriction which obviously hinders not only agricultural enterprise on the part of foreigners, but also all kinds of industrial exploitation.

Nominally, when the nations which hold by treaty the rights of extraterritoriality (legal, fiscal and disciplinary jurisdiction over their own nationals resident in China, which make it necessary for both civil and criminal actions against foreigners to be tried in a court presided over by a judge or consul of the defendant foreigner's nationality) are prepared to relinquish these rights, they will in turn receive rights of free travel and residence in the interior, together with the right to buy and lease land—at present enjoyed only by missionaries. Actually it is doubtful to what degree foreigners will ever be allowed to purchase and develop properties in China. There are precedents in various parts of the world for controlling the terms of entry and scope of enterprise of aliens, on which China may well base regulations that satisfy the already very strong prejudice against seeing Chinese land in foreign ownership. Moreover there is, apart from the prejudice against direct foreign enterprise, the patent danger that increase of direct foreign ownership and investment may lead to renewed foreign pressure. It seems to me highly probable that, *pari passu* with the modification of existing treaties, there will be continual pressure to secure rights of direct purchase

[2] For the special Japanese position in Manchuria, see below, p. 240.

and direct investment in China, that the success of any enterprise on a large scale will lead to national jealousy, and that the situation thus arising will lead to renewed demands for the protection of legitimate vested interests.

One aspect of these problems of the future may already be detected in the special problems of Japanese enterprise generally, and Korean colonization in particular, in Manchuria. In extensive regions in Eastern Manchuria, especially in what is known as the Chientao district, there is an important Korean population. The question of the extent and exercise of Japanese authority and control over these Koreans has produced various points of dispute between Japan and China, especially in regard to Japanese consular guards and the police control and frequent arrest of Koreans in Chinese territory.[3] A great proportion of these Koreans are revolutionary and anti-Japanese, having for that reason migrated from Korea into Chinese territory. Their most important occupation is rice farming. They have a technique of northern rice culture which the Chinese themselves cannot rival, and are thus able to occupy land in important numbers and with a density of population that makes them practically immune to Chinese linguistic and cultural influences.

The national status of many of these Koreans is anomalous and unsatisfactory. In the first place Koreans who are suspected by the Japanese of revolutionary propaganda may try to claim Chinese citizenship, without being able to furnish

[3] Actually the Chientao region, in which Koreans outnumber Chinese, was once in dispute between Japan and China. Finally Japan recognized a frontier between Manchuria and Korea which gave Chientao to China; and at the same time turned over the Chientao Koreans to China, willy-nilly. The Chientao Koreans are historically a rearguard; for the Koreans undoubtedly once occupied a considerable part of Manchuria, from which they were driven by the Manchus and other tribes. This and other rearguard Korean communities are, however, now being turned into advance-guards by a fresh impulse of Korean migration toward Manchuria.

adequate proof, while others, who have previously stated to Chinese officials that they have "renounced" their status as subjects of Japan, will later try to claim Japanese protection. In the second place, there appears to be occasional lack of uniformity in Chinese practice in admitting Koreans to naturalization, in respect of residence qualifications and so forth. In the third place there can be no doubt that Koreans frequently attempt to take out Chinese papers chiefly as a screen while carrying on anti-Japanese propaganda in connection with revolutionary societies across the border in Korea. In the fourth place, Koreans aspire to Chinese citizenship in order to be able to hold land. In such cases, it may be found that the Korean, naturalized as a Chinese, is actually serving as agent for a Japanese who finances him. This leads to complicated claims of jurisdiction, and the assertion of the right of consular protection for a Japanese investment.

Such claims touch a very sore point in Manchurian affairs. Under the treaty arising out of the celebrated Twenty-one Demands of 1915, the Japanese acquired the right of unrestricted residence and trade in Manchuria, including the right to lease land; a special modification of the general restrictions on foreign enterprise. This right the Chinese have, in practice, consistently obstructed, bringing strong pressure to bear on Chinese who attempt to lease land to Japanese. Although individuals are tempted by the profits of Japanese coöperation, public opinion is decidedly against it, for fear of the consequences of the extension of Japanese vested interests.

Consequently the officials, in regions where Koreans form an important element in the population, are bedeviled by a double problem. On the one hand, to uphold their own prestige, they are anxious to extend their administrative control over Koreans, to exercise their prerogative of naturalizing

Koreans, and to assert their right of protecting Koreans who have already been naturalized. Naturalization of Koreans tends to weaken Japanese claims of direct authority, and to aid the Chinese in attempts to break up the solidarity of the Korean communities and facilitate their assimilation to the Chinese. On the other hand the Koreans have thus far shown, even when naturalized as Chinese, great resistance to absorption by the Chinese, and no tendency at all to consider themselves truly Chinese. While they are glad to reside in China, they have no desire to be anything but Korean in race, language and culture. Few of them even learn to speak Chinese well, many of them speak practically no Chinese at all, and they tend to settle in strong enough groups to prevent modification of this attitude even in the second generation. Moreover there are to be found among them, besides the purely anti-Japanese revolutionaries, numbers of enthusiasts for the Russian type of revolution, who are as much disliked by the Chinese as they are by the Japanese.

Finally, there is the recurrent problem of Koreans financed by Japanese. While attempts at direct Japanese colonization have always failed, even in the Leased Territory of Kuantung under Japanese administration, there is no doubt that great and rapid development can be obtained from large estates financed and managed by Japanese, employing Korean or Chinese labor. This has been proved on a small scale in the Leased Territory, but the Chinese are anything but anxious to see demonstrations on a larger scale. Such extensions of Japanese vested interests, combining Korean colonization with Japanese investment, are regarded as a menace of the gravest kind.

The general result is a tendency to restrict all Korean colonization, although locally landlords often welcome Korean tenants because rice-cultivation by Koreans provides a bigger rent-roll than could be secured if the same land were cultivated by Chinese. The officials, however, are nervous of Korean penetration for the reasons already discussed, and the Chinese farming population dislike Koreans because no agricultural community likes to have neighbors that rival it economically, whether the competition comes from a lower standard of living or a higher technique. This feeling, on the whole, does not yet run high, because there is no serious pressure of population; but it is obviously an important potential problem of the future.[4]

Finally, there is a sort of "irredentist" problem connected especially with the region of Chientao, where numerically the Koreans are an important element in the population. Many of these Koreans are descended from the population established there before the annexation of Korea by Japan and the final determination of the boundary between Korea and Manchuria along the T'umen river. They are therefore Chinese by birth, but have no papers to show either their status as Chinese or as Japanese. There was for some time a dispute between Japan and China over the actual boundary between Korea and Manchuria in the Chientao region; this was settled by treaty in 1909, the T'umen river being established as the frontier; but, the Koreans being earlier established than the Chinese, the special Japanese interest in them has never lapsed, although they are admitted to be subject to China.

The present situation seems to be that while the already large Korean communities are if anything increasing, ob-

---

[4] Since these lines were originally written, the problem discussed has been vividly illustrated by the Wanpaoshan incident in Kirin province, where Chinese farmers opposed with violence the exploitation of land leased to Koreans. The incident led to retaliatory outrages of a much graver kind against Chinese in Korea, and has raised in an acute form all the old disputes that turn on the leasing of land to Japanese and Koreans. In fact this outbreak of trouble was as important an antecedent cause of the rupture between China and Japan as the Nakamura incident.

stacles are put in the way of new settlement. In the region of
the Ussuri, for instance, many Koreans have crossed the border
from Russian territory, to which they had originally migrated
from Korea, but where in recent years they have grown uneasy under the social and economic reforms enforced by
Soviet government.[5] These unhappy people, whose ancestors,
without doubt, occupied a great deal of what is now Manchuria and the Russian Primorsk province, and have since
become exiles successively from Korea and from the land of
their first adoption, find anything but a hearty welcome in
Chinese territory. The Chinese no more welcome incompatible minorities than do the Russians, and in addition they
fear that an important Korean population in the Ussuri region
might lead to Japanese claims similar to those advanced in
respect of Koreans elsewhere in Manchuria. Consequently,
wherever the Chinese population along the Ussuri is numerous enough, both populace and officials are extremely suspicious of Koreans, and try either to drive them back across
the frontier or to break up attempts to found separate Korean
villages.

RUSSIAN IMMIGRATION

Russian penetration is another problem altogether. There
can be no doubt that the Russians are on the move toward
the East and the Pacific; in fact theirs is by all odds the most
important combined migration of people and culture in the
modern world. Although some hold that the Russian conceptions of society and the State have yet to prove their fitness
for survival, I myself think that the major crisis has already
been decided. Russian theories will be progressively modified,
because if the new Russian social-economic organism has

---

[5] Other Koreans, however, have adapted themselves well to Russian rule.

demonstrated anything, it has proved its extraordinary vigor and faculty of growth, and no organism can grow without changing; but of the fact of its survival I think there can be no doubt.

The most significant quality of modern Russia is its extraordinary faculty of incorporating alien populations within its own organism. For this reason the Russian advance into the East is even more important as a migration of ideas than it is as the movement of a people. The eastward movement of a strictly Russian population is as yet a minor factor; what is decisive is the movement of "conversion." Russianized Buriat Mongols of the Baikal region in Siberia are important instruments of Russian policy in Outer Mongolia, and the "conversion" of natives of Outer Mongolia itself is increasingly important. Bitterly as Russian policy is detested by certain elements in Outer Mongolia, it must be conceded (though non-Russian publicists hate to concede it) that it could not be carried out at all without the fervid support of other indigenous elements. Russianized Central Asians play a similar part in the new republics of Central Asia. Russianized Mongols, and even a certain number of Koreans and Chinese, including officers, appear to have served with the Russian troops in the actions of 1929–30 on the Manchurian borders, and with great success. They were distributed among the Russian forces, not serving as separate units, except for the Mongol cavalry who marched and fought with great dash and success in the Manchuli-Hailar sector—who appear to have been deliberately employed with the idea of demonstrating the solidarity between Russians and Russian-ruled Mongols in contrast with the distrust and more or less overt hostility between Chinese and Chinese-ruled Mongols.

The secret of the Russian style of advance is that it does not merely establish an administrative order over the heads of subject peoples. Nor does it depend essentially either on Russian colonization or "colonial" administration. It interpenetrates the indigenous life with great rapidity and thoroughness, and every move is prepared in advance with great care, taking local peculiarities into account and endeavoring to give a Russian orientation without destroying local loyalties. It spreads control *through* a local population, rather than exercising it *over* them. It thus differs both from the Chinese style of expansion, which eliminates what it can and absorbs the rest, and from the Western, which proceeds by administration from the outside and above, not entering into the indigenous life—no matter how many native officials are employed—but still tending, normally to "improve" it and create "progress." The criteria of "progress," however, are Western, and the very processes of improvement imply that the people who are "progressing" are still left in the rear of the West itself.

The truth is that the Russian model of civilization is not built up so high above its foundations that to adapt it to local requirements need postulate extensive sacrifice of essential structural elements. Thus it can offer to any population a model which, while Russian in action, is largely local in structure—whereas both the Western and the Chinese models have been so specialized in the course of their own evolution that they are old and rigid, and must handle new material more inconsiderately in order to adapt it to their own requirements. Russian action can therefore more easily accomplish its effects by the dynamic use of converted minorities; for while it requires as "articles of faith" a certain creed of its own, for the assertion of which it sticks at nothing, it can yet tolerate and even encourage a type of "patriotism" of language and tradition, and local nationalisms of race and culture, that would inevitably ruin the forward movement of any Western nation, or of China.

For adequate comparison, we must look to the early Central Asian migrations, which did not *essentially* require the movement of entire populations over great distances, as is commonly supposed, but rather imparted a wavelike motion from one people to another, and often resulted in the leadership of one people by a very small minority of another people. Or we may look to the creative years of Islam, which, for all the slaughter it caused, had also an extraordinary tolerance for all kinds of diverse elements; which enlisted and carried with it as many as it slew, and which replaced its own losses with whole-hearted recruits. The spread of Russian influence is marked by the striking phenomena which attend the creative years of a new force in the world. It is so overwhelmingly confident of its own power to create that it is not for a moment ashamed to borrow freely—witness the intensive campaign for industrialization, with its use of American and German models which, however, when set in motion turn out to be surprisingly different from anything in Germany or America. True creativeness, indeed, is as much a faculty of inward digestion as it is of outward expression. There is all the difference in the world between the old type of Russian borrowing and the new. Under the old order, enterprises of all kinds were established on "the latest and most improved" European model, and thereafter, under Russian management, gradually ran down. Under the new, enterprises on "the latest and most efficient" American model turn, in Russian hands, into something startlingly un-American; but, in spite of frequent foreign accusations that things "run down" in the same old way, they are lively enough to cause excited speculation abroad. Russia is, beyond a doubt, in the affairs of its portentous Far Eastern frontier, at least abreast of Japan and a move ahead of China, which is yet in the stage which both Russia and Japan have left behind.

The Russian population in Manchuria, while important in numbers, is chiefly concentrated at one point, in Harbin. It is markedly urban, being originally derived from Russians who left Russia before the Revolution, and later strongly reinforced by exiles cast out by the Revolution. It has therefore a strong original anti-Soviet bias; but the anti-Soviet feeling is on the whole diminishing. At the same time, it has not in the least become Chinese in sympathy or point of view. Indeed, its resistance to Chinese influences is more striking than that of either Mongols or Koreans. In the Russians, the remarkable Chinese faculty for absorption, which for many centuries has disposed of a succession of alien conquerors, appears to have met its match. The Russian exile community in Manchuria is not even a victorious community; it is a community of defeat. Yet in spite of loss of prestige, and political impotence, it remains stubbornly ignorant of China and uninterested in China. To intermarry with Chinese or live like Chinese, in spite of the fact that Russians are conspicuously less influenced by "race-feeling" than are most Westerners, is a mark of failure. The more successful a Russian is, the less he is likely even to speak Chinese. On the other hand, in the sphere of Russian influence in Manchuria, the more successful a Chinese is, the more he is likely to learn Russian or to marry a Russian; while Chinese who cross the border into Siberia show a marked tendency to "go Russian" altogether. The backwash of Chinese and Koreans from Siberia is due chiefly to their own reluctance to modify their ideas of private property, not to Russian unwillingness to incorporate them within the new order. In North Manchuria, the community despises Russians, but individuals are eager to be as Russian as possible, at least socially. Among the Russians, on the other hand, the community fears the Chinese, but individuals look down on them. The general situation is perhaps a reflection of the general mutual intolerance between Chinese and foreigners. Nevertheless, it is important that the Chinese have had practically no success in absorbing or even influencing this large foreign community under Chinese rule.

While the agricultural Russian community in Manchuria is not of great importance in numbers, it is experimentally important. It has proved that Russians can settle on the land, not only without aid, but in spite of important handicaps. It has however also proved that they do not tend strongly to mix with Chinese (though they do mix with and inter-marry with Mongols and other non-Chinese tribesmen) and that they do not agree well with Chinese administration. Russian minorities on the Chinese side of the border appear, on the whole, to be worse off than Chinese minorities on the Russian side of the border. I have always been surprised at the comparatively good-humored tolerance toward Russians even of Chinese who had attempted to establish themselves in Siberia, and given it up and returned. The essential difference appears to be that while they were there, at least they circulated more freely among the Russians than Russians do among the Chinese. Russian colonists in Manchuria, indeed, tend to settle as far as possible away from Chinese officials and effective administration, whereas Chinese in Siberia very decidedly tend to establish themselves alongside of Russians, in order to turn to advantage their own superior quickness and ability, especially in bargaining. The most numerous Russian settlements are in the Hsingan range and along the upper Amur, with a few villages also near the Ussuri frontier. Their standard of living is at times very little if at all higher than that of the Chinese, but their occupations are distinctly more varied, especially in the raising of livestock. They push much farther into the wilderness; they like loneliness, and have none of the fear of the remote uninhabited wilderness that is a common characteristic of Chinese colonists.

A certain number of these villagers, as well as many townsmen, have served as mercenaries in Chinese armies, but this, far from leading to better understanding, has tended to increase mutual dislike. The Chinese are naturally fearful of giving real military authority to alien mercenaries, and being given no opportunity for a career of success and power, the Russians look on military service as an expedient nearly as desperate as banditry. A great many Russian village colonists are naturalized Chinese, and this also has led to bitter feelings. The Soviet Russians claim that on the outbreak of trouble between China and Russia in 1929, these exiles furnished "partisan" bands which, encouraged by the Chinese, raided across the Russian frontier. It is doubtful whether responsible Chinese officials encouraged such raids; but there can be no doubt that Chinese generally, at least at the beginning of the trouble, when confidence was high, the Russians were thought to be on the run, and the real power of the Soviets had not yet been categorically demonstrated, were glad to hear of any attack on Soviet Russia.

The villagers, for their part, claim that after the flight of the Chinese armies, the Soviet forces raided among the exile colonies and carried off many prisoners; and that when negotiations were opened, the Chinese officials were afraid to challenge the Russians by demanding the return of naturalized Chinese Russians together with other prisoners exchanged— the Russians having, in fact, forestalled them, by demanding the punishment, by the Chinese themselves, of "White" Russian "partisans." At any rate, one of the sequels of the Russo-Chinese conflict was an outbreak of peculiarly savage banditry among the remoter Russian settlers. These bandits kill all Chinese at sight, regardless of whether they are worth robbing or not, claiming that they were "betrayed" by the Chinese, that the protection offered them as Chinese citizens is worthless, and that there is nothing left for them but to live, fight and die as desperate outlaws. This banditry has not yet been put down, it has the tacit sympathy of many townsmen, and owing to their sparsely inhabited country, and their intimate knowledge of it, they are able to evade or hold off superior bodies of Chinese troops. Indeed, they have so much fighting spirit that they are said sometimes to take the initiative in attacking Chinese troops, from whom they capture arms and ammunition.

The divergence between exile Russians and Soviet Russians has, owing to the progress of the Revolution in Russia, become so extreme that, as I was informed and can readily believe, it is now virtually impossible for an exile to cross the frontier surreptitiously to settle down in Soviet Siberia. The extraordinary re-creation of national life in Russia has led to such changes, to such totally new manners, modes of address and deportment, conversation and even vocabulary, and to such alterations in the familiar petty details of life, that a returning exile, Russian though he be, almost immediately betrays himself a stranger. On the other hand, there are still surreptitious crossings from the Russian side to the Chinese side. Even during the months of actual military hostility, in spite of the fact that the Chinese, in dread of spies, often treated Russians very harshly, a certain number of peasants, rebelling against the Five Year Plan and the collectivization of farms, fled into Manchuria. Nevertheless—in fact, partly because of this one-way communication—the effect of Soviet Russia on the exile community is far greater than the reaction of the exiles on Siberia. Indeed every fugitive advertises, by his flight, that there is no hope of overthrowing the new order in Russia. With the steady increase of Russian prestige in the face of the world, as well as in relation to China, there is a decided tendency for the Russian exiles of Manchuria to remember that, politics apart, they are Russians after all. Indeed, were it not for the exacting demands made by the Russians themselves on exiles who wish to recover Russian citizenship, reconciliation between the exiles and the Russian Government could be made to proceed much more rapidly.

Soviet Russia is in the strong position of not having to tempt back its exiles; it can do without them, and can therefore hold up citizenship as a reward which has to be earned. It has therefore the option of opening negotiations with the exile community on favorable terms. In this respect it has the advantage over China. Neither "White" Russians nor Chinese, in the years between the collapse of the old Russia and the emergence of Soviet Russia as a power of magnitude, made the best of their opportunities, and the prospects of improved relations now are not good. The exiles went so badly to pieces as to give the impression that the only Russian group which has the power of uniting Russians is that of the Bolsheviks. The exiles were anxious to escape from Bolshevik rule; they never relished the idea of Chinese rule, and yet they were incapable of looking after themselves. Ill-armed, outnumbered, with an organization so hopelessly chaotic as to be worse than no organization at all, they have yet obstinately held on to a conviction of superiority which outfaces even the profound Chinese sense of superiority.

They consider that under Chinese rule they have been put on the same level as Chinese for taxation and administration, but not on the same level in respect of opportunities for careers; that they are used as technicians and so forth, but not granted responsible control; that it would be absurd to think of a Russian, naturalized in China, holding high office with real power; that in fact they have only a one-way equality. The Chinese, for their part, consider that the Russians under their rule are, as a community, ungrateful and unreliable: that, as uninvited step-children of the Republic they have been given ample consideration and opportunities; but that, after enjoying for years a refuge from Bolshevism they were, in the actual crisis of conflict between China and Russia, less than half-hearted in support of their country of refuge, and in fact glad on the whole (the urban population at least) to see China beaten.

If the feeling between urban Russians and Chinese is none too good, the feeling between agricultural Russian settlers and Chinese appears now to be hopeless. The Chinese were never enthusiastic about the settlement of aliens on the land, and after their recent experiences there is no likelihood that they will ever encourage it. In view of this, and in spite of the fact that the colonists fell into their present evil case largely through their own precipitancy in attacking Soviet Russia, and the fact that, as peasants, their ingrained suspicion of the newest Soviet trends is stronger than that of the urban population, there is now probably more likelihood than before that the remnants of them may eventually try to make terms with Russia.

Whether or not the Russians in Russia ever attempt to make considerable use of the Russians already in Manchuria, their position is extremely strong. If the exile Russians have been able to influence the Chinese to the extent that they have, and actually to settle on the land, make a living out of it, and even maintain themselves, however precariously, when reduced to outlawry, how much more could fresh contingents from Russia do with the backing of their own nation? Granted the inevitable historic force of the Russian attraction toward the Pacific; granted their reluctance to coöperate with Chinese under Chinese rule, but their proved talent for combination with all kinds of alien elements under their own rule; granted their ability to settle on the land itself, and their superior talent for modernization without corollary subordination to the West—it is difficult not to foresee a steady increase of Russian influence in the region roughly bounded on the south by the Chinese Eastern Railway. It is possible even to foresee actual Russian occupation to an indefinite depth south of the Amur.

Russia is overflowing, under the pressure of ideas—which the diverse examples of America, England, China, Japan and India prove, each in its own way, to be a far more potent force than that mere superfluity of numbers that we call "pressure of population." Its chief outlet is into the ancient "reservoir of the outer barbarians," which lies north of and powerfully affects the inner "reservoir" contiguous to the Great Wall frontier of China proper. The power of Russia is only precariously dammed away from Chinese Turkestan; it has overflowed into Urianghai and Outer Mongolia, where the Russians have proved that they have an ability to rule by "conversion," enlistment and amalgamation superior to that of either China or Japan.

It is difficult to see how the same pressure can be held away from the Amur-Ussuri frontier of Manchuria, which projects so awkwardly into Siberia. From the Pamirs to the Pacific Russia has, from the Chinese point of view, assumed the historic Hun-Turk-Mongol-Manchu functions of the northern barbarian, and is exhibiting in a striking manner the same historical phenomenon of the ability to enlist, recruit and lead, not driving local populations before it, but drawing them along with it. Chinese Turkestan and Mongolia are, in themselves, more important and significant in the Russian expansion than Manchuria; but Manchuria commands the gates to the Pacific, and the Pacific is an imperative factor in the destiny of Russia's eastern frontier.

CHAPTER XI

THE CITIES AGAINST THE COUNTRY

PEASANT AND TOWNSMAN

THE fact that the great mass of the Chinese population, calculated at I know not what per cent, consists of economically impotent tenant farmers, peasants and small-holders, is often and far too readily interpreted to mean that the Chinese are a nation of peasants, with a peasant culture and peasant standards. This is because, in our own world, the importance of the land and the land-fast farming population was destroyed by the Industrial Revolution. Organically, our structure has changed from one of social classes to one of occupational classes; our only valid social criteria are capital and lack of capital, technique and lack of technique. Consequently, we look down on any state in which the classes are still organically social (peasantry, bourgeoisie, aristocracy) not occupational (unskilled labor, skilled labor, labor and capital), calling it backward or even, in the loose phraseology of the day, medieval.

Now the essential characteristic of the state in which the peasant is truly a peasant is judgment by birth. Hence the English saying (now in effect outmoded; a lingering, not a vital tradition) that "it takes three generations to make a gentleman." America is proud of having no peasantry, the implication being that the farmer does not have a "feudal" relation to a landed aristocracy, but America is willfully blind to the fact that American farming, like that of China, is overweighted with "crop-sharing" farmers who ought, strictly speaking, to be classed economically as laborers, not as farmers. In truth this is, however, only another way of stating that the farm lad may, within his own lifetime, become a financier or industrialist, scientist or technician or administrator, and that his opportunities of marriage into the so-called upper classes are not limited by birth but by the accidents of occupation. The corollary of this is that we are all rootless nations; we are divorced from the land. Our occupations are no longer determined by place and class of birth but by talent and opportunity. We substitute one kind of accident for another, and call it progress, because it is congruent with our respect for the assertiveness of the individual. Our equivalent of aristocracy is no longer rooted in the land but (to continue the metaphor) in portable pots, which can be moved from one city to another; and when the plants decay, they are not thrown back on to the land, but on to the waste-heaps of the city. When a civilization reaches this point, the city looks down on the country. We no longer slight a man because he has no pedigree; but we do slight him if he is in his proper person a country bumpkin.

In these fundamental respects China has not been a peasant nation for some two thousand years. For at least that period there has been no important restriction of birth on occupational choice or promotion (except, under the Empire, for such vestigial degraded classes as barbers, actors and so on). As might be expected, also, technique concurrently assumed the place of birth as the essential social criterion, in the specialized form of literary knowledge, codified in the old examination system. It is the abandonment of the old technical standard without, as yet, the successful substitution of a new (Western) standard that differentiates China from the West—*not* the lack of the technical standard as such.

The parallel phenomenon of the flight from the country to the city, and the superior attitude adopted by city people toward country people is also fully evident in China; and, as in all cultures which have reached the city-age of their history, city-populations are comparatively rootless and transfer with comparative ease, so long as the transfer is only from one city to another. Finally, the complementary phenomenon, that of the relatively debased status of the country people, who are exploited and victimized by the city people, and fed into the bowels of the great cities, is as true of China as it is of the West.

The fact that the Western metropolis, the vast city dominating the nation and drawing to itself all the resources of the nation, has not, perhaps, an obvious equivalent in old China, is unessential. It is due primarily to the fact that the Chinese civilization never demanded the rapidity and thoroughness of communication that the West felt to be imperative. Nevertheless Sian, Nanking, Peking were all at different times characteristically megalopolitan, embodying in themselves the cultural essence and chief vitality of the nation; and in spite of the cultural preference for vague communications, the fact that they were such cities forced on them the construction of imperial arterial highways, enterprises of the magnitude of the Grand Canal, and courier systems that far outpaced the normal leisurely rate of communication. The rapid growth of Shanghai and Harbin as typically cosmopolitan cities, far in advance of the Westernization of the nation and people at large, proves that the nation is more sympathetic to the *stage* of culture represented by the great city than to the *type* of culture represented by the West.

Indeed the city-feeling, combined with sluggishness of transport, long ago led to the institution of the metropolis in miniature—scattered "great cities," each dominating its countryside. For many centuries money (which can be transferred from city to city) has been dominant over land. For as many centuries the greatest land holders have relied more on their connection with officialdom (which is quartered in the cities) than on their territorial power, and have tended, while still holding their land, to live actually in the cities; and these are metropolitan conditions. The great financial importance retained by land is due only in part to the uncertainty and frequent manipulation of currency values—in itself an index of high sophistication and "late" civilization. It is due ultimately to the lack of mechanical manufacture and speed in transfer, characteristics which the West alone among mature civilizations has developed to the point where they overshadow all the other features of the civilization; with the result that land, among Western nations, has a minimum value compared with its retained importance in any other of the great civilizations of history—whether that of Rome or that of China.

Where the "big interests," the city magnates of the West, manipulate finance and inspire government to their own benefit, but base their values on manufacturing power, the "big interests" of China also manipulate finance and work through government agencies ("power" being, first and foremost, power achieved through an official career), but continue to base their values very largely on land. Just as the highest finance of the modern West spreads its investments through different countries, the land-magnates of China, which is equivalent to a continent in itself, spread their investments over different provinces. In other words, what we call the Chinese peasantry, dominated by money values, the trade-manipulations of grain companies and city-dwelling land-lords, and the tax demands of officials, actually fulfills many of the functions of the Western working proletariat. Like the proletariats of the West, they furnish the mob. Their revolts are revolts against over-exploitation, and are regularly marked by hostility between country and city: they are, like the riots of the Western mob, risings of the "have-nots" against the "haves." They tend, in the same way, to be equalitarian, and to work by blind destruction. They do not (as in Russia) have a creative value, for they are not efforts to free society for growth, but struggles, within a society which has already fulfilled its growth, to alter the distribution of power.

It is therefore easy to understand the sophisticated, exploitational character of colonization in modern Manchuria. What Western observers, with too glib a facility, call the "land hunger of the Chinese peasant" [1] is not the primary motive power. Far from being hungry for the land in Manchuria, the great mass of the colonists are in flight from the land in China. Perhaps the commonest of all reasons for coming to Manchuria given by immigrants is that in the old home they *chan pu chu,* they "can't stick it," "can't hold on." It is the fact that they are migrants without option that throws colonization into the hands and under the control of land magnates and exploiting groups. The fact that the peasants themselves, like the city workers of the West, have no way of making themselves felt except by mass action is one reason—a reason in the background, as it were—why they want always to settle in areas contiguous to land already settled, and fearful of penetrating independently into the farther wilderness.

[1] There are two kinds of land hunger. One is that of the man who wants land because it is the only kind of wealth he likes—who would rather have land, and more land, than hard cash or business investments, and who wants to live on his land, preferring it to any city luxury. Such an affection for land is bred only in landowning, land-rooted countrymen and yeomen. This type of "land hunger" can be found in "old" communities in Manchuria. The other is the land hunger of the laboring peasant, not skilled enough to seek a trade, who must have work on the land in order to live, but who, given the chance, would rather learn a trade and move to a town. This is far the commoner type in China, and among immigrants in Manchuria. It is not, essentially, land that such men want, but employment.

The striking Manchurian phenomena which are popularly described as the juxtaposition of the "latest developments of Western civilization" and the "medieval economy of China," the clash of the primitive and the modern, are in reality phenomena of a rivalry between the methods of two highly developed but incompatible civilizations. In China proper, the West contends with the Chinese civilization as established from time immemorial. Hence the chief phenomena are those of the destruction of one civilization by another.

In Manchuria, the two styles are rivals contending for prior establishment in what is as nearly as possible a virgin country —for the area of old Chinese occupation is decidedly over-balanced by the area of former tribal country and practically uninhabited land. In this contest the West has the advantage of the comparatively great speed inherent in Western methods. Thus Westernization and industrialization, in spite of being slowed down by the rivalry of the Chinese civilization, proceed faster than in China proper. For this very reason, as has already been argued, the importance of Manchuria as a channel conducting toward China the aggression of the West is at least as great as its importance in bringing the expansive powers of China to bear on the frontier.

It must also be borne in mind that the older establishment of Chinese civilization in Manchuria had already been modified by regional characteristics, and that in the competitive effort to establish it in advance of Westernization in the course of the further spread through Manchuria, the factor of vested interest is less strong. True constructive amalgamation between East and West is therefore in certain aspects easier in Manchuria than in China proper—just as, in the past, in spite of the eagerness of the Manchus themselves to learn all they could from the Chinese, the Chinese in Manchuria took on a certain Manchu color. In the modern phase, Westernization reinforces the old regional "reservoir" importance of Manchuria to the extent that a Manchuria made strong and rich by the use of Western methods of exploitation, while it tends in an obvious manner to continue to expand outward, in no wise relaxes its tendency to bear down on and dominate China.

Manchuria, owing both to the form of Chinese colonization itself and to the pronounced focusing of Western forces, is already more "megalopolitan" than any part of China of equivalent area, and far more metropolitan in ratio of great cities to total population. Harbin and Dairen, as great cities of the modern type, are far ahead of Peking and Nanking, and tend increasingly to rival Shanghai. The drift away from the land and into the cities is as important as the colonization of land. The old pride of land, there can be no doubt, has long been defeated. The peasant and the farmer deprecate their inferiority to the townsman, and the townsman looks down on the country boor. The typical ambition of the son of a well-established landowning family is directed away from the land and the old comfortable superiorities of the "squires." The more "progressive" he is the more he wants to go to the city, where the real opportunities of promotion and power are to be found. The newly rich invest in land, but remain in the cities; their town footing is more important to them than their investments in the country, for it is in the towns that they negotiate for and keep up the power that gives them control in the countryside.

The "reservoir" itself, under the Manchus, did still represent to a certain extent, the power of the country over the city—especially the power of the landed gentry—but even so it was already a dying power. From the country, the great Banner families sent their sons to the cities to take up official careers. Gradually, as the Manchus became more Chinese, the successful families tended to move altogether into the cities. The power of the land lingered in the "reservoir" only because, being the "reservoir," it dominated China, the land of civilization. The caretakers and bailiffs of great estates, more and more neglected by absentee landlords, tended to form powerful families of their own—and in their turn migrated gradually to the cities, leaving sub-agents in charge. This was revealed at the fall of the Empire, when numbers of Peking Manchus, deprived of their subsidies and virtually shut out of the new official classes, remembered their estates in Manchuria—but found that through the lapse of time the descendants of their bailiffs (often slaves by origin) had become rich and powerful. They were in possession, they collected the revenue, they were in touch with the local officials; and they held on to the land, in defiance of the descendants of the owners. In the very act of so doing, however, they had to shift their power from a territorial to a city base. The city was essential for negotiation with officials. One of the commonest expedients for a landlord in possession but without a clear title is to place the land "in trust" with a high official, "pending fair settlement." The official thus acquires a revenue, and the title remains permanently unsettled. There are important lands in Manchuria which have been held thus "in trust," or "in chancery," as it were, passing through the hands of a succession of officials, ever since the Revolution. In the meantime the affairs of the *de facto* owners have become interlocked with those of officials, their sons have entered official careers, and they have permanently moved from the country to the city in order to handle their affairs properly.

The landed gentry, the squires and the yeomen, as masters of the country dominating the towns, have everywhere had to give way. They have had to abandon the land, leaving it, in their turn, to tenants and overseers, because if they wish to remain in touch with the springs of power and control they must live close to the officials, in the cities. Mukden, Kirin, Tsitsihar—each provincial capital—is full of city-dwelling land magnates. The flight of the rent-supported landlords from land to city is, it is true, explained by themselves usually as due to banditry and the fear of being taken for ransom if they stay in the country. This, however, is an indirect confirmation of the truth; for if their status as great landlords represented power in itself, as once it did, they could look after the bandits themselves. As it is, it is no use living in the country and depending on the troops; they must move to the cities and keep in touch with those who have authority over the troops.

While the townsman, when he becomes wealthy, invests in land but does not move to the country, the countryman, in proportion as he grows wealthy and acquires land, feels imperatively the need of moving to the city. The standards of the peasant are puritanical, compared with those of the town: at least in the old settled regions. In the regions of new settlement, because of the standard of "get rich however you can, but get rich quick," and because of the scarcity of women, morals of all kinds are looser. The greatest pride of the countryman is his ability to *kuo jih-tzu*—a highly idiomatic phrase meaning that he makes each day pay for itself, that he does not touch what he can save, that he eats for nourishment, not because he likes food. Houses that are better than necessary, the wearing of good clothes, the eating of food "above his station," all frivolity, all unnecessary expense, are moral delinquencies. But the idea, the ultimate standard that the farmer has in mind is *not* a puritan standard. The things that are wrong are not wrong in themselves. They are wrong "for the likes of him," but not for those who can afford them.

In fact, he rather admires extravagance, and even dissipation, in the rich. He himself lives with a bleak austerity. He saves because, by superhuman effort, he may one day get ahead in the bitter struggle for life. If he does, if he ever has in fact a superfluity of land and wealth, he moves first to a town and then to a city, or sends his sons there. Basing himself on the land, he works himself into trade—the grain trade and the transport trade first of all. He lives in dignity on his income. He endeavors to marry his daughters to officials or men powerful in trade, and his sons and grandsons are educated for power and prestige and anything but a puritan life.

The refugee peasant, once torn from the land in the province of his birth, commonly looks with little ambition on the land where he settles in Manchuria. His real land hunger was exhausted in the losing struggle before he migrated. He knows that the odds are against him, that the landlord and the merchant will have the whip hand over him as they did in China. To be torn from the land which at least he knew, and planted on land in what to him are barbarous surroundings, is, by his standards, bitter defeat. Consequently, there is a strong drift from country to town among those who have failed as well as among those who have succeeded. "Boom" years have decidedly a stronger effect in towns than in the countryside; for while land values *grow,* town values are *forced up.* The refugee who escapes from the land into a factory considers that he has gone up in the world. Economically, he may have become even less secure, but socially he has become more sophisticated, and with the shallow superiority of the townsman all over the world he looks down on the plodding country lout. He may later become a soldier; he may get into trade; he may get rich and buy land; but he will never go back to the land.

STANDARDS OF LIVING

The higher standard of living, which is the most important real attraction of Manchuria for immigrants from China, is in part a survival from "reservoir" days and in part a product of new Westernizing conditions. Under the Manchus, there was in fact something approaching a true peasantry in the regions of Chinese and Manchu population, with class-equivalents of serfs, yeomen and landed gentry. Social limitation by the accident of birth was fairly effective, except for the way out offered by the official examinations; but under certain conditions—notably valor in war—it was possible for the individual to rise gradually from one class to another. The countryside—except of course in Mongol and tribal regions—was agricultural, and the towns were important mainly as administrative centers and garrison points. Trade counted for comparatively little in the structure of society. Manchuria produced ample for its own needs, and neither imports nor exports were vital to its economic life. Its "invisible" imports gave it a favorable balance in the form of salaries, pay and subsidies to officials, garrisons and Bannermen, and the fortunes brought back by retired officials. Against these it exported troops and officials. Ease, plenty and security made possible a carelessness for money and the needs of the future which rather horrified the monetary sense of the Chinese. Nevertheless the Manchu open-handedness communicated itself also to Chinese living in contact with the Manchus and sharing the security of the privileged region. As a result, the people of the old settled regions to this day live in rather better houses, eat more (especially more meat), and spend more on clothing and comfort than the population of north China in general. There is the feeling that there is always more where the last lot came from. The countryman of Kirin or Eastern Liaoning, on a journey, will stop by the way when he might have reached home, and eat a good meal and pay handsomely for it, where the Shantung or Chihli man would trudge on hungry until he got home.

In trade, again, there is less close application to detail and much less of the feeling that a man should begin in early youth to master a craft or trade, rise gradually to responsibility, and stick to the same thing all his life. Safety is the dearest hope of the artisan and small trader in North China; in Manchuria, the average man wants profits that are quick as well as good. The trader who has come in from China proper has the same spirit; what, he thinks, is the good of leaving civilization if you don't make good money by it? If the profits are not good enough and quick enough, a man will cut his losses and start afresh in a manner which, in China proper, would be foolhardy. Merchants who have connections in Manchuria know that they must watch the business with care, for while the connection pays well if it pays at all, the first sign of a set-back—not necessarily a loss in the business but, often enough, a falling-off in profits—is enough to make the Manchurian correspondent default and vanish. There are the same phenomena of unlimited opportunity, combined with unscrupulous default, that characterized the period of heavy foreign investment in development projects in America, when foreign capital financed American railways, and States of enormous potential wealth defaulted on their foreign bonds. Manchuria is also "American" in the freedom with which men change their occupations, residence and interests. This is not the restlessness of primitive migration. Manchuria is to China as America is to Europe; a country to which have been transplanted not the original elements, but the late products, of a civilization already advanced, with the consequence that these late forms, comparatively unimpeded by the accumulations of the past, take on a fresh growth of their own. In China, as in Europe, sophisticated money values overrule all other values; but in Manchuria, as in America, money has a freer hand than in either China or Europe.

It is not at all uncommon in Manchuria, for instance, for a man to invest his capital in motor-road transport in Liaoning; fail, leaving heavy debts; go to Kirin and start in the timber trade with no capital, no training, nothing but confidence and (usually) an "inside" personal connection, and make a great deal of money; invest his profits in Heilungchiang in the grain and bean business, and lose everything; move back to Western Liaoning and make money again. It is common even to find a man who is known to be "wanted" for banditry or embezzlement or something else outside the law in one part of the country, and high in the councils of the chamber of commerce and allied with the private investments of officials in another.

The frontiers of expansion and colonization have peculiarities of their own. The legend of the hardy pioneer, which arises in every colonized country after the true pioneer period is safely over and done with, is largely false. The early pioneer, in Manchuria as in the American West, was bold and hardy, and quite as often as not a far from ideal citizen. Where the early period survives, as it does among the opium pioneers and bandit pioneers, the frontier is still the land of men who can look after themselves; but this period precedes the boom. When the boom comes, the "admirable bad men" move on, and their place is taken by the sly, the quick-witted and the unscrupulous, who do not work with their own hands but make other men work for them; who profit by rising values and look out for themselves by looking after other people.[2] Although wages are high as well as prices on the frontier, and big profits are made on a quick turnover, the big money is all in the hands of the middlemen. The settler himself must face a far harder standard. The long reach of the land-owner and the dealer in farm produce give them a powerful advantage. The secondary migrant, it is true, with his background of special experience and a capital provided by the sale of his old land, has only to play safe. The seasonal laborer, with no stake to lose and high pay in the short, busy season, can take his money back to China where the lower standard of living gives it a much greater buying power.

The immigrant settler, however, whether refugee or man of small capital, must either take over land at the enhanced price put on it by middlemen, or work off the price put on it by a landlord. Whether he works on terms of straightforward tenant-rental or rent-purchase, it is difficult for him to save toward his own economic independence except by reducing his standard of living. The tenant or laborer in the old settled regions has only to underlive an already comparatively high standard. For this reason the old, easy-going Manchu villages of Kirin, for instance, have each their fringe of Shantung hangers-on—market gardeners and small tenants who in a generation or two work their way up to become small-holders, firmly established. On the frontiers of new colonization, on the other hand, with their new railways, their land magnates, their powerful grain-buying and transport companies, the mass of moneyless refugees have to compete against one another and the low standard of the destitute. Their chief safeguard is the prevailing distaste for "planted"

[2] To appreciate the equivalent stage in, for instance, American colonization, in the middle of the last century, one should consult the contemporary accounts of European observers, which give an impression quite different from the now popular, non-contemporary, romanticized American version.

colonization, causing a steady drain away from the new settlements and forcing the exploiting interests to offer, sporadically, more tempting terms. It is small wonder that the line of colonization wavers; that there is always a discount, a backwash of men who give up the idea of holding land and either work as laborers for a season and go back to China, if they can, or make for the towns and employment as laborers; that in many regions of "new settlement" the villages stand within sight of abandoned villages where the attempt was made before, and failed. Nor is it surprising that the final residue of permanent settlers tends to be made up not of those of the "pioneer" spirit, but of the most docile and least independent and enterprising.

In the towns, the standard is even more "American," with its high wages in contrast with poor security. Under the old Chinese system, with its apprentice-standards, where men grow up and work all their lives in the same employment, all labor is kept on as long as possible in bad times. In Manchuria, in times of prosperity, the demand for labor is so great that wages are high and the unskilled man graduates quickly into skilled labor; but he is turned off ruthlessly the moment that trade slackens. The towns therefore are full of "floating" labor that has high standards of getting and spending, no security, no attachment to a particular business and little sense of responsibility. This class, like the new proletarian class in China itself, is of some danger politically, for in breaking away from the land and the old guild-system it has lost its roots and become to a great extent less Chinese, while, unlike the equivalent class in the West, it has not been evolved from an indigenous individualistic society and hence is incompletely Westernized. It is intellectually more active than the old "common people," and far more positive in times of discontent; but intellectually confounded by the uncomprehended issues that are being fought out between the Western order and the old Chinese order. When it strikes, it is likely to be short-sighted in its demands; when there is no use in striking it is open to the incitement of any unscrupulous political agitation that promises something for nothing; and in between whiles the wilder spirits are likely at any time to take to gang robbery and banditry.

The standard among women is a reflection of that among men. In the old settled regions, it is paradoxically at once higher and more conservative than in China proper. The early Manchu tradition, with its greater freedom for women, had a powerful effect on the Chinese who made common cause with the Manchus; just as the Manchus who went to Peking were strongly affected by Chinese standards, and tended increasingly to seclude and restrict their women. Chinese living in contact with the Manchus in Manchuria began very early to abandon the practice of binding women's feet; just as Manchus in Peking, while continuing to forbid the practice of binding the feet of their own women, adopted a form of shoe which gave their women something of the toddling gait of Chinese women with bound feet. There is a curious contrast in the readiness with which Chinese abandoned foot binding in Manchuria, and the tenacity of the practice along the Mongol frontier. I am inclined to attribute this to the ready amalgamation between Chinese and Manchus, as contrasted with the profound cleavage between Chinese and Mongols. While the Manchus were much more eager than the Mongols to adopt Chinese standards of civilization, the Chinese population in Manchuria, identifying itself politically with the Manchus, took on Manchu characteristics to a surprising extent.

At the present time the comparative social freedom of women in the old settled regions in Manchuria, in going about, joining in general conversation when men are present, and making their opinion felt in household and family affairs, gives an impression of "emancipation" when compared with old-fashioned rural China. At the same time real or rather fresh emancipation—the education of girls, freedom of choice in marriage, economic independence—probably lags somewhat behind the average in China. It is true that the endowment of schools for girls, like the endowment of all education in Manchuria, proceeds very rapidly; but I doubt if, in the general social consciousness, there is the same enthusiasm for the emancipation of women as a "cause"—perhaps for the very reason that women, in many respects, were not so backward to begin with.

The comparative scarcity of women must always have had an effect in enhancing their general value and hence their social status. This is especially noticeable in the rapidly growing towns and in regions of new settlement, where the effort to attract colonists with families has not by any means offset the surplus of men. This accounts for certain marked divergences between "old" and "new" Manchuria. In the regions of old settlement, while the proportion of women may on the whole be smaller than in China proper, there is no really pronounced lack of women. In the country and in small villages prostitution exists to a minimum extent. Owing to this, and to the custom of early marriage, venereal disease is not at all common. Country people regard it as a city disease. (This is true also of China proper.) On the frontiers of new settlement, however, and in the towns, owing to the disproportion of men to women, prostitution is a flourishing business. This is not true of villages which are merely groups of farmhouses, but it is true of the smallest villages to which men come from the countryside to trade. A village of even forty or fifty houses will have its brothel and two or three shops selling cures for venereal disease.

Women can enter brothels of their own free will, but are often placed there by husband or family. In the latter case, although money changes hands and the transaction is commonly called a "sale," it is not strictly a sale but a form of indenture. The contract provides that the money spent by the brothel represents, as it were, a capital investment. Of the money earned by the woman, a certain part is kept by her, and part goes to the brothel. This is placed, in the books, to the credit of her account. When her account is paid off, with interest, the indenture terminates, and she is free to do as she pleases, either leaving the business or remaining in it on a commission basis. Actually, it is often difficult for a woman to redeem herself, because she receives clothes and jewellery, the cost and interest being charged against her account. Owing, however, to the great demand for women, prostitutes are frequently "redeemed" by men who take them either as wives or concubines. To be thus redeemed by a rich man is their commonest ambition. The whole system, naturally, is abhorrent to the ideas of social reform which are rapidly making themselves felt in China. Immediate abolition is, however, impossible practically, in view of local social ideas; moreover the legal concepts on which it is based are very old, and generally tolerated by conservative opinion.[3] Constant efforts toward police control are made, and it appears to be generally true that a woman who has been forced into the life, and objects to it violently, can succeed in breaking the contract and getting free without "redemption."

Surprisingly enough, the number of women imported from China to be placed in brothels is not very large; though a regular, but of course surreptitious trade exists. Women born in Manchuria often take to the life because of its gayety and the chances of a fashionable life and a good match. Although the family standards of chastity in China are very high in-

[3] The situation is thus generally comparable with that in Japan.

deed—probably higher, among poor country people, than in Western nations—they are lowered locally by the pressure of the demand for women. The woman "with a past" can make a respectable marriage much more easily than in China proper. On the other hand, the same demand tends to raise the age of marriage for girls, in spite of the patriarchal tradition which encourages early marriage for the provision of as many descendants as possible, as soon as possible; for parents will wait several years on the chance of fixing up a really advantageous marriage.

In spite of the demand for women in Manchuria, the immigration of unattached women appears to be comparatively small. A certain number do come in when large numbers of refugees are being transported; some of them having, as has been said, fictitiously registered as wives and daughters. On the whole, however, the agricultural population (as everywhere else in the world) is shy of strange women. Farmers want wives who are not only farm-bred, but locally bred. Probably the most important agency in bringing women into Manchuria is the army. Whenever troops are sent into China from Manchuria, a great many of the officers, and even some of the soldiers, return with wives. The cost of marriage in China proper is very much lower, and the officer classes, at least, also think that a wife from the "old country" is smarter and more fashionable.

In the question of match-making, the influence of the drift away from the land and toward the cities and money-standards is very evident. The cost of marriage for a young farmer is not only extraordinarily high compared with the cost in China proper, but disproportionately high compared with the cost for other classes in Manchuria. I have repeatedly heard it stated, in regions of new settlement, that the young farmer just beginning to make his own way must pay at least a thousand dollars for a match of quite ordinary attractions. In other words, the cost is almost prohibitive; and the poorer the man, the more he is asked. On the other hand the merchant, and above all the official and military officer with good prospects of promotion, even if they have little capital of their own, can arrange marriages on extremely favorable terms with country families of comparative wealth; because such a marriage, to the landowner, is an alliance with power and fits in with the shift away from immobile land values to mobile values of money and position.

The standards of living reflected in education in Manchuria illustrate an acute local development of the conflict between the old order and the new that is going on throughout China. The educational endowment (controlled by the State, as everywhere else in China) is probably higher in proportion to the population than the average in China proper. Technological training, benefiting by the extra stimulus of the South Manchuria and Chinese Eastern Railways, and the excellent schools maintained by them, is also well advanced.

At the same time there is a strong conservative tradition which affects the orientation of all education. In China itself "Western education" still has many of the characteristics of a "cause," and is, as such, highly destructive of old standards. In Manchuria, because of the old and firm attraction to China, intellectual trends, in the very classes which in China are least conservative, lean toward conservatism. Here again appears the difference in the East-and-West relationships of China and Manchuria—competition, in Manchuria, to decide which standard is to be set up, as against frank opposition in China, where the problem is, how far the Chinese standard will be destroyed before it can rally and subordinate the Western standard.

Consequently, loyalty to the old tradition in China and in

Manchuria is, in certain aspects, loyalty of a different color and feeling. A profound inner discord is caused in Manchurian affairs by the higher and more rapid technical development, which assists the Manchurian pressure on China and conducts toward China the pressure of the West and of Russia, working against a counter-trend of vigorous conservatism, which endeavors to preserve the old influence of the Chinese civilization, and to increase the vitality of nationalistic Chinese expansionism in Manchuria. Nationalism and conservatism are thus identified in a way in which they are not identified in China itself.

This accounts for the existence, in competition with rapid Westernization, of an undeniably conservative ideology in social thought and government practice. While new devices are spread rapidly, new thought is under administrative suspicion. Many of the older school of officials appear to have a horror of the idea of incorporating Western thought with Chinese, and to hold that Westernization should be isolated in compartments, only to be drawn on when needed, and by no means to be granted the right of *demanding* to be used. Even the formulæ of Dr. Sun, and the doctrines of the Kuomintang, are not so freely taught as in China, and there is a decided tendency to keep the teachers of them under administrative supervision; while on the other hand the old classical curriculum is retained and taught (especially in the lower schools) to a greater extent than is common in the rest of China. The total result, as a matter of fact, appears from the foreigner's point of view to be satisfactory, in that it restrains theory from getting too far ahead of practice, and checks the spread of merely "fashionable" Westernization; for while Westernization as a fashion is very common, there is a reluctance to allow it to take practical effect until it is truly inevitable.

Intellectual circles all over China are as much concerned with the possibilities of decay and collapse in the Western civilization as they are with the suitability of Western standards for adoption in China. This is a characteristic that has already been touched on. In Manchuria this "hope of deliverance from the West" takes the form of a widespread, eager expectation that China may yet some day, from within the repository of her own traditions, produce a latent strength which can in some manner be triumphantly revived and developed to the overthrow and consternation of all foreign power and foreign standards, and enable Chinese Manchuria to vindicate its Chinese character. The very circles which are most progressive in clearing away "medievalism," in improving administration and Westernizing economic affairs, are filled with a strong and conscious pride in the Chinese point of view, the Chinese way of life and the superiority of the basic values of Chinese civilization over those of the West. This is a characteristic which deserves further consideration.

CHAPTER XII

MANCHURIA'S PLACE IN THE WORLD

MANCHURIA AND CHINA

THERE is a curious double phenomenon in the affairs of modern China. There is a stronger effort toward expansion of territory and extension of authority than at any time since the reign of Ch'ien Lung. Popular knowledge of and interest in the territories of the northwestern, northern and northeastern frontiers has grown prodigiously since the foundation of the Republic, and especially since the unification of the country under the Kuomintang. The securing of the frontiers by colonization under government control has become a definite policy. The division of Inner Mongolia into new provinces—Ninghsia, Suiyüan, Chahar and Jehol—is in effect an effort to get rid of the "reservoir" by obliterating its regional identity. The assertion of the government's interest in Chinese communities abroad (notably in the Straits Settlements and the South Seas) represents a new conception of China's functions as a State, and of the standing of China among the nations of the world. The cumulating success of negotiations for drawing up new treaties, abolishing such foreign privileges in Chinese territory as foreign-controlled concessions and extraterritorial jurisdiction, has resulted in an increase of prestige and an apparent recovery, in part at least, of the freedom of initiative in international affairs.

Yet in another aspect this interest in the frontiers is only a reflection of the fact that the frontiers threaten to have more control over China than China has over them. The fact of the matter is that China, though a nation homogeneous in culture, more homogeneous in population than most Western nations, and more united in national will than at any time since the foundation of the Republic, was never weaker than it is to-day. Foreign aggression, *potentially,* is a greater danger than it ever was. The fact that a nation depends on the good will of foreign nations, and that that good will exists and is actively exercised, does not alter the fact that it is dependent. The underlying weakness of China's position could not be better illustrated than by the fact (not as generally appreciated as it should be) that Westernization, technology, higher scientific development and higher education—all the things which Chinese leaders themselves feel to be imperatively necessary if China is to hold its own with other nations—depend to a very important extent on the remitted Boxer indemnities, and to an only less important extent on private and institutional philanthropic remittances from abroad.

It is true that the indemnities are collected from China herself; but it is none the less true that their remission for the benefit of China depends on the accident that the remitting nations happen to think that by remitting the funds they will benefit themselves as well as China, by making China a country more profitable for Western trade. The remission of these indemnities is merely another illustration of the change in form of foreign aggression; yet without them, it would be exceedingly difficult, in the present state of national finances in China, to find other funds for the purpose, owing to the disagreement of regional factions. The Boxer funds, once remitted, do not remain entirely under the control of the remitting nation, but are administered by boards on which China is represented; but this merely obscures the fact that the remission itself, under stipulated conditions, means nothing if it does not mean an option of interference.

It amounts, indeed, to a kind of permissive control over Chinese affairs; and the latest development, that of stipulating for the construction of railways and the foundation of industries, the materials for the construction of which are to be purchased in the country remitting the indemnity, approximates to the assertion of an option of control over the form that Westernization is to take in China. There is no doubt that the remitting nations think they are doing "the best thing for China"; but it is the best thing from the foreign point of view. It is no wonder that Chinese opinion does not glow with quite the same satisfied enthusiasm.

Given this weakness at the heart of domestic affairs, it is possible to understand how the expansion of Chinese frontiers by colonization is weakened by an inner conflict. In one sense it is a part of the struggle to recover internal unity by recovery of the initiative in foreign affairs. In another sense, however—illustrated by the dependence on refugee colonists —it illustrates the flight from the weak center. In this respect, the paradox that became evident in the conflict between China and Russia emerges again; the periphery of China is powerful in its domestic relations, but weak in its external relations. The provincial governments of the frontiers can intervene with immediate effect in the domestic politics of China by mere declarations of attitude; but to expand their own authority at the cost even of so weak, ill-organized and poorly armed a people as the Mongols requires a disproportionate expenditure of strength and money.

Expansion does not gain momentum without Westernization; and Westernization, at the moment, hangs uncertain between the difficulty of raising Chinese capital at all, and the difficulty of raising foreign capital except on terms which either give the lender a measure of control or—as in the case of certain railways in Manchuria, built for the Chinese by the South Manchuria Railway, on which payments have fallen into default—an uncertain but none the less dangerous option of reëntry by government action into Chinese affairs. Moreover these railways—for railways are the most dynamic single factor in Westernization simply because they increase the speed and effect of action, independent of maturely deliberated policy or the purpose of the action—tend, as has been shown, to accelerate the general pace of Westernization to a point where China alone cannot handle it, and to bear strategically on China.

The option of interference which foreign nations hold, the changing forms of foreign pressure and the disproportionate physical strength of foreign nations when it comes to decisive, rapid action, as demonstrated by Russia, and again by Japan, clearly revealed the new aspect of affairs. Incidentally, the Russian course of action also illustrated a probable future development in international affairs generally, proving that it is possible to put troops in the field, win victories and settle international disputes by virtue of military superiority, without declaring war. On the occasion of this crisis, which was in effect a test case of major importance, the immediate result of decisive Russian action was a breakdown in the theory and conduct of Chinese foreign policy. Factional leaders turned the occasion to their own account, playing on the variations which it brought about in the adjustment of provincial and national policies, and especially in the relation between regional governments and the Central Government, while the specific responsibility of dealing with the crisis itself was warily evaded. The Russians proved that they know exactly what they want from the West, and that when they have taken what they want, they cannot be made to take any

more; they outwitted several foreign offices by twisting the
Kellogg Treaty against war, which had only just been signed,
into a brilliant extempory device for conducting an entire
campaign under cover, with complete success, without declaring war and while in the act of politely debating, according
to the "rules of the game" (Western style) whether or not
the situation warranted the declaration of a war "for purposes
of self-defense" in order to regain a position of crucial offensive strategic importance. On the other side the Chinese,
caught in confusion between the Western "rules of the game"
and their own conflicting opinions of what ought to be done
and what could be done, had finally to fall back on the unsatisfactory expedient of citing the Kellogg Treaty, and their
own restraint in not declaring war, in order to cover up as
far as possible their actual defeat.

The whole situation, as far as China was concerned, was a
paradoxical reverse illustration of the aphorisms of Spengler
that "domestic politics exist simply in order that foreign politics may be possible," and that "the State's position in point
of outward power in fact completely conditions its freedom
for inward development"—a point, incidentally, well enough
appreciated in China, for on it turns the struggle to get rid
of foreign extraterritorial jurisdiction. The reassertion of the
Russian interest in the Chinese Eastern Railway both strength-
ened the position of the Japanese with regard to the South
Manchuria Railway, and weakened the position of the Chinese with regard to the railways designed to offset the hold of
the South Manchuria and Chinese Eastern systems. The
strength of the movement of independent Chinese expansion
in Northern and Northwestern Manchuria, which had augmented enormously during the period of Russian quiescence,
was immediately and noticeably curtailed.

The outcome of the struggle also threw a light on the future of "foreign privilege" in China; for while the theoretical *status* of Russian citizens in China was not altered, their *standing* in fact improved. Russians began to receive better treatment at the hands of common people, police and officials. When, in a court of law or any dispute, in the face of *theories* of "justice" and "guilt," the question "Is he a White Russian or a Red Russian" has a *practical* importance, the existence of "privilege," apart altogether from legal definition, cannot be denied. "Privilege" and "prestige" are only different formulæ for the expression of the same thing.

The only conclusion possible is that the expansion of China's land frontiers is, in large measure, a function of Western activities and Western pressure, and emphasizes the graveness of the problem of whether, in the future, China can manage to throw off its dependence on foreign good will, and define its policies (as Russia does) purely in terms of what Chinese feeling demands. Thus, in our time, the maximum Chinese colonizing expansion is in Manchuria, and is dominated in the strategy of both war and economics by Western agencies. The momentum of colonization diminishes westward along the frontiers of Inner Mongolia, in a proportion directly related to diminished railway construction, and at the western end of the northern line, in Chinese Turkestan, is practically nil, the Chinese administration there being hard enough put to it to maintain itself in the face of Russian influence. Where the line turns, along the frontiers of Tibet, colonizing expansion passes from nil to minus; for the Tibetans, during the twenty years of the Chinese Republic, have actually been encroaching on lands once conquered from them by the Chinese, and have been driving out the Chinese and establishing themselves again; and this movement appears to be spreading over an ever wider territory and to be gaining in speed.

What is more, it is evident also that the less expansive the Chinese frontier, the less the regions under Chinese administration adjacent to the frontier press inward on China itself. This is an interesting reversal of the popular theory that movements of conquest are necessarily cumulative in effect; for in that case the province of Ssuch'uan, which is losing to the Tibetans, ought to recoil on China with pronounced effect. As a matter of fact it does not; on the contrary, it has less influence on the politics of China than have the frontier provinces of the north. Thus the influence of Manchuria (including Jehol), the most progressive group of provinces, is extremely great; the influence of Chahar, Suiyüan and Ninghsia much less, and the influence of Chinese Turkestan latent. The reason why the pressure of the Ssuch'uan frontier has no important cumulative effect, while that of Manchuria has, is that the Tibetan pressure is chiefly one of population, and one that has been inherent in the situation for centuries, involving no new conceptions, the cultural pressure being unimportant, while the Manchurian pressure is coincident with that of the West and Russia.

In practice, the attempt to obliterate the "reservoir" by the formation of the new provinces of Jehol, Chahar, Suiyüan and Ninghsia, on a non-"reservoir," "normal" model, has merely resulted in a reorganization of the "reservoir" and the continuance of its functions. The process is the same as that which has preceded every important period of Northern pressure on China. All through the border regions, powers and dignities are conferred by the Central Government on the regional authorities; a device which obscures the fact that these authorities would have the same powers, whether the dignities were conferred or not. Where, however, the border authorities increase their own strength, they have a strong inclination not to put it automatically at the service of China, but to use it to emphasize their importance with respect to China. The most recent phenomenon of this kind is the conferring of important titles and subsidies on the Panch'an Lama; but (a fact not yet appreciated abroad) this only parallels a strong movement throughout Inner Mongolia to bring the different tribes, princes and ecclesiastical authorities into a policy of concerted action, based on resistance to Chinese colonization; and to coördinate the princely interest with that of the powerful Lama church and with the growing "Young Mongol" demand for regional autonomy—using the Panch'an Lama as a symbol and a rallying point.

The crux of the importance of the regional groups is that they nowhere serve primarily as tools of Chinese expansionism, directed and controlled from China itself. On the contrary, they themselves control expansion and exploitation. If it were possible to build railways fast enough, under the authority of a strong central government, it ought to be possible to extend the radial authority of the national government. As it is, however, even railways built under authority of the national government tend to fall under the power of regional authorities, who handle the rolling stock and receipts primarily for their own benefit. They themselves control expansion and exploitation. They decide how many colonists they want, and where to place them; but the fresh wealth created by exploitation is brought to bear on China, in the form of a political importance which dictates to China the terms on which the border regions participate in the federal activity of government in China.

In practice, the factor on which all action turns is the army, which in modern China constitutes a world in itself, independent of national life and feeling and turning from national to local policy and action according to the interests of its own leaders, who arise from within it. The armies of China are

the chief instruments of Western pressure, and have superseded, or rather made unnecessary in the political sense, that
foreign partition of China into "spheres of influence" which
at one time was threatened. What makes the armies more
deadly is the fact that they have become Western in armament
without becoming Western in technique. One of the first
results of successful preliminary Westernization in Japan was
the trial of the new army and navy. After an easy victory over
China, the much more serious challenge of Russia was accepted and dealt with successfully. It is frequently claimed
that the Japanese forces in these wars demonstrated no
original talent in warfare in the Western style, but adhered
woodenly to the methods of their textbooks. This unduly dis-
credits the courage of the Japanese in sticking to their own
faith in having learned their lessons adequately—a courage
which can best be appreciated by comparing these wars with
the modern wars of China, with their hopeless combination
of modern armament and traditional tactics and strategy.
Nor does it give due weight to the fact that the Russo-
Japanese War, though it may have contributed nothing original to the Western technique of warfare, was an important
stage in the development of Western military methods from
the American Civil War and the Franco-Prussian War to the
War of 1914–18; a more important stage than, for instance,
the British wars in South Africa. The study of the Russo-
Japanese War is an essential of military history for modern
soldiers, which cannot be said for the modern wars of China
with their far greater slaughter and sweep of territory.

Twenty years of civil war in China, indeed, and of government based on what are practically private mercenary armies,
have not produced a single development of interest to Western military technique. As for Russia, now a very different
nation from that which fought Japan and engaged as an

apathetic, pseudo-Western nation in the War of 1914–18, it is rapidly developing a specifically Russian, non-Western technique of warfare which is the cause of intense interest, and no little alarm, to Western nations. The Russian army is an engine of unknown power and very great importance.

In China, no matter how complete the Western armament, no campaign, even when foreign military advisors are used, is carried out in the spirit of the Western method. Thus no quarrel over domestic mastery is fought to an assertive decision, as the Western feeling would demand, and there is no question that cannot be reopened; but the definite issue, that of the relative importance of the West and China, being perpetually evaded, impends fatally over the country, paralyzing constructive effort. The weakness of China is a fundamental reluctance to choose.

The armies of the South are largely financed by Chinese abroad. The armies of the Center are umbilically dependent on the revenue of the Maritime Customs. As a large part of the foreign debt of the country is a primary charge on the Customs, the Western nations are resigned to the expenditure of the extra Customs revenue on armaments, if only the prior loan charges are met; while the Central Government is resigned to the necessity of retaining the international foreign personnel of the Customs, so long as it can impose Customs surtaxes as freely as it likes. The armies of the North, while they have at different times been under foreign influence, are the most free. That is because the North alone is in contact with undeveloped resources of its own. The armies of the South and Center destroy as they grow; they are instruments of the direct conflict between East and West. The armies of the North are financed in great measure by new expansion and the opening of new territories; they are an important factor in the race between the East, the West and Russia for priority in the development of the borders, and they are chiefly destructive when they are brought to bear in the civil wars within China proper.

It is a matter of grave difficulty for the commanders of such armies not to use them thus. An army, being an army, is not adapted to the conquest of the wilderness. It is not a natural instrument of "colonization," however well it may serve for the "colonial" conquest of a region already inhabited. A levy soldiery, based on a land-fast yeomanry, which is not on permanent professional service (like the old Manchu reserve in Manchuria, or the Cossack organization which accomplished so much in the conquest of the Siberian wilderness for Russia) can extend its frontiers by colonization even when, like the Manchus, it looks to the domination of a civilized land like China for the real exercise of its power; still more when, like the Cossacks, it is oriented by inward impulsion toward the wilderness. A professional mercenary army, however, dissociated from the land, inevitably demands a standard of pure power. It may base itself on a region, and operate by extending the power of the region, but primarily it does not demand land with room for settlement and raw materials to exploit; it demands cities to occupy, with loot and promotion for the troops and prestige and power for the commanders.

In such circumstances, policy turns on the accident of the ambition of the leader. In this respect it is true (as many Chinese think) that the present phase in China is nothing new. The political struggle, based on personal ambitions and dissociated from rival tendencies in social form and cultural growth, has been known in China ever since China passed from a civilization that was shaping its future form into a civilization that had determined its form and settled its characteristics. The Chinese civil war, as a cyclical phenomenon, is nothing new; it is the substitution of the West, as a de-

structive intruding factor in domestic affairs, partly rein-
forcing and partly replacing the old "standardized" barbarian
pressure of the North, that is new.

The Chinese of the present generation who is born with a
taste for theory can, by rational processes, arrive at any one
of a number of possible methods for the redemption of
China; but he is at the mercy of the man of action. Hence
the discontent, often disillusioned and bitter, of the intellectual classes. For the man of action in this generation gravitates
inevitably to the army. No other life in China rivals it in
scope for action. The man of thought may become an engineer or a political economist, but the man of action becomes
a general, dictating the use of railways, controlling the use of
capital in industry and decreeing the collection of taxes. Industries, to him, are sources of wealth; as long as he can arrive at wealth, he does not care for theories of industrialization. Troops, to him, are the raw material of power, and if
it is easier to achieve power by civil war than by a war against
foreign enemies, he will turn to civil war. The extension of
a frontier is, in its practical aspect, a question of the extension of his own power, and he measures his power by the
extent to which he is the master, not the servant of the nation;
hence an expansion of his outer frontier must, for him, pay
dividends in the increase of his domestic power. Western
armaments immediately and palpably increase his domestic
power; hence he does not pause in his career more than long
enough to master enough of the Western technique of
militarism to give him an advantage over his domestic op-
ponent.

Above all he does not care for the theory of the opposition
of Western and Chinese culture and civilization. If he can,
in his foreign policy, keep up enough of a front to give him
independence in his domestic policy he has, for his time and

generation, achieved the position of a strong man. Constructive foreign policy is the luxury of the man who is strong enough to spare time from domestic policies. To be properly appreciated, this has to be contrasted with the state of affairs in Russia, where domestic reconstruction is the luxury of the men who have succeeded in keeping Russia on her feet against a hostile world. The careerist, in China—above all the military careerist—is content, as a product of his own civilization, to benefit by as much of the Western civilization as he can turn to immediate profit in power and wealth, according to the standard that prevails in China, and leaving out of question the relative standard as between China and the West. The fusion of East and West is not his concern, so long as the degree of Westernization he adopts is under his own control, to be used according to his own ideas in as un-Western a manner as he pleases.

It was the good fortune of Manchuria, both as a region and as a province of China, that it should have had, in succession, two such rulers as Chang Tso-lin and his son Chang Hsüeh-liang. The older Marshal developed with great vigor the historic "reservoir" position. His son, bred to the career of the army, combined the habit of the man of action with the tastes of the man of theory. Before he was burdened with the chief responsibility, and before he had to treat with the ideas of the West practically and opportunistically, he became well acquainted with them as ideas. His own tastes gathered around him a young group with a strong tincture of theory, while the family succession secured to him the loyal support of a strong group of the men of his father's generation, men strictly of action.

Thus he was able, with an extraordinary degree of success, to maintain the indispensable regional strength of Manchuria, while using the strength of his own personality to divert Manchuria as far as possible from the fate of the pure "reservoir" policy. It was owing entirely to his personal choice, and personal courage in making the choice, that the potential power of Manchuria over China was exercised with restraint and discretion. It was because he himself chose to be guardian of China's frontier, and a leader in the expansion of China, rather than one of the claimants to power in China, that Manchuria was able to keep up its frontiers as well as it did. The successes of Manchuria—notably in the rapid expansion into Inner Mongolia—stand to his personal credit, while such failures as that of the stand against Russia and the disaster of the Japanese blow of September 1931 resulted in part from the historic weaknesses in the material at his command (such as the inherent distaste for northward campaigns, as against the enthusiasm for southward campaigns) but in the main from the lack of a strong nation behind him in the south.

The measure of his success was that by his personal influence he made Manchuria, potentially China's most dangerous frontier, into an outpost that, in spite of difficulties, was strong and confident. So formidable was the development that the Japanese, after being afforded a pretext by too cavalier treatment at the hands of the Kuomintang and "young China" group, thought themselves forced to take the grave risk of direct intervention in September 1931, in order to cut short the rapid growth of Chinese power. Fundamentally the Chinese error in allowing events to go so far was the old error of pressing too far their old land-frontier technique against a sea-power.

The hope of a rally within China lies, after all, not with the men of action but with the men of thought, and especially with what is called the "Chinese Renascence" movement. For the present, the men of action exclude its leaders from any real control in affairs; and this is to the good, for it turns the movement inward, into the life of the nation, giving it a chance to spread widely before breaking into the sphere of action. The Chinese Renascence is a movement toward the rediscovery, reëxperiencing, revaluation and reinterpretation of the basic values of the indigenous culture of China. If it has the vitality to spread (and it has many signs of such a vitality) from literature and academic discussion into the world of life and action, it may yet reanimate China. The movement involves, in certain aspects, the application of Western criteria, by Chinese, to Chinese values of thought and experience. Nevertheless its constructive power comes from within, for it demands the prior mastery of the Western criteria themselves by Chinese.

In such processes, though they have yet to spread from the cities and from intellectual circles into the life of the nation at large, there is real hope, because they make possible a true integration of Western elements. In this way they are superior to schematized programs of "reform," which begin in the world of politics, not of life and inward experience, and represent in the ultimate analysis (even the "Three People's Principles" of Dr. Sun, for instance) merely proposals of maximum voluntary surrender on the part of China; and in so far as the Renascence movement replaces compromise by integration, *digestion* of the West by China, it tends to break the present stalemate of ruinous makeshifts. The very slow-ness of the spread of the Chinese Renascence from the world of thought to the sphere of action may prove ultimately a source of strength, through making possible a more thorough antecedent integration of thought and feeling with practice.

THE PLACE OF MANCHURIA IN WORLD AFFAIRS

The two views of the "Manchurian Question" most commonly held are that, on the one hand, Manchuria is destined to be a Flanders or Alsace-Lorraine of the Far East; or that, on the other hand, Chinese colonization in Manchuria is the vanguard of a Chinese advance that will one day throw the dominating shadow of China over all the territories of the North Pacific seaboard.[1] According to this view, Japan is destined to become a Far Eastern Belgium, dominated by the continental mass of China as Belgium is dominated by Europe; while China is also destined to intervene between Russia and the Pacific as Western Europe intervenes between Russia and the Atlantic.

Whatever the outcome may be, there can be no doubt that the fate of Manchuria turns not only on the population movements of our own generation, but on the policies that are now being formulated by China, Russia and Japan. Chinese colonization may or may not, in the end, settle the question; in the meantime, what it has definitely brought about is the necessity of a considered change of policy on the part of all the nations immediately affected.

The period of more or less vague wariness and policies of precaution is at an end, and all depends now on policies of action. The policy of Japan in Manchuria, ever since the Washington Conference, appears at the first glance to have been essentially defensive. This quality of defensiveness it shares,

---

[1] These concluding pages were written before the Japanese intervention in September 1931. Rather than try to amend them by bringing in references to a crisis not yet settled when this book goes to the printer, I let them stand, for I think that thus they may more clearly bring out the underlying situation, and so less quickly go out of date.

I have only to add that any attempt to establish a Japanese leadership over the Manchurian Chinese and the neighboring Mongols, comparable to the Manchu power over the "reservoir," is not likely to work smoothly. The Japanese are utterly alien to the "reservoir" tradition—as are all Western nations. At the best they could create only another Korea or a new India. The possibility of a recrudescence of the "reservoir" power lies with the Russians, and with them alone; for only the Russians are true "northern barbarians"; the Japanese and all the Westerners are "sea barbarians." What the Japanese action has already accomplished, however, is a staggering blow to that typical myth of the late Western culture—which however is indestructible—the belief that good intentions can produce peace throughout the world.

indeed, with the China policies of all the Western nations. Nevertheless I do not believe that Japan and the Western nations generally are, in the ultimate analysis, easing up in their pressure on China. The apparent relaxation is, in reality, as I have tried to indicate, due to a change in the form of the pressure. There is no doubt that there is an *intention,* among the different foreign offices, to keep out of Chinese politics as far as is physically possible, and that public opinion supports government policy, and is even anxious to assist, wherever possible, the growth of a Chinese nation with a complete freedom of initiative of its own.

The question is, how far the logic of events (if it can be called a logic) will favor the aspirations of Chinese patriots and foreign altruists. We are, in short, living in the last phase of the mixed doctrines of national self-determination, internationalism and, so to speak, super-national government, and aspiration for world peace, which gained currency during the period of exhaustion and mental lassitude after 1918. In the West itself, the conflict of these doctrines is leading toward bitter disappointment, the failure of national self-determination as a basis for a sound internationalism, and loss of hope for the ideal of a permanent international peace ruling throughout the world with the force of law. How far can the West, which is failing tragically in the West itself, succeed in the East; and how far can China, dependent as it is on the West, succeed where the West is failing?

The nations of the West are quite as dependent as China on the accidents of individual leadership. The leader is now more important than the nation. This is true of Japan also, where the political party tends more and more to be identified with the individual personality of the leader. Policies are no longer inherent to the same extent in the nation itself, irrespective of parties and leaders. Yet the enormous physical powers we have created continue to operate. Our nations are now the tools of our manufactures, industries, and stock exchanges, and these now produce our leaders.

Hence, while individual nations may, for instance, desire a weak China or a strong China, our industries and our finances continue to operate as independent powers, irrespective of whether China is weak or strong, and the pressure of the West, accordingly, is changing from the pressure of separate national policies to the pressure of a civilization which cannot be controlled by any nation, or group of nations. The specific internationalism of the West, with its characteristics of good will in intention and helplessness in action, is an index of the fact that the nations of the West no longer guide the civilization which they created. Yet the old Western passion for individualism, responsibility and assertive control lives on; our leaders only last so long as they can keep up the illusion of controlling the uncontrollable.

There seems to be no conclusion but that the West has exhausted its powers of creativeness, and left behind the period when the party meant more than the leader and the nation meant more than the party. It can be said, of the Europe of the French Revolution, that if it had not produced Napoleon it must have produced someone else who would have had much the same career. To that extent, he was a man of destiny. The phase was inevitable. On the other hand it cannot be said of American or British politics of the present day that a Harding, a Coolidge, a Hoover, or a Lloyd George, a Baldwin or a Macdonald, are "men of destiny." They wield enormous powers, but they are not created or demanded by the situation; they are thrown up more or less accidentally out of the whirl of politics, and the accidents of their countries' policy follow the accidents of their individual careers. Important as they are in person, it is not inevitable, but accidental, that one should succeed the other. Our modern tendency to create commissions and delegate committees is a confession of subconscious loss of confidence in the inevitability of our leaders.

Russia appears to be the only nation of the modern world that is "young" enough to have "men of destiny." It creates its Lenin and its Stalin; they follow each other with the certainty of fate. Russia, more than China and more than any nation of the West, is launched on a career of growth, and grow it will, irrespective of the leader. Russia, of all countries, is the one of which it can be said not only that something new *may* happen, but that something new is *bound* to happen.

The *activity* of Russia (which is more important than its *policy*) not only in Manchuria but in Mongolia and Central Asia, illustrates this with a deadly clearness. Chinese policies in Manchuria, irrespective of whether the Manchurian Government *wishes* to engage in the politics of civil war in China or to devote itself to the colonization and exploitation of its own territory, is *inevitably* conditioned by the balance between the domestic affairs of China and its foreign relations. The Japanese policies in Manchuria, irrespective of political programs of "forward policy" or "policy of conciliation and cooperation," are *inevitably* controlled by the struggle between Western civilization as a whole and Chinese civilization. Above all, however, the policies of Russia are conditioned by historic forces. In the early Russian eastward expansion, forces from within the nation itself, the instinctive efforts of pioneers and adventurers, overrode the considered policies of the government. This power from within the nation itself is as active as ever, and is chiefly responsible for the fact that, apart altogether from the difference in government, in social structure and in declared international policy between Imperial Russia and Soviet Russia, the actual Russian expansion, the type of action taken on the spot, is essentially what it always was. It is a continuation of what went before. It still carries on an imperative eastward drift, and still demonstrates the knack of incorporating non-Russian elements in the Russian advance. This genius of conquest is more potent than methods of subjugation or obliteration, for it recruits at least as fast as it destroys. Of Russia, more than of any nation, it might be said that there is enough to do at home, without being active abroad; but there is no point in saying it, for the nation is oriented outward, and is bound to thrust outward. The government can only organize what the people of themselves accomplish.

The main front of Russian advance is not Manchuria, but Mongolia and Central Asia. Nevertheless Manchuria is the pivot on which turns the main advance, because it commands the Pacific outlet which is imperative if the main advance is to be turned into a permanent occupation and given facilities of continued growth. Power in the North Pacific, however, is as vital to Japan and China as it is to Russia. Hence the importance of Manchuria as a front on which not only Russia and China are opposed, and Japan and China, but on which Japan and Russia have in the past been opposed and may yet be opposed again. It is inevitable that China, as the weakest of the three nations in the sphere of foreign action, should endeavor to play off Russia and Japan against each other. It is also inevitable, however, that, given a certain degree of weakness on the part of China, Russia and Japan should endeavor to defer issues of direct rivalry between themselves, by concessions to each other at the expense of China.

These are the elementary factors of the situation, well enough known since the end of the last century, when it had become evident that China was disproportionately weak as a military power, that Japan had made itself over into a strong nation of Western type, and that Russia was piling itself up all along the edge of the old buffer region, north of the Chinese "reservoir" frontiers, and must, unless stopped by military measures, overflow into them.

The success of Japan in the Russo-Japanese War deferred the final issue, and was, beyond a doubt, of immediate benefit to China in terms of the northern frontier as a whole, though it increased the pressure on the much shorter Manchurian frontier proper. The final issue was again deferred by the implication of Russia in the War in Europe, and by the temporary collapse of Russian expansion during the Revolution. The problem is now, however, returning to all its old importance—and more.

In this connection, the living force of history is demonstrated in one very curious and interesting respect—the comparative cordiality of relations between Russia and China, as against the acrimony that repeatedly recurs in relations between China and Japan. There is, to my mind, only one satisfactory explanation of this. The territories in which Russia operates are, historically, the territories of the northern barbarians; Russian policies are, from the Chinese point of view, a recurrence of the old barbarian pressure. Deep in the Chinese consciousness there is a feeling that these processes are normal; at the very least, they are familiar.

This type of feeling is of enormous importance. It is a parallel to that between Frenchmen and Germans. No matter what the individual intellectual capacity of a Frenchman or a German, they conform to a certain type of action when in international negotiation with each other. It is the same with Russians and Chinese. Rooted in the Chinese consciousness there is a peculiar contempt for Russians. There is a feeling that they are to be feared, but only within limits, and that in spite of being dangerous they can always be used. When it comes to a blunt opposition of force, it may be necessary to yield to them. It may be necessary to grant them special powers in the north, just as the old barbarian chiefs were granted special titles, and their power disguised under the assumption that it was a power delegated by China. Apart from direct military conflict, however, the Chinese have never been afraid of them and are not now. They are profoundly sure of their superiority in negotiation; they are sure that they know always what kind of thing the Russians will do next, and that they will be able to prepare counter measures. Chinese negotiators, even when being forced to yield, appear to be much more at their ease, and sure of themselves, in dealing with Russia than in dealing with any other nation. Defeat by Russia has never caused anything like the same consternation as defeat by any other power. The loss of Outer Mongolia, and its virtual inclusion in the Soviet Union of Republics, aroused only a fraction of the feeling and comment caused by any advance of Japanese railway policy in Manchuria. There is a sure feeling (whether justified or not) that it is only those violent but stupid northern barbarians again, and that as soon as they calm down they can be handled.

In respect of Japan the feeling is quite different. Military defeat from the seaward side, in spite of the history of the nineteenth century, is still novel and terrifying to the consciousness of the people at large. There is no buffer territory between the sea and the heart of China; there are no non-Chinese "reservoir" tribes to graduate the shock; and the tradition of the sea-going population itself is one of exploiting, not of being exploited. The impact of Western nations, the alien standards of the West, treaties dictated by the West, have always aroused a reaction of terror and hate far greater than any defeat in the vague buffer territories of the north. There is no underlying tradition to prescribe a method of dealing with aggression from over the sea. The methods applied in the eighteenth and nineteenth centuries were, generally speaking, colored by the traditions applying to the northern land-frontier barbarians. They did not work well; in fact, they tended to bring on disasters. Hence a feeling, which has now penetrated very deep, that the Western nations are incalculable, that they are always likely to spring a fresh surprise, something quite outside of experience and the "rules of the game."

Indeed, this feeling is likely to be justified afresh by the change in the form of Western pressure. At any rate there is a pronounced tendency for Western nations, when they are triumphant over China, to be visited with a much greater vindictiveness, because of an underlying terror of the strangeness and unpredictability of Western action, than is visited on Russia. In the Manchurian theater this hostility is concentrated on Japan. A minor defeat in negotiation by Japan causes more baffled rancor throughout the population both of Manchuria and China, than a major military defeat by Russia. In the same way, sporadic outbreaks of race-feeling between Russians and Chinese die down and are forgotten, by both sides, much more quickly than similar "incidents" between Chinese and Japanese.

In the circumstances, whatever the temporary formal relation between Russia and China, there is a recurrent tendency on the part of China to hope and work for help from Russia against Japan, rather than help from Japan against Russia. There is, I think, a feeling that when Russia can be "used" at all, the method of the use is plain and the results calculable; but that any attempt to "use" Japan is profoundly dangerous, because the tool, however carefully studied, is never really familiar and may turn at any moment in the user's hand. Whatever the momentary incidents of the future, I cannot but foresee a prevailing tendency for China to align itself with Russia against Japan; although whether this will be justified in the upshot by ability to handle Russia as well is another question. In any case, history is here again on the side of Russia's Pacific aspirations.

When the great background of history is taken into consideration, and the strife of civilizations, the actual migration into Manchuria cannot, I think, be considered the major factor in the destiny of Manchuria, although it may prove to be an important determining factor. Racial stocks, in the ordinary physical sense, do not create cultures; they are the material in which a culture works itself out. It may be that cultures are born of land and people together; that they demand, for their origin, a given people in a given setting. However that may be, once they are launched they have a life and career of their own.

There is little difference, in physical racial type, between the majority of Northern Chinese and the majority of Mongols. Such differences as do exist cannot be divided into satisfactory categories of measurements. It is often possible to mistake a Chinese in Mongol costume for a Mongol, or a Mongol in Chinese costume for a Chinese. On the other hand, when it is possible to tell them apart, it is possible not because of differences in stature, dimensions, proportions, of which one can say definitely "this is Chinese and that is Mongol"; it is only possible because of differences in stance, movement, expression, manner, which are intangible in the material sense, but unmistakable. They are not differences of the physique itself, but of the life within the physical structure. Yet these intangibles, which belong to outlook, culture, feeling and the way of life, establish a cleavage as marked as that between the most pronounced Latin and the most obvious German.

Theoretically, perhaps, Chinese and Mongols ought to fuse by amalgamation, as the different European stocks are fusing in America. Actually, their effect on each other is one of conflict. In the past, the Mongols invaded China, where some turned Chinese and some remained Mongol, to be driven out by the rise of the next Chinese dynasty; but even so, they had their effect—as in emphasizing the cleavage between North and South in China. In the present, the Chinese invade Mongolia, where the first wave tends to a large extent to turn Mongol, but the second wave drives out and practically obliterates the Mongols; but even so they feel the effect of Mongolia—as in taking over the border tradition.

The future of Manchuria is not by any means only a question of the prevalence of a Chinese population over Russian, or Japanese and Korean efforts to plant colonies of settlers. There is decisive action as well in the rivalry between the Chinese way of life, the Russian way of life, and the Japanese-Western way of life. It is possible, perhaps probable, that any attempt at Russian settlement, even in northernmost Manchuria, would be smothered by an incoming Chinese population; or that, as some hold, Chinese colonization may thrust into Siberia and overwhelm the Russian element. On the other hand it is also at least possible—far more possible than is generally realized—that the Chinese population adjacent to Siberia might be caught up in the Russian advance toward the Pacific and so Russianized that its Chinese qualities would become secondary characteristics, like the secondary Mongol characteristics of the Buriats in Siberia. It is even possible that Korean migration might result in a Japanese-Korean advance across the Yalu (rivers always being highly unsatis-

factory frontiers of population and culture) and the establishment of a new frontier aligned on the Ch'angpaishan
range. The underlying struggle in Manchuria is, and will be
throughout our century, caused by the conflicting migration of
cultures and peoples, and the effort of cultures to assert themselves over peoples. In such a struggle, generals and statesmen are the accidents of history; tradition, the way of life,
the effort of race and region to assert themselves in the face
of culture and nation, and the effort of nation and culture to
impose themselves on race and region, are history itself.

CHAPTER XIII

MANCHUKUO: THE STATE AND THE THEORY

THE events of the 18th September, 1931, at Mukden, had been preceded by a period of increasing tension, not only as between China and Japan, but as between China, Japan, and the Soviet Union. Chinese expansion, working from within the "core" of Chinese railways in the central plain of Manchuria, enclosed on the north by the Chinese Eastern Railway and on the east by the South Manchuria Railway, was within sight of success in changing the whole political balance in Manchuria. On the west it was extending Chinese power into Mongolia, thus outflanking the position of the Soviet Union and shutting off Japanese interests from direct penetration westward through Manchuria. At the same time, the Chinese of Manchuria had broken through the fence of alien-controlled railways both in Kirin, east of the South Manchuria Railway and in Heilungchiang, north of the Chinese Eastern Railway.

The time when alien economic domination could be squeezed out was at hand. Manchuria could be made thoroughly Chinese. The population was already about 95 per cent Chinese. It was badly distributed, for it did not occupy anywhere near 95 per cent of the habitable land, but through spread and increase by colonization, it could soon have been distributed to make the territorial balance conform more satisfactorily to the balance of population. The last vestiges of foreign control would then have been the foreign investments in railways and other enterprises, and here the Chinese in Manchuria, as in China itself, could eventually have regained full control and initiative by the perfectly normal method of avoiding a frontal attack on "foreign privilege" as a whole, while concentrating on the recovery of control in one particular sphere after another.

This period of successful advance met its first check in 1929, in a conflict with the Soviet Union over the Chinese Eastern Railway. The conflict arose when the provincial authorities of Manchuria took action to assert Chinese authority over the railway, overriding the interest and authority of the Soviet Union. The causes of this conflict are now, however, of little interest. What is important is that the Chinese authorities abandoned negotiation in favor of direct action, and that the Soviet Union met action with action. In a "war" or "undeclared war" which amounted to little more than a display of Soviet military strength all along the Manchurian frontier, the Chinese forces broke up in disorder. Peace was finally dictated, on Soviet territory, according to terms laid down by the Soviet Union.

This incident, now little regarded, completely altered the complexion of all international affairs in Manchuria. To begin with, it raised the prestige of the Soviet Union, for the time being, above that of Japan; the center of gravity of Manchuria was unsettled, and began to move from the region of Mukden toward the region of Harbin. Still more important, it made quite plain the fact that the apparently increasing strength of China in Manchuria did not rest on secure foundations of a really increased strength in China itself, but on an unstable balance of international factors. The great gains in unification and the recovery of national initiative in China were largely due, it was now clear, to the general international policy of abstaining from intervention in China.

To this policy, partly documented by the Washington Treaties of 1922, the Soviet Union was not fully committed, not being a signatory of those treaties. Nevertheless the Soviet action made it dangerously evident that a bold stroke of intervention in Manchuria, if applied at a strategic point and a well-chosen time, could not be successfully countered. There did not exist in either China or Manchuria sufficient strength to resist such intervention; the international policy of nonintervention, being only in part a policy and in part merely a tendency, a convention that was beginning to become recognized, was fatally weak, because there existed no prompt and inescapable method which could be invoked to prevent direct action by the direct, compulsory use of force. In the dangerous world of "realistic politics" there was clearly nothing to prevent a signatory of the Washington Treaties from acting on the precedent set by a non-signatory. The startling possibilities of the new method of resorting to military action without declaring war, thus short-circuiting all anti-war treaties, had been sufficiently demonstrated.

This was in effect the character of the paralyzing original military action at Mukden on the night of September 18, 1931. It is generally believed that this action was not the result of considered Japanese national policy, but was brought off by a comparatively small military group with the deliberate but at the moment unauthorized intention of forcing a political crisis in Japan and launching a new military-political policy in Manchuria. This at any rate was the result of the action. The success of the interventionists in convincing the Japanese nation that intervention could not be repudiated resulted in a complete reorientation of Japanese national and international policy. The Mukden Incident developed with phenomenal rapidity into a general occupation of Manchuria. The almost incredible paralysis not only of action but of thought among other nations, together with a fatal tendency to deal with Chinese affairs as if they were merely an extension of European and American affairs, and an invincible unwillingness to deal with the deeper currents of Far Eastern history, allowed control of all Manchuria to fall into Japanese hands more quickly than even the most optimistic Japanese could have predicted.

As a result, however, of the suddenness with which Japan secured a free field of action in Manchuria, it was necessary to develop not only a complete machinery of administration but a complete new theory of Manchurian affairs, under extreme pressure. Control had actually to be established more rapidly than a theory of control could possibly be thought out, set up, and recognized. The fundamental character of the new relation between Japan and Manchuria had been established by the nature of the intervention. Behind intervention lay the theories and ideals of a well-integrated group of military officers who had for years been working out and debating among themselves a whole new system of thought, applying both to the domestic affairs and to the international relations of Japan. It was comparatively easy to diffuse the new ideas from a group within the army throughout the army as a whole. It was also comparatively easy to rouse the entire nation to a spirit of faith in the army and loyalty to the army. It was impossible, however, to convert all the different economic, political, and social interests within the nation, rapidly and completely, to unanimous agreement with the policies and methods of the dynamic group which had launched the new Manchurian undertaking. It was inevitable therefore that while the establishment of control proceeded rapidly, there should be a struggle, none the less intense because all parties were anxious to conceal it as far as possible, over the exercise of control and the direction of higher policy.

The intricacies of this internal struggle can probably not be fully comprehended except by those with a penetrating knowledge of Japanese affairs. The Westerner whose acquaintance is primarily with China and Manchuria can certainly not hope to appreciate all the more obscure workings of the forces involved. It is probably adequate to say, however, that two main issues have been in question. One concerns the structure of the new continental empire—whether it should take the form of direct extension of Japanese rule and administration, of the type seen in Korea, or whether it should take the form of a state—potentially a group of states—representing a Japanese hegemony but not a Japanese empire, and managed by indirect control but not by direct rule.

The second question concerns the alternative between centralization, with direct political and economic exploitation of the new sphere of control concentrated in Japan—an extractive, colonial imperialism, as one might say—and decentralization, with control and exploitation distributed over a group of federation of states, coöperating but not competing with each other—what might be called a "dominion" imperialism. This, the second alternative, is that of the "economic bloc." If it is to be effective, it demands the ruthless subordination of Manchurian economy to forms that will supplement but not compete with the interests of Japan; but it also demands the disciplined suppression of interests in Japan which have a natural appetite for exploiting a region like Manchuria by extracting its wealth and transferring it to Japan.

Such interests are instinctively opposed to the idea of in-

terdependence between Japan and Manchukuo, and in favor
of the dependence of Manchukuo on Japan. Partly because
of the close association between Government and national
economy in Japan, developed during the period when the
creation of new industry and trade was fostered by Government action, Japanese interests have often both a monopolistic tendency and a habit of Government association. The
ideas of federation and interdependence, on the other hand,
appear to be much more closely associated with the political-
military group whose theories point toward the creation of a
Japanese hegemony, with Japan leading, directing, and controlling, but not actually ruling, an allied state or group of
states on the mainland of Asia, than with the vested interests of Japanese industry and trade.

Both the structure and the policy of Manchukuo appear
to show the results of conflict and compromise between these
two major tendencies, but with the balance in favor of the
army school of continental expansion and interdependence.
Thus the form of the State decreed for Manchukuo is definitely not of the Korean pattern. It is frequently assumed
that the arbitrarily organized form of government in Manchukuo predicates an intention of future annexation; that
as in the case of Korea, the first stage is to be a protectorate,
and the final form direct incorporation with the Japanese
Empire. On the other hand, the careful resurrection of
Imperial forms modeled closely on the old dynastic ideas
of China, which in turn are closely related to the ideas of
empire and dynasty in Japan, indicates that there was a
deliberate and genuine intention not to follow the Korean
precedent. In Korea, at the time of annexation, Japan had
of necessity to deal with the fact that a genuine Korean
dynasty was already in existence. So long as it survived, it
was a focus for resistance against Japanese policy.

In Manchuria, on the other hand, the new dynasty, being itself created (or in theory restored) by Japan, is not a focus of resistance to Japan but a fulcrum for the exercise of further Japanese policy. Moreover the dynastic ideas inherent in the older Chinese culture, and still vigorous in Japan itself, would recoil with the greatest distaste from the device of setting up an emperor only to remove him later without scruple. Even apart from these dynastic considerations, which are much more real in the Far East than in the West, it is obvious that in the present unstable world it would be unwise for Japan, the last strong monarchy in Asia, to encourage any idea that monarchies can be set up and removed in an irresponsible way, for reasons of temporary convenience. It seems quite justifiable, therefore, to assume that the inauguration of a dynasty in Manchukuo was intended as an assurance of the maximum degree of stability, permanence, and responsibility—the strongest possible assurance that the destiny of Manchuria, while it was to be linked with that of Japan, was not to be similar to the fate of Korea.

There is, however, one element in the situation which makes it still possible to alter the Manchurian policy of Japan from a "Manchukuo" form to a quasi-Korean form. The Emperor of Manchukuo has no heir. If he should continue to have no heir, and if by the end of his reign the Manchukuo policy had not fulfilled expectations, it would be possible to change to a policy of annexation. Certain considerations, however, make it fairly clear that annexation would actually mark a retreat from, or modification of, the present policy of expansion, and that therefore it would not be the culmination of a plan previously prepared. The idea of a dynastic system in Manchuria offers a number of political facilities which confirm the supposition that it was adopted not for temporary use but in order to suit long-term policies. The chief of these facilities is the possibility of extending the federative method in order to form new states either in Mongolia or actually in China. This factor cannot be properly understood without reference to the history of the original Manchu dynasty in China. The average Westerner finds it hard to grasp some of the concepts involved, because for many years—beginning long before the fall of the Manchu dynasty—it has been customary to speak of the Chinese Empire and to ignore the nature of the relation existing between dynasty and empire.

Actually, the empire ruled over by the Manchus was not a Chinese empire. It included more territory than had ever been ruled by any dynasty of Chinese origin, and far more territory than had been controlled by the Ming dynasty—the last purely Chinese dynasty, and the dynasty which, in 1644, the Manchus had succeeded. It should also be remembered that before the Manchus entered China they had already founded, and successfully maintained for a number of years, a separate empire in Manchuria and Eastern Mongolia, the forms of which were closely modeled on the Chinese imperial system. It is not possible to assume that this was simply a rival dynasty laying claim to the throne of China, although in some respects the Manchu conquest was equivalent to sweeping success in a Chinese civil war, or that the nature of its claims were comparable to, for instance, the old claim of the Kings of England to the throne of France. Nor is it justifiable to assume either that the Manchus, by conquest, annexed China to Manchuria, or that, by transferring their capital from Mukden to Peking, they removed the center of sovereignty and so annexed Manchuria, in a manner of speaking, to China. It is, indeed, extremely unwise to believe that the complex body of ideas which we associate with such words as "dynasty," "empire," "nation," "sovereignty," can be translated term for term into Chinese and made to apply, function for function, to the world of Chinese-Manchu-Mongol-Central Asian statecraft.

What actually happened when the Manchus entered China was that the sphere of the already existing and already very "Chinese" Manchu Empire was enlarged, by a kind of civil war, and its center of gravity changed; but its nature was not changed. It was still a Manchurian Empire, but no longer a Manchurian Empire only. It was still a Manchu Empire, and from 1644 it became also a Chinese Empire; but this enlargement was accomplished by addition, not by fusion. China was not annexed to Manchuria, and Manchuria certainly was not annexed to China. Without going into details, it may be stated that this principle was gradually applied throughout the territories ruled by the Manchus. It was most clearly defined in China, Manchuria, and Mongolia, less clearly defined in such territories as Tibet and Chinese Turkestan, and never very strenuously asserted in Korea. The essence of the principle was that a kind of federated empire, known as "all under heaven," belonged to the Manchu dynasty; but within it China did not belong to Manchuria, nor Manchuria to China, nor Mongolia to China, nor China to Mongolia, and so for each of the constituent regions and peoples.

These older concepts were gradually obscured during the second half of the nineteenth century, partly because the dynasty, by long association with China, came to look upon the outer territories as possessions which they held as Emperors of China. A most important influence, however, was that of the international relations of the Manchu dynasty. Because the Western nations treated the Manchu Empire as, essentially, the Empire of China, to which outer possessions were attached, the policy of the dynasty itself was increasingly warped away from the original idea of federation and toward the idea of a sovereign Chinese power with a possessive relation toward a periphery of outer territories. The older federative structure was certainly never generally understood by Western statesmen; and indeed its type of federation was not the same, point for point, as such Western federations as the Austro-Hungarian Empire, the German Empire, or the United States.

Because of the overwhelming importance of foreign relations in their reaction on Chinese domestic affairs, during this period of foreign domination, Chinese who undertook the study of government and statecraft were increasingly influenced by Western concepts of nationality, sovereignty, and so forth, and their understanding of the older concepts inherent in their own history was weakened accordingly. The Chinese Republic, in its early years, wavered for a while between recognition of the older federative relation and outright acceptance of Western concepts of the State and its sovereignty. It was not long before the newer theories prevailed, however, and it is now perfectly natural for Chinese to look on China as a State to which the outer territories "belong"; to which they are, or ought to be, "subject." Only among such peoples as the Tibetans and Mongols can one find at the present day a perfectly clear and general understanding of the distinction between Tibetan or Mongol nationality and Chinese nationality.

A knowledge of these older concepts is necessary to understand the almost archaeological precision with which the principles of the State of Manchukuo have been enunciated. At point after point they reveal the knowledge and understanding of statesmen thoroughly versed not only in the dynastic history of China but in the history of frontier conquests in general and the Manchu conquest in particular. The older ideas are not yet lifeless. It may not be possible to revive them satisfactorily, but the attempt is being directed with skill. It is handicapped by the obvious difficulty, in a rapidly expanded administration, of finding in the requisite numbers men who can execute the principles as skillfully as they have been thought out. Bureaucratic and military administrations are not noted either for historical insight or for executive tact. Even more, however, the type of thought inherent in the principles of the new State is obstructed by the tide of world history as a whole. Its dynastic concepts can appeal only with the greatest difficulty to a generation which automatically looks on monarchies as anachronistic. In Japan, monarchy can be appealed to as a noble survival; in Manchuria, or at least among the Chinese of Manchuria, it can hardly appear to be anything but violent reactionary dogma.

Even with this disadvantage, however, a State of Manchukuo has potentialities which make it one of the most formidable enterprises in contemporary statecraft. Socially, it is reactionary in the extreme, but in its regional and historical assumptions it is not so much an attempt at reaction against new principles as an attempt to return to principles which still have a genuine importance. Politically, moreover, it is adaptable to several alternatives, and this increases its effectiveness as a weapon of Japanese policy. It is, for instance, obviously possible to extend its principles to the formation of a new Mongol nation, by combining the present Mongol regions of Manchuria with the part of Inner Mongolia adjacent to Manchuria; and this Mongol nation could again be expanded by a reactionary movement against the present revolutionary Government of Outer Mongolia. It would also be possible to form a "Hua Pei Kuo" or "State of

North China"; and such states could be federated either with Manchukuo, or directly with Japan. If they were federated with Japan, the relation could be either "colonial" or one of nominal alliance; if with Manchukuo, there would be nothing in the dynastic structure, as such, to hinder the organization of States distinct from each other but under a common sovereign.

In its administrative, as distinct from its dynastic structure, there is also scope under Manchukuo for alternative policies. The Government is at present much more highly centralized than was the Chinese Government of the Northeastern Provinces; but this does not prevent the possibility of new forms of decentralization of great significance. The uneven distribution of the Chinese population, and its heavy concentration toward the south, especially in the provinces of Fengt'ien and Kirin in their now reduced form, has already been pointed out. This obviously affords the possibility of using comparatively small but specially organized populations, by strengthening the Mongols in the west and using Japanese and Koreans in the north and east, to hold down the solidly Chinese and "irredentist" south.

Such problems are inseparable from the problem of the land. The lack of a true public domain in Manchuria has already been discussed, together with the close interconnection between landlords, officials, the military superstructure, railways, grain companies and other exploiting interests. This closely knit alliance was destroyed by the Japanese occupation, but the system itself was not destroyed. Since many of the landlords were also officials, or closely connected with officials, and since many of them fled from Manchuria, there must be many and complicated cases in which the allotment or reallotment of land deeds affects the basic economic position of individuals and whole communities. Currency reform, being merely a rearrangement of the symbols of wealth, cannot be regarded as in itself a sufficient stabilization of the agricultural economy which includes the great majority of the Manchurian population. If the control of land and of the trade in grain and beans is merely to be transferred from the protected interests of the old Government to the protected interests of followers and supporters of the new Government, then it will be impossible for the theoretically stated principles of the new order to send healthy roots down into the mass of the people.

Questions of land tenure and land administration must also be connected with the antagonism against Japanese colonization. There have been cases where, it is stated, lands were to be purchased from Chinese holders and turned over to Japanese colonists, whereupon the peasants have risen against the Japanese. This may have been due, as Japanese reports claim, to an unjustified fear that the lands would not be paid for; but it may well have been due to the fact that they actually were not paid for. In many regions, land deeds are rarely clear, and are interpreted as much by local custom as by legal construction. In such cases, especially if an absentee landlord has disappeared, and if land administration is manipulated by the connivance of the petty officials who are nearest to the land and farthest from the superior authorities of government, it is easy to see that the peasants in actual tenure could be evicted with no compensation. In addition it must be remembered that to peasant smallholders, land means more than money. The market value of the land, paid over in cash, does not necessarily enable the peasant to find, move to, and settle on an equal or equivalent amount of land elsewhere.

On the other hand, the same basic problems of the peasant, his land, and his money, must mean that a sudden restoration of Chinese sovereignty would be dreaded by a large part of the population. They would fear more scrambling from the top to get down to the land and get hold of it, another wave of ruthless internecine competition in the upper levels of the agricultural economy, in which the interests of the peasant who actually works on the land would be disregarded by the rent-collectors and traders who control the use of the land. This means that the Manchurian peasant, like many a peasant in China, has not sufficient economic resources to be able to afford patriotism. If his interests are fostered to the point where he can afford to think about patriotism, he is more likely to develop a local, regional, "Manchurian," or Manchurian-nationalist patriotism than either a specifically Chinese patriotism or a genuinely pro-Japanese political conviction. If his interests are disregarded, then his present racial and cultural group-feeling is more likely to turn into class-consciousness than it is to turn into patriotism of any kind.

Other economic questions in Manchuria, while really of less pressing importance than the agrarian problem, are a good deal more likely to attract attention. In social, political, and administrative matters the military-political group in Japan appears on the whole to have overborne the influence of the groups associated with Japanese industry and trade. In the trade of Manchuria (which of course profoundly affects agriculture) and in the exploitation of resources other than agriculture, Japanese interests appear to have been given compensating advantages. It is here, however, that the widest margin of dispute between different schools of Japanese opinion appears to exist.

Two basic approaches to the Japanese exploitation of Manchurian resources are possible. One is the use of cheap raw material, and cheap labor. Japanese industry can use Manchurian resources for the factories of Japan; but on the other hand Japanese finance can also invest in factories in Manchuria, using Chinese labor to undercut the labor and prices of Japan itself. A laissez-faire economy in Manchuria would be extractive and exhaustive; it would drain off the wealth of Manchuria, and keep down the standard of living, partly by using Manchurian products on which Japan would take the profit of manufacture and trade, and partly by drawing off dividends for Japanese investors in factories in Manchuria. The people of Manchuria would be sacrificed to the competition between conflicting Japanese interests.

As against this there are the possibilities of a highly artificial but conceivably workable "federative" development of Manchurian economy, to suit its federated political relation to Japan. This would mean a cold-blooded determination to make the Manchurian economy supplement that of Japan, refusing to allow the development of Manchurian manufactures or trade competing with established interests in Japan, but at the same time refusing to allow Japanese enterprise to forestall or exploit at will any and every form of economic activity in Manchuria. A balance would have to be established, allowing Manchuria to take profits out of Japan, as well as Japan to take profits out of Manchuria.

An essential element in the success of any such controlled economy would be the raising of the Manchurian standard of living, so that the standard of Manchuria should not drag down the average standard of Japan, while giving added wealth to limited groups in Japan. At the same time protection of Manchurian agriculture and trade against the highly organized finance of Japan would be necessary, so as to prevent Japanese interests from gaining control of the land in Manchuria, and thus to save the Manchurian Chinese from what happened to the Koreans.

It is not apparent that any final balance has been struck as between the extremes of controlled, interacting economy and uncontrolled Japanese exploitation. Because, however, a controlled economy must mean a rise in the standard of living, and uncontrolled exploitation must mean full use of the cheapest labor available, it is probable that figures of emigration from China into Manchuria will provide an approximate index of Japanese economic policy. The standard of living cannot be raised if free immigration is permitted. Free immigration means the immigration of famine refugees and other financially helpless individuals, who keep down the cost of labor. Restricted immigration means that the agricultural output can only be kept up by increased mechanization, to take the place of the seasonal labor formerly supplied from China. This in turn would in time mean that the machine-using Manchurian farmer, with a relatively high standard of living to protect, would himself support restriction of immigration. An economic barrier would thus be created between the Chinese of Manchuria and the Chinese of China, which would favor the development of a separatist regional feeling.

Free Japanese exploitation, on the other hand, would create a political demand for unrestricted immigration, in order to make the maximum use of cheap labor. This question, however, is really subordinate to the question of whether the continental policy of Japan intends to stop short, or indeed is able to stop short, at the creation and maintenance of Manchukuo, or whether it aims at, or must be drawn into, the creation of a wider sphere of action. This involves major considerations of history which need to be separately examined.

Chapter XIV

PACIFIC OCEAN AND GREAT WALL

It has been common, since 1931, to speak of Chinese and Japanese "rivalry" in the exploitation of Manchurian natural resources; of Japanese and Russian "rivalry" over the Chinese Eastern Railway; of Manchukuo as a "puppet" State, a device to shield future Japanese annexation. No acute diagnosis, however, can fail to discern that much more serious phenomena underlie the superficial symptoms. Manchuria is in fact a nexus of all the most important problems in the dynamics of both Far Eastern history and world history. Problems of this kind, if attacked by any self-consistent method of criticism, will yield convincing answers. One may deal in the logic of power-politics, in the logic of materialistic determinism, the class war, and imperialistic expansionism, in the logic of geographical history, or in the logic of history as form, the idea that cultures and civilizations are organic bodies, subject to the laws of youth and age, growth and decay. Perhaps the most satisfactory approach is that through geography and history, because of the acrid controversies attaching to different schools of political interpretation.

In examining the history of the border regions of China— the regions from Manchuria in the east to Chinese Turkestan and Tibet in the west—it is impossible to escape three conclusions. In the first place, frontier history, north of the Great Wall, is indisseverable from the history of China within the Great Wall, but at the same time it is, within its own limits, quite distinct from Chinese history. The two histories interlock, and neither can be fully understood without the other; but each at the same time has its own laws and characteristics.

In the second place, for many centuries in the interaction of the two histories, the frontier was in general the positive pole, the focus of action, while China within the Great Wall was the negative pole, the focus of reaction. Frontier history is tied to Chinese history primarily because the frontier peoples repeatedly made conquests in China and were affected by the reactions of their own conquests. Chinese history is tied to frontier history because China, while it was able to react repeatedly to conquest and to adapt conquest by the frontier to the rhythm of Chinese history, was never able to master the frontier as such, and so to eliminate the factor which prevented fusion between China and the frontier. In the modern period, however, this relation was changed, and very suddenly changed. China became the pole of positive action; China began to master the frontier, and the resultant changes in the balance of the whole Asiatic continent particularly affected Russia, the nearest great power on the continental side, and Japan, the nearest maritime power. These changes therefore must be closely connected with the "Manchurian crisis."

In the third place, finally, the characteristic history of the frontier regions is essentially a continental history. For many centuries, from the dawn period of Chinese history almost until the contemporary period, the relation between China and the frontier was defined by the line of the Great Wall. The building of the Great Wall—centuries after the processes had begun to operate—was itself an acknowledgment of the importance of these processes. The power of China was a land power, as much as was the power of the mounted barbarians of the north. The change in relation between China and the frontier followed closely on the rise of oversea Western influence in China, and was made possible by factors, like railways and modern armaments, which were introduced from overseas and reflected the power of the maritime Western nations. The factors involved in the "Manchurian crisis" must therefore be closely connected with the relation between continental and maritime history, land power and sea power. The mere existence of Manchukuo embodies the paradox of power on the Great Wall frontier exercised by a maritime nation. For this reason the "Manchurian crisis" cannot possibly be restricted to the Far East, and must continue to be a matter of world importance.

In relating Manchurian history to world history one must therefore go far back of the year 1931. Even the Manchu conquest of 1644 cannot be taken as the point of origin of Manchurian history; for it was no more than a modern episode in a history which already for many centuries had had an unmistakable rhythm. The rise of the Manchus was only the repetition of a phase which had already occurred under the Mongols in the thirteenth century; the Mongols themselves had merely reënacted the rhythm of the rise and fall of the Nüchen or Juchen Tartars of the Chin dynasty. This rhythm can be traced right back to the period when the power of the Han dynasty in China made headway against the Hsiung-nu in the trans-frontier region, and Chinese and Barbarians, in campaigns that swept over thousands of miles of territory, collided against each other along the line of the Great Wall that still stands today. That was in the period immediately before and immediately after the beginning of the Christian era; and even then the phenomenon was not new, for it had been known already for something like two thousand years.

It is not too much to say that Columbus had a more novel and far-reaching effect on Manchurian history than did Nurhachih, the initiator of the Manchu conquests. While the Central Asian and Far Eastern world—with the exception of the islands beyond the coast of Asia—had from the beginning of time moved in a rhythm of migration and conquest radiating from a focus somewhere near the Altai range between Mongolia and Chinese Turkestan, the history of the Mediterranean world had been dominated by sea-power, as exercised in the closed Mediterranean Sea, between Africa, Asia, and Europe. In spite of such migrations as those of the Vikings, significant history at the time of Columbus had not yet emerged from the Mediterranean into the Atlantic. Europe still gravitated toward the Mediterranean. These two worlds of history, that of the Mediterranean Sea and that of the Asiatic continent, finally met and came to a deadlock with the Turkish conquest of Constantinople in 1453. The influence of the Mediterranean, which had once reached out through the Near East to India, Central Asia and even China, was thrown back; the power of the Turks, after threatening to break into Europe, was also checked, although not finally checked until the seventeenth century.

Thus it was about a hundred years before the rise of the Manchus that the way between the Mediterranean and Central Asia and the Far East was closed. It was this that led to efforts to find a way by sea to the Orient, and it was the fact that Columbus discovered America before Vasco da Gama found the way around Africa that gave the new age a totally novel character. It was not only a new way to the East that was discovered, but simultaneously a new East and a new West. Because the routes opening up this abruptly expanded universe were sea-routes, the dynamics of the new age which we call "modern history" were from the beginning dynamics of maritime power.

This meant that the Manchu Empire was to be the last conquest of the old type reaching from the trans-frontier into China. Even before it was established, the Western nations had begun to approach China from the sea. The first Portuguese vessel appeared at Canton in 1510. The Manchu conquest was actually delayed for a while by cannon cast for the Ming armies by Jesuit missionaries; a history of the Manchu Conquest was published, in Latin, by a Catholic missionary, exactly ten years after the occupation of Peking; and the Manchus in their turn used artillery cast by the Jesuits, to put down the rebellion of Wu San-kuei in 1674–78. Accurate mapping of the new empire was due primarily to the skill and energy of Catholic missionaries. There was a temporary check to Western activity in China when the influence of the Catholics declined, after a controversy over rites which brought the Church into conflict with the Emperor. This, however, really signified little more than that the Catholics lost their advantage of priority in the penetration of China; but since the next wave from the West was impelled by the forces of the industrial revolution and expansive trade, the influence of Protestant Western Europe would in any case have become dominant over that of Catholic Southern Europe.

The maritime power of the West, in other words, increased in China as the power of the Manchus first matured and then began to wane. The decay of the Manchus cannot be attributed to Western influence; it sprang from inner causes and followed a course already well known from the history of a score of other dynasties before it, both Chinese and "barbarian." Western influence, indeed, actually upheld the dynasty when it was already tottering, in the years of

the Taiping Rebellion. It was at this point that the interference of the maritime West began to affect the established
processes of Chinese history.

Economically, the West was interested in the exploitation
of China; politically, while not averse from profiting by
the weakness of the Manchu dynasty to begin the partition-
ing of China into spheres of influence, it yet demanded
"peace and order" to ensure stable conditions for exploitation. Even while it demanded peace and order, however, the
West was destroying the old economic structure of China,
the major trend of which had been in lines running from
south to north. The West broke across these lines, to draw
all trade toward the east and the coastal ports. Politically,
and simultaneously, it interfered with the normal processes
governing the fall of one dynasty and the rise of another.
The injection of Western ideas brought about the founding
of a republic instead of a new dynasty, while insistence
on "law and order" brought political pressure to bear on the
new Republic from the very beginning.

Thus neither the economic nor the political forms of the
old China remained untouched. At the same time, the
international affairs of China were perforce deflected from
a northern focus to a maritime focus. The great northward
extension of the power of China, partly through the building of railways and promotion of colonization and partly
through international recognition of the principle that China,
in the new period, should occupy the whole of the territory
of the Manchu Empire, was merely a paradoxical reflection
of the fact that the northern frontier had lost importance.
Huge territories like Outer Mongolia, which had never been
directly ruled by any purely Chinese dynasty, and territories
like Inner Mongolia, Chinese Turkestan, Tibet and even
the northern and western part of Manchuria, which China

had never occupied either permanently or strongly, could be assigned to China simply because their impact on China was no longer decisive. They could now, on the contrary, be themselves for the most part reached and "opened up," as the saying went, by penetrating to them from the coast of China through the hinterland.

Russia also suffered from the reach inland of maritime power. Russia alone, of the major Western nations, had no need of the sea power and maritime trade which for other nations were the keys to the exploitation of China. For Russia alone the older structure of the Far East had a plain meaning. For the Russians, the Central Asian Turks were not a barbarous kind of Chinese, but Turks. To them, it was not at all obvious that Mongolia was a part of China; it seemed quite plain that it was the country of the Mongols, who might soon become part of the Russian conglomerate of peoples. While other nations, long before the end of the nineteenth century, had formed the habit of speaking of the Manchu Emperor as the Chinese Emperor, it remained quite normal for Russians to use the term Bogda Khan, the Manchu and Mongol title of the Emperor.

For the Western nations in general, the change from the period of influence to the period of control was marked by the Treaty of Nanking, in 1842; but the Russians could look back as far as the Treaty of Nerchinsk, in 1689, which nominally gave a check to the eastward advance of the Russians, but actually marked the completion of the first stage in the annexation of all the eastern, tribal territory of Siberia, including the Tungus territory from which the Manchus derived. In the Western pressure on China, control had from the beginning been more important than annexation; but the Russian advance, both in the seven-

teenth century and in the nineteenth, was one of outright annexation.

When the Russians were finally checked, it was not by
the Chinese but by the maritime nations. The Open Door
policy of 1899–1900, commonly supposed by Americans to
have been a policy of chivalry and altruism, can better be
described as an assertion of American determination to be
a Great Power in the Far East, and has since become, partly
because of changes in the Far East, partly because of changes
in the West itself, a policy of intervention.[1] Specifically, the
Open Door policy at the time of its enunciation acted in
restraint of Russian ambitions in the Far East. This was the
first stage in bringing maritime pressure to bear on the
continental expansion of Russia. The next step was taken by
Japan, in the Russo-Japanese War, and here again it was the
intervention of America, through Theodore Roosevelt's
mediation and the Treaty of Portsmouth, that persuaded
Russia to conclude peace.

At this point, a new period began. It had been foreshadowed when Russia, Germany, and France, in 1895, had
prevented Japan from gaining a foothold in Southern Manchuria after victory over China. This was the beginning of
the opposition between modern land-power and sea-power,
and of the opposition of all maritime nations to any one
maritime nation which might attempt to transfer its power
from the sea, the basis of "equal opportunity," to the land,
the sphere of "special position." From the time when Japan,
after defeating Russia, finally broke into Manchuria, American policy in the Far East—a purely maritime policy—has
definitely been opposed to Japanese policy. It was American

[1] See Tyler Dennett, "The Open Door," in *Empire in the East* (New York:
Doubleday, 1934).

initiative which led to the Washington Conference of 1921, the surrender by Japan of many of the advantages gained under the Twenty-one Demands of 1915, and the conclusion of a new group of treaties intended to dominate Japan at sea and prevent further Japanese expansion on the mainland.

Yet it was impossible, by any such means, to do more than delay the development of the new period. History has its own equivalent for the economic law of diminishing returns; and sea-power, as the gauge of world power, had begun to reach the point of diminishing returns. The margin of expansion in sea-power and the exploitation of sea communications had, by the beginning of the twentieth century, been virtually exhausted. A change of emphasis from oceanic to continental factors was already foreshadowed, and uncertainty over the time and place at which the change would begin to manifest itself contributed to the tension of the years before 1914. "Colonial" rivalry alternated between Africa and Asia; the German navy challenged the supremacy of the British navy, and at the same time the German project of a Berlin to Baghdad railway, thrusting into Asia by land, challenged the new grouping of continental power which the drawing together of French and Russian interests attempted to establish.

When war broke out, in 1914, the opposition between land-power and sea-power was perfectly clear. Although, from the French point of view, it was primarily a Franco-German war, fought to reverse the decision of 1870, the rest of the world never doubted that the main issue was between Great Britain and Germany. As between these two, Germany was the dynamic factor, because Germany was at the same time the most aggressive land-power in Europe and the most aggressive sea-power threatening the supremacy of Great Britain. At the end of the war, therefore, in spite of the triumph of France and in spite of the greatly increased importance of the United States, Great Britain was the major world power, and certainly the power with the greatest interest in stabilizing the balance of world forces. Russia, as one of the primary continental powers, was apparently reduced to helplessness for many years to come. The power of Germany had been broken both on land and at sea. If, therefore, the policy of Great Britain toward Germany and Austria were modified so as to prevent France from becoming too powerful in Europe, all that remained was to avoid rivalry with America in naval power and far-reaching over-sea policies.

The Treaty of Versailles, therefore, while it left many issues within Europe confused, was clear in its determination of major world issues. The possibility of great continental combinations of land-power had to all appearances been removed. Great Britain and the United States were the two dominant world powers, and both of them, in their relations to each other and to other nations were, in the first instance, sea-powers. They could, by combination, exercise a control by restraint over the second-line naval powers, such as Japan and France. It was assumed that sea-power had finally disposed of the challenge of land-power, and that if the categories of sea-power could be permanently determined, the whole structure of world power could be stabilized.

The Washington Treaties of 1922, accordingly, were an attempt at a permanent codification of world power. Being based fundamentally on the concept of sea-power, they naturally confirmed the older "Open Door" policy of America, which tended to prevent the unsettling of Far Eastern conditions by barring all attempts to set up specifically continental interests in Asia. Unfortunately, however, it is axiomatic that makers of treaties are weak in the understanding of history. A treaty, especially a treaty based on victory in war, is in the nature of things an attempt to make permanent the conditions obtaining at a particular point in history: but history itself is dynamic and works in phases, which cannot be surgically separated and arrested. The vice in all agreements intended to obviate conflict is that if the major dangers are all guarded against, pressure is transferred to points previously obscure. The perfectly genuine cautiousness of the great powers in the years before 1914 made them unwilling to resort to war on the main issues; whereupon the thwarted pressure inherent in European conditions finally broke out of control in the Balkans. In the same way, the Washington Treaties brought under control the pressure on the continent of Asia from the maritime side; whereupon the pressure inherent in the situation itself broke out of control on the Siberian front of Manchuria. The Russo-Chinese conflict of 1929–30 was the preliminary landslip of the avalanche of 1931.

International precautions based on a balance of sea-power had not been able to influence the development of continental power from the continental side. Indeed, the possibility of such a development had been underestimated. The power-politics disguised under the phraseology of the Washington Treaties had not counted on the ability of the Soviet Union to recuperate inwardly within ten years and become, in its outward relations, a major world power. The structure of the Washington Treaties depended, for its efficacy, on the absence of any real power on the continent of Asia. The creation of a genuine Russian power knocked the props from under it.

Once the structure had begun to give way, however, emphasis was transferred from the Soviet Union to Japan;

for Japan in 1931, like Germany in 1914, was the nation that was off balance, divided between its maritime and its continental commitments. The policy of other nations had necessarily to follow the decision of Japan either to put its continental policy before its naval policy, or its naval policy before its continental policy. The further consequence was that when Japan did in fact succeed in improving its continental position to the point of being able to hold the Soviet Union in check by land and dominate China, naval questions once more became of crucial importance, it being necessary for Japan to make sure, if possible, that there would be no attempt from overseas to interfere with the now very definite connection between the fate of Japan and the fortunes of the Japanese policy on the mainland of Asia.

The Japanese position in Manchuria is now so much more important than either the British position at Hongkong or the French influence in Yunnan that Japan may be regarded as the only maritime nation definitely committed to an active policy on the mainland of Asia. The Indian empire of the British is not an expanding empire. Its Tibetan, Chinese Turkestan, and Afghan frontiers alike are defensive frontiers. The Soviet Union is the only nation whose position in Asia challenges that of Japan; and this not only by reason of Asiatic Siberia, but by reason of the actual Soviet influence in Outer Mongolia and potential Soviet control of Chinese Turkestan. It is for this reason that the fate of China cannot be decided in China proper. The Japanese policy on the mainland is essentially a China policy, it is true, inasmuch as the degree of success in controlling China will determine the success of the policy as a whole; but because of the divided front as between Siberia and China, the point of balance is not in China itself, but between the Great Wall and Siberia.

It is in this region that the basic relation between Europe and Asia must be determined. In the nineteenth century Europe, and to a lesser extent America, reached out overseas to divide and control the world. In the twentieth century it is more likely that the geographical frame of history will be continental. The economic processes of our time, the "Americanization" of the world, favor the development of large areas within which raw products, manufacture, and distribution to consumers can be brought into close adjustment and made as nearly as possible independent of other "autarchic" areas. Domains like those of the United States, Brazil, and the Soviet Union are well adapted to these processes; Western Europe is ill adapted. One of the structural weaknesses underlying the political unrest of Western Europe is the lack of adequate territorial space and economic range; political independence clashes with economic interdependence.

Power in the air, as yet almost unexploited, is also closely related to the opposition between land-power and sea-power. The political continuity of such territories as the United States, China, and the Soviet Union gives them full scope for the development of air communication. Germany and France are handicapped by the fact that the potential range of their aircraft is choked by the limited range of their territory. Great Britain above all is at a disadvantage. The British air route to India and Australia is dependent on the political friendliness of a number of States; while Russian pilots can fly unhindered from the Arctic Circle to the frontiers of Persia, Afghanistan, and China. There is no equivalent, in the air, for the "high seas" in which no national jurisdiction is recognized; nor is there likely to be. Over the high seas, which belong to no nation, major naval powers like America, Great Britain, or Japan can exercise control in time of emergency; but the primary need of aircraft is for safe landings, and therefore they cannot fly at will over the sea.

The land mass reaching from the Atlantic to the Indian and Pacific Oceans is the most important in the world. It has at present no center of gravity; but when that center is determined, it will affect the whole character of world history. A world whose forces have been coördinated to great land masses will be very different from the present world of reticulated forces coördinated to sea-routes and the extension overseas of interests that are at once vulnerable and irreconcilable. When the consolidation of continental groupings has reached its natural limits, and unwieldy land-powers in North and South America, Africa, and the Eurasiatic continent look out once more at each other across the oceans, the employment of sea-power may once more offer an escape from the restrictions of the land. In our own time, however, the continents of the world offer more scope for novel developments of power than do the oceans.

Japan hangs on the flank of Asia as England hangs on the flanks of Europe, and it would seem that such insular maritime powers must decline to minor importance in a continental age. It cannot be assumed, however, that sea-power will give place by natural decline to the vigorous unimpeded growth of land-power. The continental policy of Japan is in part a supreme effort actually to translate sea-power into land-power; but in part it is the Asiatic equivalent of the British policy, now matured through several centuries of skillful application, of balance of power in Europe. The stultification of land-power, in order to give full scope for the use of sea-power, is the balance-wheel of British foreign policy. With a League of Nations at Geneva, split across and across by national animosities, Great Britain can negotiate; but the United Empire of Europe which Napoleon nearly created could only be countered with war.

A solid Japanese Empire of Asia would subordinate Japan to China as completely as a British Empire over Europe would subordinate Great Britain to Germany. For this reason Japan has always flinched from the possibility of the unification of China and a genuine extension of the power of China into Manchuria, Mongolia, Chinese Turkestan, and Tibet. The division of the Far East into separate nations of South and North China and Manchukuo, and the formation of new independent nations in Mongolia, Tibet, and Chinese Turkestan would on the contrary create a Europe of the Far East. An "Asiatic culture" could be at least as homogeneous as the "Western civilization" of Europe, and the power of Japan could be made at least as essential to the balance of Asia as the power of Great Britain is to the balance of Europe.

Such a division of the Far East inevitably conflicts with the continental tendency toward cohesion and the formation of very large territorial units. Moreover a continental policy, rapidly and drastically carried out, naturally tends to make it necessary to apply methods of direct administration where methods of indirect control would be preferable. There is thus an inner contradiction between the continental policy and the maritime interests of Japan. It is on the resolving of this inner contradiction, and on the conflict between maritime control and continental trend of history, not only in Manchuria but in the continental land mass to which Manchuria is one of the gates, that the structure of Asia and in large measure the balance of the world now depend.

If the first real challenge to Japanese expansion should come from the naval powers of the West, it would mean only an attempt to restore the older forms of maritime control in the Far East. If the challenge should come from the Soviet Union, it would mean a major decision in the history of the world, for it would bring to a head all the issues latent between land-power generally and sea-power generally. The interests of all nations would be involved, and the efforts of individual nations, or even groups of nations, to limit the sphere of conflict might be futile, for the true field of conflict would range from Atlantic to Pacific. The westward trend of history from the Mediterranean to the Atlantic and from the Atlantic to the Pacific would reach the land again. The five centuries of oceanic history since Columbus would complete the interlude between the ancient Asiatic migrations and a new Asiatic age; and the Great Wall would mark the meeting of still stubborn maritime forces and resurgent continental forces.

LOCATION MAP
OF
MANCHURIA

0   50   100   200 MILES
0   50   100   200 KILOMETERS

SIBERIA

Argun R.

Manchuli

Hailar

GREAT HSINGAN

LITTLE HSINGAN

Nonni R.

Mergen

Upper Amur R.

Middle Amur R.

S I B E R I A

Lower Amur R.

HEILUNGCHIANG

Suiyüan

T'ungchiang
(Lahasusu)

OUTER
MONGOLIA

SOUTHERN HSINGAN

Solun

Tsitsihar

T'ailai

Tao R.

T'aoan

T'aonan

Anda

Anda Station

Middle Sungari R.

Harbin

Ashiho

Nonni R.

Shuangch'eng

Lalin

Petuna

Sanhsing

Lower Sungari R.

Fuchin

Hulin

Ussuri R.

PRIMORSK PROVINCE

CHAHAR

Dalai Nor

K'aitung

Mutan or Hurkha R.

K I R I N

Upper Sungari R.

Ninguta

Hsink'ai
Lake
(Hanka L.)

K'ailu

West Liao R.

East Liao R.

Kuanch'engtze

Kirin

JEHOL

Dolonnor

Ch'ihfêng

Shira Muren (Upper Liao)

T'ungliao
(Baiyantala)

Chengchiat'un

Hungchou

Tunhua

Vladivostok

Fak'umen

Tungchiangtze

Changwu

L I A O N I N G

Hsinmint'un

Ch'aoyang

Tahushan

Olchou

Liao R.

Fengtien
(Mukden)

Tiehling

Hailung

(FENGTIEN)

Hsingching

CH'ANGPAISHAN RANGE

Ch'angpaishan

Tumen

Ch'engte
(Jehol)

Koupangtze

Chinchou

Haich'eng

K O R E A

S E A
O F
J A P A N

Hulutao

Newchwang

Fenghuangch'eng

Yalu R.

Antung

Ch'inwangtao

GREAT WALL

INNER GT. WALL

Shanhaikuan

Gulf of

Liaotung

HOPEI

KUANTUNG
LEASED
TERRITORY

Ryojun (Port Arthur)

Dairen

Korea Bay

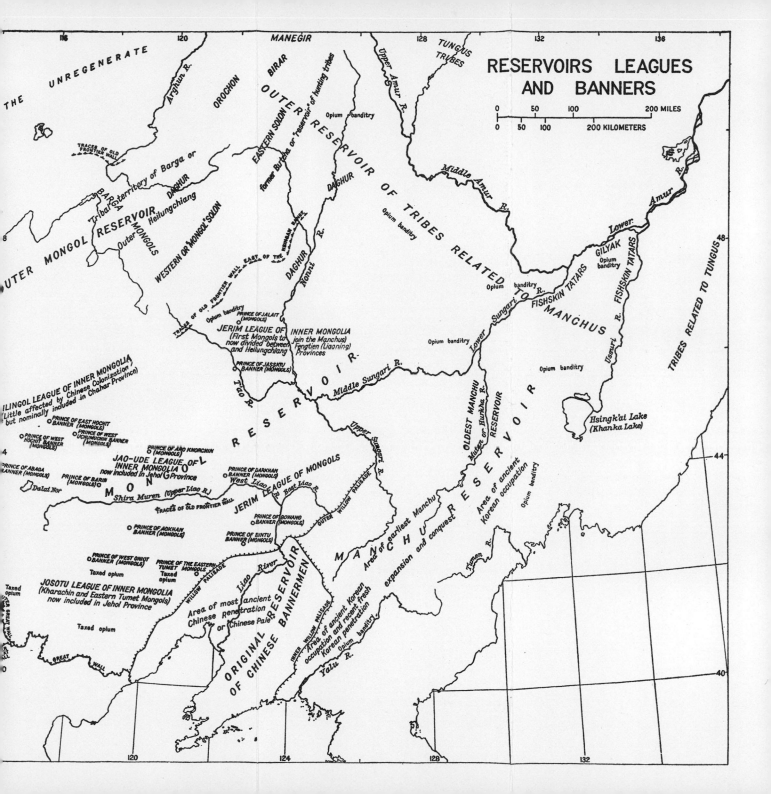

RESERVOIRS LEAGUES
AND BANNERS

THE UNREGENERATE

MANEGIR

TUNGUS
TRIBES

200 MILES
200 KILOMETERS
0   50   100

Arghun R.

OROCHON

BIRAR

Upper Amur R.

Middle Amur R.

Lower

TRACES OF OLD
FRONTIER WALL

EASTERN SOLON

former Butcha or "reservoir" of hunting tribes

RESERVOIR OF TRIBES RELATED TO MANCHUS

Amur R.

Tribal Territory of Barga or

DAGHUR

OUTER MONGOL RESERVOIR

BARGA

Outer Mongols

DAGHUR

WESTERN OR MONGOL SOLON

Heilungchiang

Opium banditry

Opium banditry

Opium banditry

Opium banditry

GILYAK

FISHSKIN TATARS

FISHSKIN TATARS

TRIBES RELATED TO TUNGUS

Opium banditry

Daghur

Nonni R.

Nunbaing Range

DAGHUR

TRACES OF OLD FRONTIER WALL EAST OF THE

Opium banditry

PRINCE OF JALAIT (MONGOLS)

JERIM LEAGUE OF INNER MONGOLIA
(First Mongols to
now divided between
join the Manchus)
and Heilungchiang
Fengtien (Liaoning)
Provinces

RESERVOIR

Lower Sungari R.

Ussuri R.

Opium banditry

ILINGOL LEAGUE OF INNER MONGOLIA
(Little affected by Chinese Colonization
but nominally included in Chahar Province)

PRINCE OF JASSATU
BANNER (MONGOLS)

Tao R.

Middle Sungari R.

OLDEST MANCHU
Mutgo or Hurkha R.

Area of ancient
Korean occupation

Opium banditry

PRINCE OF EAST HOCHIT
BANNER (MONGOLS)
PRINCE OF WEST
UCHUMUCHIN BANNER
(MONGOLS)

PRINCE OF WEST
HOCHIT BANNER
(MONGOLS)

PRINCE OF ARO KHORCHIN
(MONGOLS)

MON

RESERVOIR

Hsingk'ai Lake
(Khanka Lake)

PRINCE OF ABAGA
BANNER (MONGOLS)

JAO-UDE LEAGUE OF
INNER MONGOLIA
now included in Jehol Province

Upper Sungari R.

MANCHU

PRINCE OF BARIN
(MONGOLS)

PRINCE OF DARKHAN
BANNER (MONGOLS)

Dalai Nor

Shira Muren (Upper Liao R.)

West Liao R.

East Liao R.

JERIM LEAGUE OF MONGOLS

G

Area of earliest Manchu

expansion and conquest

Tumen R.

TRACES OF OLD FRONTIER WALL

JERIM

OUTER WILLOW PALISADE

PRINCE OF BOWANG
(MONGOLS)

PRINCE OF AOKHAN
BANNER (MONGOLS)

PRINCE OF BINTU
BANNER (MONGOLS)

Liao River

RESERVOIR

PRINCE OF WEST ONIOT
BANNER (MONGOLS)

PRINCE OF THE EASTERN
TUMET MONGOLS

Taxed opium

Taxed opium

JOSOTU LEAGUE OF INNER MONGOLIA
(Kharachin and Eastern Tumet Mongols)
now included in Jehol Province

Taxed
opium

Taxed opium

WILLOW PALISADE

Area of most ancient
Chinese penetration
or Chinese Pale

ORIGINAL RESERVOIR
OF CHINESE BANNERMEN

INNER WILLOW PALISADE

Area of ancient Korean
occupation and recent fresh
Korean penetration

Opium banditry

Yalu R.

GREAT WALL

GREAT WALL

———

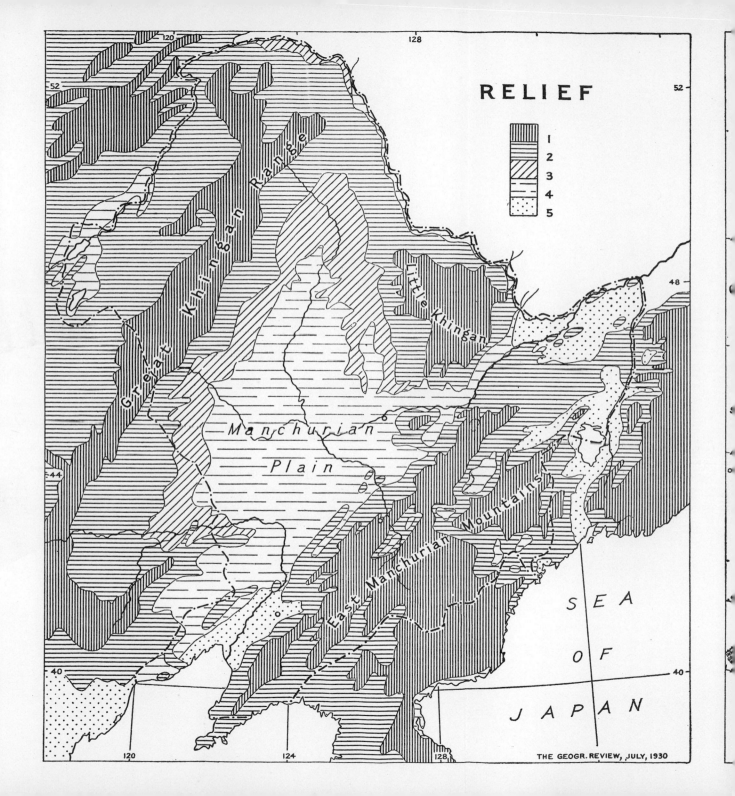

RELIEF

1
2
3
4
5

Great Khingan Range

Little Khingan

Manchurian

Plain

East Manchurian Mountains

SEA

OF

JAPAN

INDEX

335